ERNESTO 'CHE' GUEVARA was born in Argentina in 1928. He trained as a doctor and travelled extensively around Latin America. He played a key role, alongside Fidel Castro, in the revolution in Cuba and, after the three-year guerrilla war, became Minister for Industry. He also established a guerrilla base in Bolivia. He was captured and killed in 1967.

By the same author

The Motorcycle Diaries
Guerrilla Warfare
The Bolivian Diary

ERNESTO 'CHE' GUEVARA

Reminiscences of the Cuban Revolutionary War

Preface by Aleida Guevara

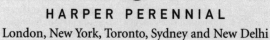

HARPER PERENNIAL

London, New York, Toronto, Sydney and New Delhi

Harper Perennial
An imprint of HarperCollins*Publishers*
77–85 Fulham Palace Road
Hammersmith
London W6 8JB

www.harperperennial.co.uk
Visit our authors' blog at www.fifthestate.co.uk

This Harper Perennial edition published 2009

1

This version of the text first published by Ocean Press in 2006

Published in Spanish as *Pasajes de la Guerra Revolucionaria*

A catalogue record for this book
is available from the British Library

ISBN 978-0-00-727721-6

Printed and bound in Great Britain by Clays Ltd, St Ives plc

Mixed Sources
Product group from well-managed
forests and other controlled sources
www.fsc.org Cert no. SW-COC-1806
© 1996 Forest Stewardship Council

CONTENTS

EDITORIAL NOTE

This edition of *Reminiscences of the Cuban Revolutionary War* has been divided into two parts. Part One replicates exactly the format in which the book was originally published, in 1963, by the Cuban publishing house Union. Many chapters of that book had already appeared in serial form in the magazine of the Cuban armed forces, *Verde Olivo*. After it was published, Che Guevara edited the pages of the printed book, making additions, deletions, and corrections (see the photographs of these pages reproduced here). These corrections were never included in subsequent printings. When Aleida March, Che's *compañera* and director of the Che Guevara Studies Center, discovered the marked-up book many years later, his additions were finally incorporated. They appear here for the first time.

Part Two contains essays and episodes of the revolutionary war written by Che after 1963. In these pieces, he revisits old battles, describes new ones, and provides a more reflective, political analysis of the epic war which lasted from the December 2, 1956, arrival of the *Granma* on Cuban shores, to the triumph of the Cuban Revolution on January 1, 1959.

Authorized and meticulously revised by the Che Guevara Studies Center of Havana, Cuba, with extraordinary photographs of the period, this edition of *Reminiscences of the Cuban Revolutionary War* is the most authoritative ever to be published.

Ocean Press

BIOGRAPHICAL NOTE ON ERNESTO CHE GUEVARA

One of *Time* magazine's "icons of the century," Ernesto Guevara de la Serna was born in Rosario, Argentina, on June 14, 1928. He made several trips around Latin America during and immediately after his studies at medical school in Buenos Aires, including his 1952 journey with Alberto Granado, on the unreliable Norton motorbike described in his earlier journal *The Motorcycle Diaries*.

He was already becoming involved in political activity and living in Guatemala when, in 1954, the elected government of Jacobo Árbenz was overthrown in a CIA-organized military operation. Ernesto escaped to Mexico, profoundly radicalized.

Following up on a contact made in Guatemala, Guevara sought out the group of exiled Cuban revolutionaries in Mexico City. In July 1955, he met Fidel Castro and immediately enlisted in the guerrilla expedition to overthrow Cuban dictator Fulgencio Batista. The Cubans nicknamed him "Che," a popular form of address in Argentina.

On November 25, 1956, Guevara set sail for Cuba aboard the yacht *Granma* as the doctor to the guerrilla group that began the revolutionary armed struggle in Cuba's Sierra Maestra mountains. Within several months, he was appointed by

Fidel Castro as the first Rebel Army commander, though he continued ministering medically to wounded guerrilla fighters and captured soldiers from Batista's army.

In September 1958, Guevara played a decisive role in the military defeat of Batista after he and Camilo Cienfuegos led separate guerrilla columns westward from the Sierra Maestra (which he later described in *Reminiscences of the Cuban Revolutionary War*).

After Batista fled on January 1, 1959, Guevara became a key leader of the new revolutionary government, first as head of the Industrial Department of the National Institute of Agrarian Reform; then as president of the National Bank. In February 1961 he became minister of industry. He was also a central leader of the political organization that in 1965 became the Communist Party of Cuba.

Apart from these responsibilities, Guevara represented the Cuban revolutionary government around the world, heading numerous delegations and speaking at the United Nations and other international forums in Asia, Africa, Latin America, and the socialist bloc countries. He earned a reputation as a passionate and articulate spokesperson for Third World peoples, most famously at the conference at Punta del Este in Uruguay, where he denounced US President Kennedy's Alliance for Progress.

As had been his intention since joining the Cuban revolutionary movement, Guevara left Cuba in April 1965, initially to lead a Cuban-organized guerrilla mission to support the revolutionary struggle in the Congo. He returned to Cuba secretly in December 1965, to prepare another Cuban-organized guerrilla force for Bolivia. Arriving in Bolivia in November 1966, Guevara's plan was to challenge that country's military dictatorship and eventually to instigate a revolutionary movement that would extend throughout the continent of Latin America. The journal he kept during the Bolivian campaign became known as *The Bolivian Diary*. Che was wounded and captured by US-trained and run Bolivian counterinsurgency troops on October 8, 1967. The following day he was murdered and his body hidden.

Che Guevara's remains were finally discovered in 1997 and returned to Cuba. A memorial was built at Santa Clara in central Cuba, where he had won a major military battle during the revolutionary war.

El libro de los pasajes, por si otra
vez se puede editar, corregido y aumentado

"Here is the book *Reminiscences*, corrected and expanded, if at some other time it is to be republished." —Che Guevara

PREFACE

Aleida Guevara

Organizing Che's personal files a while back, my mother—searching for a document—found among my father's papers a hand-written note that said, "Here is the book *Reminiscences*, corrected and expanded, if at some other time it is to be republished."

The history of these recollections begins on May 8, 1963, when, for the first time, readers were able to get their hands on a book containing a collection of reminiscences written by Che about the Cuban revolutionary war (1956–59). The book itself was based on notes Che had made in his campaign diary. This was also the case with *The Motorcycle Diaries*, the young Ernesto's first book of recollections. Although written in a more distinctive, refined style, *Reminiscences of the Cuban Revolutionary War* maintained Che's early sparkle and dynamism. In the process, these reminiscences became a chronicle with considerable testimonial value and a document of priceless historical significance.

Che later corrected this text, with minor additions and editing and style changes, in case the decision was ever made to republish the book. Years later, the book was in fact reissued, and expanded with other material by Che—also from the same period—that had been published in magazines and newspapers. The new edition, however, appeared without the changes and corrections earlier indicated by Che.

In its work of recovering historical memory, and taking into account the inadequacies of previous editions, the Che Guevara Studies Center of Havana, Cuba, has decided to reissue the book. This time, the recommended changes have been duly incorporated, and the wishes Che expressed in that hand-written note have been fulfilled.

The book you hold in your hands is, therefore, much more precise and complete than previous editions. It also contains reproductions of Che's own marked-up copy of the original book.

The Che Guevara Studies Center takes great pleasure in presenting this book, considered one of Che's classics, that allows the reader to delve into extraordinary moments in the life of a legendary figure. The book is written in a clear and direct manner, highly characteristic of Che's narrative technique, and provides accounts of key moments in the guerilla struggle, led by men and women of Cuba immersed in their battle to conquer the future.

If Che is able to communicate with you through these singular sketches of revolutionary warfare, and especially with young readers who have not had the opportunity to read Che previously, then when you finish this book you will surely better understand the Cuban people and one of the most important periods in our revolutionary process. Above all, you will gain a sense of the human quality of those who fought in the struggle [against Batista], their fears and limitations, and, accordingly, their grandeur.

Reading each episode, we can actually feel ourselves alongside these fighters, sense their concerns, and enjoy their successes. We can discover a first-hand analysis of how the struggle developed and the diligence with which Che's guerrilla fighters undertook critical and self-critical analysis when they saw the need. Such an analysis will undoubtedly provide a message for those who seek to make revolutionary struggle their weapon of combat, and may also help them avoid the same errors.

From the first moment I read this book, the episode titled "The Murdered Puppy" has remained deeply etched in my memory. I have never been able to forget it; I can hear the puppy's yelp and feel the guilt of the guerrilla fighters. It cannot be denied that in combat decisions must be made in a matter of seconds; often the lives of many *compañeros* depend on the speed with which they are carried out. You can be sure you made the correct choice, but you cannot ignore the pain those decisions often inflict. All this remains with those who fight; indeed, they are human beings like you or me, or any other person, with all the complex feelings that make us individuals and allow us to feel part of the human community.

I hope that you enjoy and learn from this book, written as it was by someone who could be described as the chronicler of the final phase of my people's war of liberation. Face the ambushes, make the decisions, and fight for freedom alongside the combatants through the experiences of one of their most battle-hardened and beloved leaders. But when finishing this book, don't lay down your weapons. Today, the most useful weapons are knowledge and understanding — let us continue to fight, together, for a better world.

¡Hasta la victoria siempre! Ever onward to victory!

Aleida Guevara March
Havana, June 2005

Part 1

Reminiscences of the Cuban Revolutionary War

PROLOGUE

For a long time we have wanted to write a history of our revolution, illustrating its many and varied aspects. Many of the revolution's leaders have often expressed, privately or publicly, their desire to write such a history. But the tasks are many, the years go by, and the memory of the insurrection is dissolving into the past. These events have not yet been properly described, events which already belong to the history of the Americas.

For this reason, I present here a series of personal reminiscences of the skirmishes, attacks, and battles in which we all participated. I do not wish that this fragmentary history, based on memories and a few hasty notes, should be regarded as a full account. On the contrary, I hope that those who lived through each event will further elaborate.

The fact that during the entire struggle, I was limited to fighting at a given point on Cuba's map, evidently prevented me from participating in battles and events in other places. Still, I believe that to bring to life our revolutionary actions, and to do this with some order, I can best begin with the first battle—the only one Fidel Castro fought in that went against our forces—the surprise attack at Alegría de Pío.

There are many survivors of this battle and each of them is encouraged to fill out the story by contributing what they remember. I ask only that such a narrator be strictly truthful. They should not pretend, for their own aggrandizement, to have been where they were not, and they should be wary of inaccuracies. I ask that after writing a few pages — to the best of their ability, according to their disposition and education — they seriously criticize them, in order to remove every word not corresponding strictly with fact, or those where the facts are uncertain. With this intention, I myself begin my reminiscences.

Ernesto Che Guevara
[1963]

ALEGRÍA DE PÍO

Alegría de Pío is in Oriente province, Niquero municipality, near Cape Cruz, where on December 5, 1956, the dictatorship's forces surprised us.

We were exhausted from a trek that was not so much long as painful. We had landed on December 2, at a place known as Las Coloradas beach. We had lost almost all our equipment, and wearing new boots had trudged endlessly through saltwater swamps. Almost the entire troop was suffering open blisters on their feet; but boots and fungal infections were not our only enemies. We reached Cuba following a seven-day voyage across the Gulf of Mexico and the Caribbean Sea, without food, in a poorly maintained boat, almost everyone plagued by seasickness from not being used to sea travel. We left the port of Tuxpan on November 25, a day with a stiff wind when all sea travel was prohibited. All this had left its mark on our troop made up of raw recruits who had never seen combat.

All we had left of our equipment for war was nothing but our rifles, cartridge belts, and a few wet rounds of ammunition. Our medical supplies had vanished, and most of our backpacks had been left behind in the swamps. The previous night we had passed through one of the cane fields of the Niquero sugar mill, owned at the time by Julio Lobo. We had managed to satisfy our hunger and thirst by eating sugarcane, but lacking experience we had left a trail of cane peelings and bagasse. Not that the guards following our steps needed any trail, for it had been our guide—as we found out years later—who betrayed us and brought them to us. When we stopped to rest the night before, we let him go—an error we were to repeat several times during our long struggle until we learned that civilians whose backgrounds we did not know could not be trusted in dangerous areas. In the circumstances, we should never have permitted that false guide to leave.

By daybreak on December 5 only a few could take another step. On the verge of collapse, we would walk a short distance and then beg for a long rest. Thus debilitated, orders were given to halt on the edge of a cane field, in some bushes close to dense woods. Most of us slept through the morning hours.

At noon we noticed unusual activity. Piper planes as well as other small army and private aircraft began to circle. Some of our group continued peacefully cutting and eating sugarcane, not realizing they were perfectly visible to those flying the enemy planes, which were now circling at slow speed and low altitude. I was the troop physician and it was my duty to treat everyone's blistered feet. I recall my last patient that morning: his name was *compañero* Humberto Lamotte and it was to be his last day on earth. In my mind's eye I see how tired and anguished he was as he walked from my improvised first-aid station to his post, carrying in one hand the shoes he could not wear.

Compañero [Jesús] Montané and I were leaning against a tree talking about our respective children, eating our meager rations—half a sausage and two crackers—when we heard a shot. Within seconds, a hail of bullets—at least that's how it seemed to us, this being our baptism of fire—descended on our group of 82 men. My rifle was not one of the best; I had deliberately asked for it because I was in terrible physical condition due to a prolonged asthma attack I had endured throughout our whole maritime voyage, and I did not want to be held responsible for wasting a good weapon. I can hardly remember what followed; my memory is already hazy. After the initial burst of gunfire, [Juan] Almeida, then a captain, approached requesting orders, but there was no one to issue them. Later I was told that Fidel had tried in vain to gather everybody into the adjoining cane field, which could be reached just by crossing a boundary path. The surprise had been too great and the gunfire too heavy. Almeida ran back to take charge of his group. A *compañero* dropped a box of ammunition at my feet. I pointed to it, and he answered me with an anguished expression, which I remember perfectly, and which seemed to say, "It's too late for ammunition." He immediately took the path to the cane field. (He was later murdered by Batista's henchmen.)

This might have been the first time I was faced, literally, with the dilemma of choosing between my devotion to medicine and my duty as a revolutionary soldier. There, at my feet, was a backpack full of medicine and a box of ammunition. They were too heavy to carry both. I picked up the ammunition, leaving the medicine, and started to cross the clearing, heading for the cane field. I remember Faustino Pérez, on his knees in the bushes, firing his submachine gun. Near me, a *compañero* named [Emilio] Albentosa was walking toward the cane field. A burst of gunfire hit us both. I felt a sharp blow to my chest and a wound in my neck; I thought for certain I was dead. Albentosa, vomiting blood and bleeding profusely from a deep wound made by a .45-caliber bullet, screamed something like, "They've killed me," and began to fire his rifle although there was no one there. Flat on the ground, I said to Faustino, "I'm fucked," and Faustino, still shooting, looked at me and told me it was nothing, but I saw in his eyes he considered me as good as dead.

Still on the ground, I fired a shot toward the woods, on an impulse like that of my wounded companion. I immediately began to think about the best way to die, since in that minute all seemed lost. I remembered an old Jack London story in which the hero, aware that he is about to freeze to death in Alaskan ice, leans against a tree and prepares to die with dignity. That was the only thing that came to my mind. Someone, on his knees, shouted that we should surrender, and I heard a voice — later I found out it belonged to Camilo Cienfuegos — shouting, "No one surrenders here!" followed by a swear word. [José] Ponce approached me, agitated and breathing hard. He showed me a bullet wound that appeared to have pierced his lungs. He told me he was wounded and I replied, indifferently, that I was as well. Then Ponce, along with other unhurt *compañeros*, crawled toward the cane field. For a moment I was alone, just lying there waiting to die. Almeida approached, urging me to go on, and despite the intense pain I dragged myself into the cane field. There I saw the great *compañero* Raúl Suárez, whose thumb had been blown away by a bullet, being attended by Faustino Pérez, who was bandaging his hand. Then everything blurred — low-flying airplanes strafing the field, adding to the confusion — amid scenes that were at once Dantesque and grotesque, such as an overweight combatant trying to hide behind a single sugarcane stalk, or a man who kept yelling for silence in the din of gunfire, for no apparent reason.

A group was organized, headed by Almeida, including

Commander Ramiro Valdés, in that period a lieutenant, and *compañeros* [Rafael] Chao and [Reynaldo] Benítez. With Almeida leading, we crossed the last path among the rows of sugarcane and reached the safety of the woods. The first shouts of "Fire!" were heard from the cane field and columns of flame and smoke began to rise. But I can't be sure about that. I was thinking more of the bitterness of defeat and the imminence of my death.

We walked until darkness made it impossible to go on, and decided to lie down and go to sleep huddled together in a heap. We were starving and thirsty, the mosquitoes adding to our misery. This was our baptism of fire, December 5, 1956, on the outskirts of Niquero. Such was the beginning of forging what would become the Rebel Army.

THE BATTLE OF LA PLATA

An attack on a small army garrison at the mouth of the La Plata river in the Sierra Maestra produced our first victory. The effect was electrifying and traveled far beyond that rough region. It was like a call to attention, proving that the Rebel Army did in fact exist and was disposed to fight. For us, it reaffirmed our chances for final victory.

On January 14, 1957, a little more than a month after the surprise attack at Alegría de Pío, we came to a halt by the Magdalena river, which separates La Plata and a ridge beginning in the Sierra Maestra and ending at the sea. Fidel gave orders for target practice as some sort of training for our people — some of the men were using weapons for the first time in their lives. We bathed there as well — having ignored matters of hygiene for many days — and those who were able to do so changed into clean clothes. At that time we had 23 working weapons: nine rifles equipped with telescopic sights, five semiautomatic machine guns, four bolt-action rifles, two Thompson submachine guns, two submachine guns, and a 16-gauge shotgun.

That afternoon we climbed the last hill before reaching the environs of La Plata. We were following a narrow track, traveled by very few people, which had been marked out by machete especially for us by a peasant named Melquiades Elías. He had been recommended by our guide Eutimio [Guerra], who at that time was indispensable to us and seemed to be the epitome of the rebel peasant. He was later apprehended by [Joaquín] Casillas, however, who, instead of killing him, bought him off with an offer of $10,000 and a rank in the army if he managed to kill Fidel. Eutimio came close to fulfilling his part of the bargain, but lacked the courage to do so. He was nonetheless very useful to the enemy, informing them of the location of several of our camps.

At the time, Eutimio was serving us loyally. He was one of the many peasants fighting for their land in the struggle against the big landowners, and anyone who fought them also fought the Rural Guard, who did the landowners' bidding.

That day we took two peasants prisoner, who turned out to be relatives of our guide. One of them was released but we kept the other one as a precautionary measure. The next day, January 15, we sighted the La Plata army barracks, under construction and with zinc roofs. A group of half-dressed men were moving about, but we could nevertheless make out their enemy uniforms. Just before sundown, about 6 p.m., a boat came in; some soldiers got out and others climbed aboard. Because we could not quite figure out the maneuver, we postponed the attack to the following day.

We began watching the barracks from dawn on January 16. The coast-guard boat had withdrawn during the night and although we searched the area, no soldiers could be seen. At 3 p.m. we decided to approach the road along the river leading to the barracks and take a look. By nightfall we crossed the very shallow La Plata river and took up position on the road. Five minutes later we apprehended two peasants; one of them had a record as an informer. When we told them who we were and assured them that if they did not speak our intentions could not be guaranteed, they gave us some valuable information: the barracks held about 15 soldiers. They also told us that Chicho Osorio, one of the region's three most notorious foremen, was about to pass by; these foremen worked for the Laviti family estate. The Lavitis had built an enormous fiefdom, maintaining it through a regime of terror with the help of individuals like Chicho Osorio. Shortly afterward, the said Chicho showed up drunk, astride a mule, with a small Afro-Cuban boy riding behind him. Universo Sánchez, in the name of the Rural Guard, gave him the order to halt and Chicho rapidly replied, "mosquito." That was the password.

We must have looked like a bunch of pirates, but Chicho Osorio was so drunk we were able to fool him. Fidel stepped forward and in an indignant tone said he was an army colonel who had come to investigate why the rebels had not yet been liquidated. He bragged about having gone into the woods, which accounted for his beard. He added that what the army was doing was "trash." In a word, he cut the army's efficiency to pieces. Sheepishly, Chicho Osorio admitted that the guards spent all their time inside the barracks, eating and doing nothing but firing occasional useless rounds. He readily agreed that the rebels must be wiped out. We carefully began asking about who was friendly and unfriendly in the area and noted his replies, naturally reversing the roles: when Chicho called somebody a bad man we knew he was one of our friends, and so on. We had some 20 names and he was still jabbering away. He told us how he had killed two men, adding, "But my General Batista set me free at once." He spoke of having slapped two peasants who were "a little bad-mannered," adding that the guards were incapable of such action; they let the peasants talk without punishing them. Fidel asked Osorio what he would do if he ever caught Fidel Castro, and Osorio, with an explicit gesture, said that he would cut his ... off, and that the same went for Crescencio [Pérez]. "Look," he said, showing us his shoes, which were the same Mexican-made kind our troops wore, "these shoes belonged to one of those sons of ... we killed." There, without realizing it, Chicho Osorio signed his own death sentence. At Fidel's suggestion, he agreed to accompany us to the barracks in order to surprise the soldiers and prove to them they were badly prepared and were neglecting their duties.

Nearing the barracks, with Chicho Osorio in the lead, I was still not certain he had not wised up to our trick. But he kept on ingenuously, so drunk he could not think straight. After crossing the river again to approach the barracks, Fidel said that established military rules called for a prisoner to be tied up. Osorio did not resist and he went on, unwittingly, as a real prisoner. He explained to us that the only guards posted were at the entrance to the barracks under construction, and at the house of one of the other foremen named Honorio. Osorio guided us to a place near the barracks on the road to El Macío. *Compañero* Luis Crespo, now a commander, went on to scout around and returned saying that the foreman's report was correct. Crespo had seen the two barracks and the fiery ends of the guards' cigarettes.

We were just about ready to approach the barracks when we had to hide to let three soldiers on horseback go by. The men were driving a prisoner on foot like a mule. They passed close by me, and I remember the words of the poor peasant, "I'm just like one of you," and the answer by one of the men we later identified as Corporal Basol, "Shut up and keep walking or I'll whip you." We thought the peasant would escape danger by not being in the barracks when we attacked with our bullets, but the following day, when the soldiers heard of the attack, they brutally murdered him at El Macío.

We had 22 weapons ready for the attack. It was an important occasion, and we had very little ammunition. We had to take the army barracks at all costs, for failure meant wasting our ammunition, leaving us practically defenseless. *Compañero* Lieutenant Julio Díaz — who later died heroically at the battle of El Uvero — Camilo Cienfuegos, Benítez, and Calixto Morales, armed with semiautomatic machine guns, were to surround the palm-thatched quarters on the right side. Fidel, Universo Sánchez, Luis Crespo, Calixto García, [Manuel] Fajardo — today a commander with the same last name as our physician, Piti Fajardo, who was [later] killed in the Escambray — and myself, would attack the center. Raúl [Castro] with his squadron and Almeida with his would attack from the left.

We approached within 40 meters of the barracks. By the light of a full moon, Fidel initiated the gun battle with two bursts of machine-gun fire and all available rifles followed. Immediately, we demanded the enemy's surrender, but with no results. The murderer and informer Chicho Osorio was executed as soon as shooting broke out.

: The attack had begun at 2:40 a.m., and the guards put up a much fiercer resistance than we had expected. A sergeant, armed with an M-1, responded with fire every time we demanded their surrender. We were given orders to use our old Brazilian-type hand grenades. Luis Crespo threw his, and I mine, but they did not detonate. Raúl Castro threw a stick of dynamite and nothing happened. We then had no choice but to get close to the quarters and set them on fire, even at the risk of our own lives. Universo Sánchez made the first, futile attempt and Camilo Cienfuegos also failed. Finally, Luis Crespo and I got close to one of the buildings and this *compañero* set it alight. The light from the blaze showed us it was simply a storeroom full of coconuts, but we had intimidated the soldiers and they gave up the fight. One of them, trying to escape, ran right into Luis Crespo's rifle; Luis shot him in the chest, took the man's rifle, and continued firing into the house. Camilo Cienfuegos, sheltered behind a tree, fired on the fleeing sergeant and ran out of ammunition. The soldiers, almost defenseless, were being wounded mercilessly by our bullets. Camilo Cienfuegos was first into the quarters, on our side, where shouts of surrender could be heard.

We quickly took stock of our takings: eight Springfields, one Thompson machine gun, and about 1,000 rounds; we had fired approximately 500 rounds. In addition, we now had cartridge belts, fuel, knives, clothing, and some food. Casualties: they had two dead, five wounded, and we had taken three prisoners. Some, along with the informer Honorio, had fled. On our side, not a scratch.

We withdrew after setting fire to the soldiers' quarters and tending to the wounded as best we could — three of them were seriously wounded and we left them in the care of the prisoners. We were told after the final victory that they had died. One of the soldiers later joined the forces under Commander Raúl Castro, was promoted to lieutenant, and died in a plane accident after the war.

Our attitude toward the wounded was in stark contrast to

that of Batista's army. Not only did they kill our wounded men, they abandoned their own. Over time this difference had an effect on the enemy and it was a factor in our victory. Fidel ordered that the prisoners be given all available medicine to take care of the wounded. This decision pained me because, as a doctor, I felt the need to save all available medicine for our own troops. We freed all the civilians and at 4:30 a.m. on January 17 started for Palma Mocha, arriving at dawn and searching out the most inaccessible zones of the Sierra Maestra.

Our eyes met with a pitiful spectacle: the day before, an army corporal and one of the foremen had warned all the families in the area that the air force was going to bomb the entire zone, and an exodus — almost all the peasants — toward the coast had begun. No one knew of our presence in the area, so it was evidently a maneuver on the part of the foremen and the Rural Guard to take the land and belongings away from the peasants. But their lie had coincided with our attack and now became a reality. Terror reigned among the peasants and it was impossible for us to stop their flight.

This was the first victorious battle of the Rebel Army. This battle and the one following it were the only occasions in the life of our troop when we had more weapons than men. Peasants were not yet ready to join in the struggle, and communication with the urban bases was practically nonexistent.

THE BATTLE OF ARROYO DEL INFIERNO

The Arroyo del Infierno is a narrow, shallow river flowing into the Palma Mocha river. Walking along it, away from the Palma Mocha, and mounting the slopes of the bordering hills, we reached a small circular clearing where we found two peasant huts. Here we made camp, naturally leaving the huts unoccupied.

Fidel presumed that the army would come after us, locating our approximate position. With this in mind, he planned an ambush to capture some enemy soldiers, and to this end he posted the men.

Fidel watched our lines vigilantly, and checked and re-checked our defenses. Contour lines were marked irregularly every five or so meters up the hill. On the morning of January 19 we were reviewing the troops when there was an accident that could have had serious consequences. As a trophy from the battle of La Plata, I had taken a helmet from one of Batista's corporals, and I wore it with great pride. But when I went to inspect the troops, walking through open woods, the forward guards heard us coming in the distance and saw that someone wearing a helmet was leading the group. Fortunately, at that moment they were cleaning their weapons, and only Camilo

Cienfuegos's gun was working. He opened fire on us, and immediately realized his mistake. His first shot missed and then his machine gun jammed, preventing him from firing further. This incident was symptomatic of the state of high tension that prevailed as we waited for the relief that battle would bring. In such moments, even those with the strongest nerves feel a certain faint trembling in the knees, and everyone longs for the stellar moment of war: battle. None of us, however, wanted to fight; we did so out of necessity.

At dawn on January 22 we heard a few single shots from the direction of the Palma Mocha river, and this forced us to maintain even stricter discipline in our lines, to be more cautious, and to wait for the imminent arrival of the enemy.

Believing the soldiers to be nearby, we ate neither breakfast nor lunch. Some time before, the *guajiro* Crespo and I had found a hen's nest and we rationed the eggs, leaving one behind as is customary so the hen would continue to lay. That day, in light of the shots we had heard during the night, Crespo decided we should eat the last egg, and we did so. It was noon when we saw a human figure in one of the huts. At first we thought that one of the *compañeros* had disobeyed the order not to approach the huts. That was not the case: one of the dictatorship's soldiers was looking around. Then about six others appeared; some of them left, three remained in view. We saw the soldier on guard look about, pick a few weeds, put them behind his ears in an attempt at camouflage, then sit calmly in the shade; his face, clearly visible through the telescopic sight, showed no signs of fear. Fidel's opening shot shattered him; he managed to shout out something like, "*Ay, mi madre!*" then he fell over dead. The gun battle spread and the unfortunate soldier's two comrades fell. Suddenly, I noticed that in the hut closer to me another soldier was trying to hide from our fire. I could only see his legs, since from my elevated position the roof of the hut concealed his body. I fired at him and missed; the second shot caught the man full in the chest and he fell, leaving his rifle pierced in the ground by the bayonet. Covered by the *guajiro* Crespo, I reached the house and saw the body; I took his bullets, his rifle, and a few other belongings. The man had been struck full in the chest, the bullet probably piercing his heart, and his death had been instantaneous; he already showed the first signs of rigor mortis, perhaps because of the exhaustion of his last day's march.

The battle was extraordinarily fast and soon, our plan successfully executed, we all withdrew.

Taking inventory, we found that we had spent approximately 900 bullets and had retrieved 70 from a full cartridge case. We also acquired a machine gun, a Garand, which was given to Commander Efigenio Ameijeiras, who used it for a good part of the war. We counted four enemy dead, but months later, after capturing an informer, we learned that five had actually been killed. It was not an absolute victory, but neither was it Pyrrhic. We had matched our forces against the enemy, in new conditions, and we had passed the test.

This improved our spirits greatly, and enabled us to continue climbing the whole day toward the most inaccessible reaches in order to escape pursuit by larger enemy groups. We reached the other side of the mountain. We were walking parallel to Batista's troop, also withdrawing, both groups having crossed the same mountain peak to reach the other side. For two days our troops and those of the enemy marched almost side by side without realizing it. Once, we slept in a hut that was barely separated from another housing the enemy, by a small river like the La Plata and a couple of bends in the road. The lieutenant commanding the enemy patrol was Sánchez Mosquera, whose name had become infamous throughout the Sierra Maestra in the wake of his pillaging. It is worth mentioning that the shots we had heard several hours before the battle had killed a peasant of Haitian descent who had refused to lead the troops to our hideout. If they had not committed this murder they would not have alerted us and found us waiting for them.

Once again, we were carrying too much weight; many of us had two rifles. Under these circumstances, it was not easy to walk, but clearly morale was different from what it had been after the disaster of Alegría de Pío. A few days earlier we had defeated a group smaller than ours, entrenched in a barracks; now we had defeated a column on the march, superior in numbers to our forces. We could all verify the importance of this type of battle to eliminate the enemy's forward guard, for without a forward guard, an army is paralyzed.

AIR ATTACK

After the victory over Sánchez Mosquera's forces, we walked along the La Plata's banks, and later, crossing the Magdalena river, returned to the already familiar region of Caracas. But the atmosphere was different from what we had experienced that first time, when we had been in hiding and the villagers had supported us. Now, Casillas's troops had passed through, sowing terror throughout the region. The peasants had gone, leaving only their empty huts and a few animals, which we sacrificed and ate. Experience had taught us it was not smart to stay in the houses, so after spending the night in one of the more isolated huts, we climbed back to the woods and pitched camp beside a small spring almost at the summit of Caracas peak.

It was there that Manuel Fajardo came to me and asked me if it were possible that we could lose the war. My response, quite aside from the euphoria of victory, was always the same: the war would unquestionably be won. He explained that he had asked me because the *gallego* Morán had told him that winning the war was impossible, that we were lost; he had urged Fajardo to abandon the campaign. I made Fidel aware of this, who told me that Morán had already let him know he was covertly testing the morale of the troops. We agreed that this was not the best approach, and Fidel made a short speech urging greater discipline and explaining the dangers that might arise if this discipline were disregarded. He also announced three crimes punishable by death: insubordination, desertion, and defeatism.

Our situation was not particularly happy in those days. The column lacked that spirit which is forged only through battle, and it was without a cohesive political consciousness. On one day, a *compañero* would leave us, on the next day another, and many requested assignments in the city that often entailed much more risk but that meant an escape from the rough conditions in the countryside. Still, our campaign continued on its course; the *gallego* Morán demonstrated indefatigable energy looking for food and making contact with the peasants in the immediate vicinity.

Such were our spirits on the morning of January 30, [1957]. Eutimio Guerra, the traitor, had earlier asked permission to visit his sick mother and Fidel had granted it, also giving him some money for the trip. According to Eutimio, his trip would last some weeks. We had not yet caught on to a series of incidents, but this man's subsequent behavior clearly explained them. When he rejoined the troop, Eutimio said that he had almost reached Palma Mocha when he realized government forces were on our trail. He had tried to get back to warn us but found only the bodies of the soldiers in Delfín [Torres's] hut, one of the peasants whose land became the scene of the battle of Arroyo del Infierno. Eutimio said he had followed our trail across the Sierra Maestra until he finally found us; but what had actually happened was that he had been taken prisoner. After being bribed with money and a military rank in exchange for murdering Fidel, he was now working as an enemy agent.

As part of this plan, Eutimio had left the camp the previous day and on the morning of January 30, after a cold night, just as we were getting up, we heard the roar of planes. We could not quite locate them since we were in the woods. Our field kitchen was some 200 meters below us near a small spring, where the forward guard was stationed. Suddenly, we heard the dive of a fighter plane, the rattle of machine-gun fire, and after a moment, the bombs. Our experience was very limited and we seemed to hear shots from all sides. Fifty-caliber bullets explode when they hit the ground and, although what we heard was machine guns firing from the air, as the bullets exploded near us they gave the impression of coming from the woods. Because of this, we thought we were being attacked by ground troops.

I was instructed to wait for members of the forward guard and to gather up some of the supplies we had dropped during the air attack. We were to meet the rest of the troop at the Cueva del Humo. My *compañero* was Chao, a veteran of the Spanish Civil War, and though we waited quite a while for some of the missing men, no one came. We followed the column along an indistinct track, both weighed down, until we came to a clearing and decided to rest. After a while, we noticed some noise and movement, and saw that our column's tracks were also being followed by Guillermo García (today a commander) and Sergio Acuña, both from the forward guard, who were trying to rejoin the group. After some deliberation, Guillermo García and I returned to the camp to see what was happening since the noise of the planes had faded. A desolate spectacle awaited us: with an eery precision that fortunately was not repeated during the war, the field kitchen had been attacked. The hearth had been smashed to pieces by machine-gun fire, and a bomb had exploded exactly in the center of the forward guard camp, just moments after our troops had left. The *gallego* Morán and a *compañero* had gone out to scout and Morán had returned alone, announcing that he had seen five planes in the distance but that there were no ground troops in the vicinity.

The five of us, with heavy loads, continued to walk through the bleak scene of our friends' burned-out huts. We found only a cat that miaowed at us pitifully and a pig that came out grunting when it heard us. We had heard of the Cueva del Humo, but did not know exactly where it was, so we spent the night in uncertainty, waiting to see our *compañeros* but fearing we would meet the enemy instead.

On January 31 we took up position on the top of a hill overlooking some cultivated fields, where we thought we would find the Cueva del Humo. We scouted around without finding anything. Sergio, one of the five, thought he saw two people wearing baseball caps, but he was slow in telling us and we could not catch up with them. We went out with Guillermo to explore the bottom of the valley near the banks of the Ají river, where a friend of Guillermo gave us something to eat, but the people there were very fearful. Guillermo's friend told us that all of Ciro Frías's merchandise had been taken by the guards and burned; the mules had been requisitioned and the mule driver killed. Ciro Frías's store was burned down and his wife taken prisoner. The men who had passed through in the morning were under Major Casillas's orders, who had slept somewhere near the house.

On February 1 we stayed in our little camp, practically in the open air, recovering from the exhaustion of the previous day's march. At 11 a.m. we heard gunfire on the other side of the hill and soon, closer to us, we heard desperate shouts, like someone crying out for help. With all this, Sergio Acuña's nerves seemed to snap, and silently, he left his cartridge belt and rifle, deserting the guard post he was assigned to. I noted in my campaign diary that he had taken with him a straw hat, a can of condensed milk, and three sausages; at the time we felt deeply for the can of milk and the sausages. A few hours later we heard some noise and prepared to defend ourselves, not knowing whether the deserter had betrayed us or not. But Crescencio appeared with a large column of almost all our men, and also some new people from Manzanillo led by Roberto Pesant. Missing from our forces were Sergio Acuña, the deserter, and *compañeros* Calixto Morales, Calixto García, and Manuel Acuña; also a new recruit [Evangelista Mendoza] who had been lost on the first day in the cross fire.

Once again we descended to the Ají river valley, and on the way some of the supplies from Manzanillo were distributed, including a surgical kit and a change of clothes for everyone. It moved us greatly to receive clothes which had [our] initials embroidered on to them by the girls of Manzanillo. The next day, February 2, two months after the *Granma* landing, we were a reunited, uniform group; 10 more men from Manzanillo had joined us and we felt stronger and in better spirits than ever. We had many discussions on what had caused the surprise air attack, and we all agreed that cooking by day and the smoke from the fire had guided the planes to our camp. For many months, and perhaps for the duration of the war, the memory of that surprise attack weighed heavily on the spirits of the troop. Right to the end, fires were not built in the open air during the day, for fear of unfavorable consequences.

We would have found it impossible to believe, and I think it did not enter anyone's mind, that the traitor and informer Eutimio Guerra had been in the observation plane, pointing out our location to Casillas. His mother's illness had been a pretext to leave us and join the murderer Casillas.

For some time to come, Eutimio played an important adverse role in the development of our liberation war.

SURPRISE ATTACK AT ALTOS DE ESPINOSA

After the surprise air attack described previously, we abandoned Caracas peak and attempted to return to familiar regions where we could establish direct contact with Manzanillo, receive more help from the outside, and better follow the situation in the rest of the country.

We turned back, crossing the Ají, and returned through territories familiar to all of us, until we reached the house of old Mendoza. With machetes, we had to open up paths along the ridges of the hills that had not been walked for many years, and our progress was very slow. We spent the nights in those hills, practically without food. I still remember, as though it were one of the great banquets of my life, when the *guajiro* Crespo turned up with a can of four pork sausages—a result of earlier savings—saying that they were for his friends. The *guajiro*, Fidel, myself, and someone else enjoyed the meager ration as if it were a lavish feast. The march continued until we reached the house, to the right of Caracas peak, where old Mendoza prepared us something to eat. Despite his fear, his peasant loyalty meant he welcomed us each time we passed through; such were the exigencies of friendship with Crescencio Pérez and other peasants who were his friends in the troop.

For me the march was excruciating—I was suffering a bout of malaria. Crespo and the unforgettable *compañero* Julio Zenón Acosta helped me complete the anguished march.

We never slept in the huts in that area; but my state and that of the famous *gallego* Morán, who took every opportunity to fall sick, meant that we had to sleep beneath a roof, while the rest of the troop kept watch in the vicinity, coming to the house only to eat.

We were forced to reduce the troop's size, as a group of men were suffering very low morale, and one or two were seriously wounded; among the latter were Ramiro Valdés (today minister of the interior), and one of Crescencio's sons, Ignacio Pérez, who later died heroically with the rank of captain. Ramirito [Ramiro Valdés] had been badly wounded in the knee, the same knee that had already been hit during the [1953] Moncada attack, so we had no choice but to leave him behind. A few other men also left, to the advantage of the troop. I remember one of them had an attack of nerves and began to shriek, there in the solitude of mountains and guerrillas, that he had been promised a camp with abundant food and antiaircraft defenses, but that now the planes were hounding him and he had neither a roof over his head, nor food, nor even water to drink. More or less, this was the impression new guerrillas had of campaign life. Those who stayed and survived the first tests grew accustomed to the dirt, the lack of water, food, shelter, and security, and to a life where the only things one could rely on were a rifle and the cohesion and resistance of the small guerrilla cell.

Ciro Frías arrived with some new recruits, bringing news that today makes us smile, but which at the time filled us with confusion. Díaz Tamayo was on the verge of switching allegiance and "making a deal" with the revolutionary forces; and Faustino had collected thousands and thousands of pesos. In short, subversion was spreading throughout the entire country and chaos was descending on the government. We also heard some sad news, but with important lessons in it. Sergio Acuña, the deserter of some days before, had gone home to some relatives. He began to brag to his cousins about his feats as a guerrilla. A certain Pedro Herrera overheard and denounced him to the Rural Guard. The infamous Corporal Roselló arrived, tortured him, shot him four times, and apparently hanged him. (The assassin's identity has never actually been verified.) This taught the men the value of cohesion and the futility of attempting to flee a collective destiny alone. But it also made it necessary for us to change camps, for presumably the young man had talked before being murdered, and he knew we were at Florentino's house.

There was a curious incident at that time and only later when we were fitting the evidence together did things become clear: Eutemio Guerra told us he had dreamed Sergio Acuña's death, and that in his dream, Corporal Roselló had killed him. This sparked a long philosophical discussion about whether dreams could really predict things to come. It was part of my daily work to explain cultural or political-type things to the men, so I tried to explain that it was not possible. Perhaps the dream could be explained by a huge coincidence, and anyway, we had all believed Sergio Acuña might meet his fate that way; we all knew Roselló was the man pillaging the region at that time. Universo Sánchez provided the key, suggesting that Eutimio was a "storyteller," and that the previous day when he had left the camp to get 50 cans of milk and a military lamp, someone had obviously told him about it.

One of those who insisted most strongly on the premonition was a 45-year-old illiterate peasant I have already mentioned: Julio Zenón Acosta. He was my first student in the Sierra Maestra; he was working hard to learn to read and write, and every time we stopped I would teach him a few letters of the alphabet; at that point we were learning the vowels. With great determination, not dwelling on past years but looking at those to come, Julio Zenón had set himself the task of becoming literate. Perhaps his example may be useful today to many peasants, to *compañeros* of his during the war, or to those who know his story. For Julio Zenón Acosta was another of our great *compañeros* at that time; he was a tireless worker, familiar with the region, always ready to help a combatant in trouble, or a combatant from the city who did not yet have the necessary reserves to get out of tight spots. He was the one to cart water from distant springs, the one to take a quick shot, the one to find dry kindling on days of rain and quickly build a fire. He was, in fact, our jack-of-all-trades.

One of the last nights before his treachery became known, Eutimio complained that he did not have a blanket, and asked Fidel if he would lend him one. It was cold in the heights of those mountains that February. Fidel answered that if he did so, they would both be cold, and suggested that they sleep under the same blanket and Fidel's two coats to keep warm. So Eutimio Guerra spent the whole night next to Fidel, with a .45 pistol from Casillas with which to kill him. He also had a pair of grenades to cover his retreat from the peak. He spoke to Universo Sánchez and me, both always near Fidel, about Fidel's guards, "I'm very concerned about those guards; it's so important to be careful."

We explained that there were three men posted nearby. We ourselves, veterans of the *Granma* and Fidel's trusted men, relieved each other through the night to protect Fidel personally. Thus, Eutimio spent the night beside the revolution's leader, holding his life at the point of a gun, awaiting the chance to assassinate him. But he could not bring himself to do it. That whole night, the fate of the Cuban Revolution depended, in large measure, on the twists and turns of a man's mind, on a balance of courage and fear, and, perhaps, on conscience, on a traitor's lust for power and wealth. Luckily for us, Eutimio's inhibitions were stronger, and the day broke without incident.

We had left Florentino's house and were camped in a ravine in a dry creek bed. Ciro Frías had gone home, relatively close by, and had brought back some hens and food, so that the long night of rain, virtually without shelter, was offset in the morning by hot soup and food. The news came that Eutimio had passed through as well. Eutimio came and went, for he was trusted by everyone. He had found us at Florentino's house and explained that after he had left to see his sick mother he had seen what had happened at Caracas, and had come after us to see what else had happened. He explained that his mother was now well. He was taking extraordinary, audacious risks. We were in a place called Altos de Espinosa, very close to a chain of hills—El Lomón, Loma del Burro, Caracas—which the planes strafed constantly. With the face of a soothsayer, Eutimio said, "Today, I tell you, they will strafe the Loma del Burro." The planes did in fact strafe the Loma del Burro, and Eutimio jumped for joy, celebrating his keen prediction.

On February 9, 1957, Ciro Frías and Luis Crespo left as usual to scout for food, and all was quiet. At 10 a.m., a peasant boy named [Emilio] Labrada, a new recruit, captured someone nearby. He turned out to be a relative of Crescencio and an employee in [León] Celestino's store where Casillas's soldiers were stationed. He informed us that there were 140 soldiers in the house; from our position we could in fact see them in the distance on a barren hill. Furthermore, the prisoner said he had talked with Eutimio who had told him that the following day the area would be bombed. Casillas's troops had moved, but he could not say exactly which direction they were going in. Fidel became suspicious; finally, Eutimio's strange behavior had come to our attention and speculation began.

At 1:30 p.m., Fidel decided to leave the area and we climbed to the peak, where we waited for our scouts. Ciro Frías and Luis Crespo soon arrived; they had seen nothing strange, everything was normal. We were talking about this when Ciro Redondo thought he saw a shadow moving, called for silence, and cocked his rifle. We heard one shot and then another. Suddenly the air was full of the shots and explosions of an attack, concentrated on our previous camp. The new camp emptied rapidly; afterward I learned that Julio Zenón Acosta would live for eternity at that hilltop. The uneducated peasant, the illiterate peasant, who had understood the enormous tasks the revolution would face after victory, and who was learning the alphabet to prepare himself, would never finish that task. The rest of us ran. My backpack, my pride and joy, full of medicine, reserve rations, books, and blankets, was left behind. I managed, however, to pick up a blanket from Batista's army, a trophy from La Plata, and ran.

Soon I met up with a group of our men: Almeida, Julito [Julio] Díaz, Universo Sánchez, Camilo Cienfuegos, Guillermo García, Ciro Frías, Motolá, Pesant, Emilio Labrada, and Yayo

[Reyes]. (There was one other in this group, though now I don't remember who it was.) We followed a circuitous path, trying to escape the shots, unaware of the fate of our other *compañeros*. We heard isolated explosions following on our heels; we were easy to follow since the speed of our flight meant we could not erase our traces. At 5:15 p.m., by my watch, we reached a rocky spot where the woods ended. After vacillating for a while we decided it was better to wait there until nightfall; if we crossed the clearing in daylight we would be spotted. If the enemy had followed our tracks, we were well placed to defend ourselves. The enemy, however, did not appear and we were able to continue on our way, guided unsurely by Ciro Frías who vaguely knew the region. It had been suggested that we divide into two patrols in order to ease the march and leave fewer signs. But Almeida and I were opposed to this, wanting to maintain the unity of the group. We realized we were at a place we knew called Limones, and after some hesitation, for some of the men wanted to continue, Almeida — who as a captain led the group — ordered us to continue to El Lomón, which Fidel had designated as our meeting point. Some of the men argued that Eutimio knew about El Lomón and that the army would therefore be waiting for us. We no longer had the slightest doubt that Eutimio was a traitor, but Almeida decided to comply with Fidel's order.

After three days of separation, on February 12, we met Fidel near El Lomón, at Derecha de la Caridad. There it was confirmed for us that Eutimio Guerra was the traitor, and we heard the whole story. It began after the battle of La Plata, when he was captured by Casillas and, instead of being killed, was offered a certain sum of money for Fidel's life. We learned that he had been the one to reveal our position in Caracas and that he had also given the order to attack the Loma del Burro by air, since that had been our itinerary (we had changed plans at the last minute). He had also organized the attack on the small hollow in the river canyon we were sheltered in, from which we saved ourselves with only one casualty because of the opportune retreat Fidel had ordered. Further, we had confirmation of the death of Julio Acosta and at least one enemy soldier. There were also a few wounded. I must confess that my gun caused neither deaths nor wounds, for I did nothing more than beat a high-speed "strategic retreat." We were once again reunited, our 12 (minus Labrada who had gone missing) and the rest of the group: Raúl, Ameijeiras, Ciro Redondo, Manuel Fajardo, [Juan Francisco] Echeverría, the *gallego* Morán, and Fidel—a total of 18 people. This was the "Reunified Revolutionary Army" of February 12, 1957. Some *compañeros* had been scattered, some raw recruits had abandoned us, and there was the desertion of a *Granma* veteran named Armando Rodríguez, who carried a Thompson submachine gun. In the last days, whenever he heard shots closing in from the distance, his face filled with so much horror and anguish that later we termed his the "hunted face." Each time a man revealed the face of a terrified animal, possessed by the terror our ex-*compañero* had shown in the days before Altos de Espinosa, we immediately foresaw an unfortunate outcome, for that "hunted face" was incompatible with guerrilla life. Someone with such a face "shifted into third," as we said in our new guerrilla slang; Rodríguez's machine gun later showed up in a peasant hut some distance away: his legs must have been blessed.

DEATH OF A TRAITOR

After this small army was reunited, we decided to leave the region of El Lomón and move to new ground. Along the way, we continued making contact with peasants in the area and laying the necessary groundwork for our subsistence. At the same time, we were leaving the Sierra Maestra and walking toward the plains, where we were to meet those involved in organizing the cities.

We passed through a village called La Montería, and afterward camped in a small grove of trees near a river, on a farm belonging to a man named Epifanio Díaz, whose sons fought in the revolution.

We sought to establish tighter contact within the July 26 Movement, for our nomadic and clandestine life made impossible any exchange between the two parts of the July 26 Movement. Practically speaking, these were two separate groups, with different tactics and strategies. The deep rift that in later months would endanger the unity of the movement had not yet appeared, but we could already see that our ideas were different.

At that farm we met with the most important figures in the urban movement. Among them were three women known today to all the Cuban people: Vilma Espín, now president of the Federation of Cuban Women and Raúl [Castro's] *compañera*;

Haydée Santamaría, now president of Casa de las Américas and Armando Hart's *compañera*; and Celia Sánchez, our beloved *compañera* throughout every moment of the struggle, who in order to be close to us later joined the guerrillas for the duration of the war. Another figure to visit was Faustino Pérez, an old acquaintance of ours, and a *compañero* from the *Granma*, who had carried out several missions in the city and came to report to us, before returning to continue his urban mission. (A short while later he was taken prisoner.)

We also met Armando Hart, and I had my only opportunity to meet that great leader from Santiago, Frank País.

Frank País was one of those people who command respect from the first meeting; he looked more or less as he appears in the photographs we have of him today, though his eyes were extraordinarily deep.

It is difficult, today, to speak of a dead *compañero* I met only once, whose history now belongs to the people. I can only say of him that his eyes revealed he was a man possessed by a cause, who had faith in it, and that he was clearly a superior kind of person. Today he is called "the unforgettable Frank País"; and for me, who saw him only once, that is true. Frank is another of the many *compañeros* who, had their lives not been cut short, would today be dedicating themselves to the common task of the socialist revolution. This loss is part of the heavy price the people have paid to gain their liberation.

Frank gave us a quiet lesson in order and discipline, cleaning our dirty rifles, counting bullets, and packing them so they would not get lost. From that day, I made a promise to take better care of my gun (and I did so, although I can't say I was ever a model of meticulousness).

That same grove of trees was also the scene of other events. For the first time we were visited by a journalist, and a foreign journalist at that — the famous [Herbert] Matthews, who brought to the conversation only a small box camera, with which he took the photos so widely distributed later and so hotly disputed in the stupid statements of a Batista minister. Javier Pazos acted as interpreter; he later joined the guerrillas and remained for some time.

Matthews, according to Fidel, for I was not present at the interview, asked unambiguous questions, none of them tricky, and he appeared to sympathize with the revolution. To the question of whether he was anti-imperialist, Fidel said he replied in the affirmative, and also that he objected to the [US] arms deliveries to Batista, insisting that these would not be used for continental defense but rather to oppress the people.

Matthews' visit was naturally very brief. As soon as he left us we were ready to move on. We were warned, however, to redouble our guard since Eutimio was in the area; Almeida was quickly ordered to find him and take him prisoner. Julito Díaz, Ciro Frías, Camilo Cienfuegos, and Efigenio Ameijeiras were also in the patrol. It was Ciro Frías who overcame Eutimio easily, and he was brought to us. We found a .45 pistol on him, three grenades, and a safe conduct pass from Casillas. Once captured with this incriminating evidence, he could not doubt his fate. He fell on his knees before Fidel and asked simply that we kill him. He said he knew he deserved to die. He seemed to have aged; there were a good many grey hairs at his temple I had never noticed before.

The moment was extraordinarily tense. Fidel reproved him harshly for his betrayal, and Eutimio wanted only to be shot, recognizing his guilt. None of us will forget when Ciro Frías, a close friend of Eutimio, began to speak. He reminded Eutimio of everything he had done for him, of the little favors he and his brother had done for Eutimio's family, and of how Eutimio had betrayed them, first by causing the death of Ciro's brother — who Eutimio had turned over to the army and who had been killed by them a few days before — and then by trying to destroy the whole group. It was a long, emotional tirade, which Eutimio listened to silently, his head bent. He was asked if he wanted anything and he answered that yes, he wanted the revolution, or better said us, to take care of his children.

The revolution has kept this promise. The name Eutimio Guerra resurfaces today in this book, but it has already been forgotten, perhaps even by his children. They go by another name and attend one of our many schools; they receive the same treatment as all the children of the country, and are working toward a better life. One day, however, they will have to know that their father was brought to revolutionary justice because of his treachery. It is also just that they know that the peasant — who in his craving for glory and wealth had been tempted by corruption and had tried to commit a grave crime — had nevertheless recognized his error. He had not even hinted at asking for clemency, which he knew he did not deserve. They should also know that in his last moments he remembered his children and asked our leader that they be treated well.

A heavy storm broke and the sky darkened. In the midst of the deluge, lightning streaking the sky, and the rumble of thunder, one lightning bolt struck followed closely by a clap of thunder, and Eutimio Guerra's life was ended. Even those *compañeros* standing near him could not hear the shot.

I remember a small episode as we were burying him the following day. Manuel Fajardo wanted to put a cross over his grave, but I didn't let him because such evidence of an execution would have been very dangerous for the owners of the property we were camped on. So he cut a small cross into the trunk of a nearby tree. And this is the sign marking the grave of the traitor.

The *gallego* Morán left us at that time; by then he knew how little we thought of him. We all considered him a potential deserter (he had disappeared once for two or three days with the excuse that he had been following Eutimio and had got lost in the woods). As we prepared to leave, a shot sounded and we found Morán with a bullet in the leg. Those who were nearby later sustained themselves with many heated discussions on this: some said the shot was accidental and others that he shot himself so he wouldn't have to follow us.

Morán's subsequent history — his treachery and his death at the hands of revolutionaries in Guantánamo — suggests he very probably shot himself intentionally.

When we had left, Frank País agreed to send a group of men in the first days of the following month, March. They were to join us at Epifanio Díaz's house, in the vicinity of El Jíbaro.

BITTER DAYS

The days following our departure from the house of Epifanio Díaz were for me, personally, the most grueling of the war. These notes are an attempt to give an idea of what the first part of our revolutionary struggle was like for all combatants. If, in this passage, more than any other, I have to refer to my own involvement, it is because it is related to later episodes. It would not be possible to separate the two without losing the continuity of the narrative.

After leaving Epifanio's house, our revolutionary group consisted of 17 men from the original army, and three new *compañeros*: Gil, Sotolongo, and Raúl Díaz. These three *compañeros* came on the *Granma*; they had been hiding for some time near Manzanillo and, hearing of our presence, had decided to join us. Their stories were the same as ours: they had been able to evade the Rural Guard by seeking refuge in the house of one peasant after another; they had reached Manzanillo and hidden there. Now they joined their fate to that of the whole column. In that period, as has been described, it was very difficult to enlarge our army; a few new men came, but others left. The physical conditions of the struggle were very hard, but the spiritual conditions even more so, and we lived with the feeling that we were constantly under siege.

We were walking slowly in no fixed direction, hiding among bushes in a region where the livestock had won out over the foliage, leaving only remnants of vegetation. One night on Fidel's small radio we heard that a *compañero* from the *Granma*, who had left with Crescencio Pérez, had been captured. We already knew about this from Eutimio's confession, but the news was not yet official; now at least we knew he was alive. It was not always possible to emerge with your life from an interrogation by Batista's army.

Every so often, from different directions, we heard machine-gun fire; the guards were shooting into the trees, which they often did. But although they expended considerable ammunition, they never actually entered these areas.

In my campaign diary I noted, on February 22, [1957], that I had the first symptoms of what could develop into a serious asthma attack, as I was without asthma medicine. The new date for the rendezvous was March 5, so we were forced to wait for a few days. We were walking very slowly, simply marking time until March 5, the day Frank País was to send us a group of armed men. We had already decided that first we had to fortify our small front before increasing it in numbers, and therefore, all available arms in Santiago were to be sent up to the Sierra Maestra.

One dawn found us on the banks of a small stream where there was almost no vegetation. We spent a precarious day there, in a valley near Las Mercedes, which I believe is called La Majagua (names are now a little vague in my memory). By night we arrived at the house of old Emiliano, another of the many peasants who in those days felt the shock of fear each time they saw us, but who nevertheless risked their lives for us valiantly, contributing to the development of our revolution. It was the wet season in the Sierra Maestra and we were soaked every night, which is why we entered the homes of peasants, despite the danger, because the area was infested with soldiers.

My asthma was so bad I could not move very well, and we had to sleep in a little coffee grove, near a peasant hut, where we regrouped our forces. On the day I am describing, February 27 or 28, censorship in the country was lifted and the radio streamed news of everything that had happened during the past months. They spoke of terrorist acts and of the Matthews interview with Fidel; it was then that [Batista's] minister of defense made his famous statement that the Matthews interview had never taken place, and challenged him to publish the photos.

Hermes, the son of old Emiliano, was a peasant helping us with meals and pointing out paths we should take. But on the morning of February 28 he did not appear as he usually did, and Fidel ordered us to evacuate immediately and post ourselves where we could overlook the roads, as we did not know what would happen. At about 4 p.m., Luis Crespo and Universo Sánchez were on watch, and the latter saw a large troop of soldiers coming along the road from Las Vegas, preparing to occupy the crest. We had to run quickly to the top of the hill and cross to the other side before the troops blocked our path, which was not difficult, given that we had seen them in time. The mortars and machine guns were beginning to sound in the direction we came from, proving that Batista's army was aware of our presence. Everybody was able to reach the peak easily, and pass over it; but for me it was a tremendous effort. I made it to the top, but with such an asthma attack that each step was difficult. I remember how much work Crespo put in to help me when I could not go on and pleaded they leave me behind. The *guajiro*, in that particular language among the troops, said to me, "You Argentine son of a ...! You'll walk or I'll hit you with my rifle butt." With everything he was already carrying, he virtually carried both me and my pack, as we made it over the hill with a heavy downpour against our backs.

That is how we reached a small peasant hut and learned we were in a place called Purgatorio. Fidel passed himself off as Major [Armando] González of Batista's army, supposedly searching for the insurgents. The owner, coldly courteous, offered us his house and waited on us. But there was another man there, a friend from a neighboring hut, who was an extraordinary groveler. Because of my physical state I could not fully enjoy that delicious dialogue between Fidel in the role of Major González and the peasant, who offered him advice and wondered aloud why that *muchacho*, Fidel Castro, was in the hills fighting.

We had to make a decision, because it was impossible for me to continue. When the indiscreet neighbor had left, Fidel told the owner of the house who he really was. The man embraced him immediately, saying he was a supporter of the Orthodox Party, that he had always followed [Eduardo] Chibás, and was at our service. We had to send the man to Manzanillo to establish contact or at least to buy medicine, and I had to be left near the house without his wife knowing or suspecting I was there.

The last combatant to join our group, of doubtful character but great strength, was assigned to stay with me. Fidel, in a generous gesture, gave me a Johnson repeater, one of the treasures of our group, to defend ourselves with. We all pretended to leave in one direction, and after a few steps my companion (who we called "El Maestro") and I disappeared into the woods to reach our hiding place. News of the day was that Matthews had been interviewed by telephone and announced that the famous photographs would be published. Díaz Tamayo had countered that this could never happen, since no one could ever have crossed the army lines surrounding the guerrillas. Armando Hart was in prison, accused of being second-in-command of the movement. It was February 28.

The peasant carried out his task and brought me sufficient adrenalin. Then came 10 of the most bitter days of struggle in the Sierra Maestra: walking, supporting myself from tree to tree or on the butt of my rifle, accompanied by a frightened *compañero* who trembled each time we heard shots and who became nervous each time my asthma made me cough in some dangerous spot. It was 10 long days of work to reach Epifanio's house once again, which normally took little more than one. The date for the meeting had been March 5, but it had been impossible for us to get there. Because of the army line and the impossibility of rapid movement, we did not arrive at Epifanio Díaz's welcoming house until March 11.

The inhabitants of the house informed us of what had happened. Fidel's group of 18 men had mistakenly split up when they thought they were going to be attacked by the army, in a place called Altos de Meriño. Twelve men had gone on with Fidel and six with Ciro Frías. Later, Ciro Frías's group had fallen into an ambush, but they all came out of it unhurt and met up again nearby. Only one of them, Yayo, who returned without his rifle, had passed by Epifanio Díaz's house on his way toward Manzanillo. We learned everything from him. The troop Frank was sending was ready, although Frank himself was in prison in Santiago. We met with the troop's leader, Jorge Sotús, who held the rank of captain. He had not made it on March 5 because news of the new group had spread and the roads were heavily guarded. We made all the necessary arrangements for the rapid arrival of the new recruits, who numbered around 50 men.

REINFORCEMENTS

On March 13, [1957], while we waited for the new revolutionary troop, we heard over the radio that there had been an attempt to assassinate Batista; they listed the names of some of the patriots killed in the assault. First, there was the student leader José Antonio Echeverría; then there were others, like Menelao Mora. People not involved in the attempt also died. The following day we learned that Pelayo Cuervo Navarro, a militant from the Orthodox Party who had always stood firmly against Batista, had been assassinated and his body abandoned in the aristocratic residential area of the country club known as El Laguito. It is worth noting, as an interesting paradox, that the murderers of Pelayo Cuervo Navarro, and the sons of the dead man, joined together in the failed [1961] Bay of Pigs invasion to "liberate" Cuba from "communist disgrace."

Despite the veil of censorship, some details of this unsuccessful attempt on Batista's life—which the Cuban people remember well—got through. Personally, I had not known the student leader, but I had known his friends in Mexico, when the July 26 Movement and the Revolutionary Directorate had agreed to joint action. These *compañeros* were Commander Faure Chomón, who today is ambassador to the Soviet Union, Fructuoso Rodríguez, and Joe Westbrook, all of whom participated in the attack. As is well known, the men had almost made it to the dictator on third floor, but what could have been a successful takeover instead became a massacre of all those who could not escape the trap the presidential palace had become.

Our reinforcements were scheduled to arrive on March 15. We waited long hours in the agreed place, a river bend in the canyon. It was an easy wait in hiding, but no one arrived. Afterward they explained that there had been some difficulties. They arrived at dawn on March 16, so tired they could barely walk the few steps to the trees where they could rest until daybreak. They came in trucks owned by a rice farmer from the area who, frightened by the implications of his act, went into exile in Costa Rica. He later returned by plane flying arms into Cuba, transformed into a hero; his name was Hubert Matos.

The reinforcement was about 50 men, of whom only 30 were armed. They brought two machine guns, one Madzen, and one Johnson. After a few months of living in the Sierra Maestra, we had become veterans, and we saw in the new troop all the defects those who came on the *Granma* had displayed: lack of discipline, inability to adjust to the bigger hardships, lack of decision, incapacity to adapt to this life. The group of 50 was led by Jorge Sotús, with the rank of captain, and was divided into five squadrons of 10 men, whose leaders were lieutenants; they had been assigned these ranks by the movement in the plains, and these still awaited ratification. The squadron leaders were a *compañero* named Domínguez, who I believe was killed in Pino del Agua a little while later; *compañero* René Ramos Latour, an urban militia organizer, who died heroically in battle during the last days of the dictatorship's final offensive; Pedrín Soto, our old *compañero* from the *Granma*, who finally managed to join us and who also died in battle on the "Frank País" Second Eastern Front, and who was posthumously promoted to commander by

Raúl Castro; also, *compañero* Pena, a student from Santiago who reached the rank of commander and took his own life after the revolution; and Lieutenant Hermo, the only squadron leader to survive the almost two years of war.

Of all the new troop's problems, difficulty marching was one of their greatest. Their leader, Jorge Sotús, was one of the worst, and he constantly lagged behind, setting a bad example for the troop. I had been ordered to take charge of the troop, but when I spoke about this with Sotús, he argued that he had orders to turn the men over to Fidel, and that as long as he was leader, he could not turn them over to anyone else, etc., etc. I still had a complex then about being a foreigner, and did not want to take extreme measures, although I noticed a great uneasiness in the troop. After several short marches, which nevertheless became very long due to the men's poor preparation, we reached a place at La Derecha where we were to wait for Fidel. There we met the small group of men who had been separated from Fidel earlier: Manuel Fajardo, Guillermo García, Juventino, Pesant, the three Sotomayor brothers, and Ciro Frías.

The enormous difference between the two groups was clear: ours was disciplined, compact, war-practiced; that of the raw recruits was still suffering the sickness of the first days. They were not used to eating one meal a day, and if the ration did not taste good they would not eat it. Their packs were full of useless things, and if they weighed too heavily on their backs they preferred, for example, to give up a can of condensed milk than a towel (a crime of lèse-guerrilla). We took advantage of this by collecting all the cans of food they left along they way. After we were installed in La Derecha the situation became highly tense because of constant friction between Jorge Sotús—an authoritarian spirit who had no rapport with the men—and the troop in general. We had to take special precautions and René Ramos, whose nom de guerre was Daniel, was put in charge of the machine-gun squadron at the entrance of our refuge so we had a guarantee nothing would happen.

Some time later, Jorge Sotús was sent on a special mission to Miami. There he betrayed the revolution by meeting with Felipe Pazos, whose immeasurable ambition for power made him forget his obligations, and who set himself up as provisional president in a cooked-up intrigue in which the US State Department played an important role.

With time, Captain Sotús showed signs of wanting to redeem himself and Raúl Castro gave him the opportunity, which the revolution has denied no one. He began, however, to conspire against the revolutionary government and was condemned to 20 years in prison, escaping thanks to the complicity of one of his guards who fled with him to the ideal haven of *gusanos* [right-wing Cuban exiles]: the United States.

At the time, however, we tried to help him as much as possible, to iron out his disagreements with the new *compañeros*, and to explain to him the need for discipline. Guillermo García went to the region of Caracas in search of Fidel, while I made a little trip to pick up Ramiro Valdés, more or less recovered from his leg wound. On the night of March 24, Fidel arrived with 12 *compañeros* who at that time stuck firmly by his side, and the sight was impressive. There was a notable difference between the *barbudos* [bearded men], with packs made of any available material and tied together whichever way possible, and the new combatants with clean uniforms, clean-shaven faces, and clean backpacks. I explained the problems we had encountered to

Fidel and a small council was established to decide on future plans. The council was made up of Fidel, Raúl, Almeida, Jorge Sotús, Ciro Frías, Guillermo García, Camilo Cienfuegos, Manuel Fajardo, and myself. Fidel criticized my behavior in not exercising the authority conferred on me, but leaving it in the hands of the recently arrived Sotús, against whom there was no animosity but whose attitude, in Fidel's opinion, should not have been tolerated. The new platoons were also organized, integrating the entire troop and forming three groups under the direction of captains Raúl Castro, Juan Almeida, and Jorge Sotús; Camilo Cienfuegos would lead the forward guard and Efigenio Ameijeiras the rear guard; I was general staff physician and Universo Sánchez functioned as general staff squadron leader.

Our troop reached a new excellence with these additional men. We had also received two more machine guns, although they were of doubtful efficiency since they were old and poorly maintained. Nevertheless, we were now a considerable force. We discussed what action we should take immediately; my feeling was that we should attack the first possible enemy post in order to temper the new men in battle. But Fidel and all the other council members thought it better to march for some time so they could get used to the rigors of life in the jungle and the mountains, and the long marches through rugged hills. So we decided to move eastward and walk as much as possible, looking for a chance to surprise a group of soldiers after having some elementary training in guerrilla warfare.

The troop prepared itself enthusiastically and left to fulfill its tasks. Its baptism of blood was to be the battle of El Uvero.

TEMPERING THE MEN

The months of March and April 1957 were months of restructuring and apprenticeship for the rebel troops. After receiving reinforcements at La Derecha, our army had some 80 men and was organized as follows: The forward guard, directed by Camilo, had four men. The next platoon was led by Raúl Castro and had three lieutenants; they were Julito Díaz, Ramiro Valdés, and Nano Díaz, each of whom had a squadron. (The two *compañeros* named Díaz, both of whom died heroically at El Uvero, were not related. One was a native of Santiago; today, the Díaz Brothers refinery in that city honors the memory of Nano and his brother who fell in Santiago de Cuba. The other, a *compañero* from Artemisa, a veteran of the *Granma* and of Moncada, completed his final mission at El Uvero.) With Captain Jorge Sotús were lieutenants Ciro Frías (later killed on the "Frank País" Second Eastern Front), Guillermo García (today head of the western army), and René Ramos Latour (who died after attaining the rank of commander in the Sierra Maestra). Then came the general staff or command post, which was made up of Fidel as commander-in-chief, Ciro Redondo, Manuel Fajardo (today a commander in the army), Crespo (commander), Universo Sánchez (commander), and myself as doctor.

The platoon that customarily followed in the column's line

was Almeida's, then a captain, whose lieutenants were Hermo, Guillermo Domínguez (killed in Pino del Agua), and [Hermes] Peña. Efigenio Ameijeiras, a lieutenant, and three men, closed the column and made up the rear guard.

In light of our group's dimensions, squadrons began to cook for themselves and to distribute food, medicine, and ammunition. In almost all the squadrons, and certainly in all the platoons, veterans taught new men the art of cooking, or getting the best flavor out of the food available; the art of packing a backpack; and how to march in the Sierra Maestra.

The road between La Derecha, El Lomón, and El Uvero can be covered by car in a few hours, but for us it meant months of slow, cautious walking, pursuing our principal mission of preparing the men for combat and life after it. That was how we again passed through Altos de Espinosa, where veterans formed a guard of honor around the grave of Julio Zenón, who had fallen there some time before. There I found a piece of my blanket, tangled in the brambles as a reminder of my "strategic retreat" made at full speed. I put it in my pack, firmly resolving never again to lose my equipment in that manner.

I was assigned a new recruit, Paulino [Fonseca], as an assistant to carry the medical supplies. This eased my task a little so that for a few minutes each day after our long marches I could attend to our troop's health. We again passed through the Caracas peak, site of such a disagreeable encounter with enemy planes, thanks to Guerra's treachery. We found a rifle, left behind by one of our men after the battle of La Plata, in order to retreat more easily. By now we had no extra rifles; on the contrary, we were short. We were in a new phase. There had been a qualitative change; the enemy now avoided an entire zone for fear of encountering us, although it's true we also showed little interest in clashing with them.

The political situation in those days was pregnant with the nuances of opportunism. The well-known voices of Pardo Llada, Conte Agüero, and other vultures of the same ilk specialized in demagogic outbursts calling for harmony and peace, and criticizing the government—timidly. The government had spoken of peace; the new prime minister, Rivero Agüero, indicated that if necessary he would go to the Sierra Maestra to gain peace for the country. Nevertheless, a few days later, Batista declared it was not necessary to speak with Fidel or the insurgents; that Fidel Castro was not in the Sierra Maestra and neither was anyone else; and that, therefore, there was no reason to talk with "a bunch of bandits."

So Batista's group showed its willingness to continue the fight, the only thing on which we easily agreed, for it was also our intent to continue at any price. A new chief of operations was named, Colonel [Pedro] Barrera, well known for embezzling army rations funds. He later calmly watched the destruction of the Batista phenomenon from Caracas, Venezuela, where he was military attaché.

We had some nice characters with us then, useful in creating almost commercial-scale advertising for our movement in the United States. Two of them in particular brought a few inconveniences as well. Three Yankee *muchachos* had escaped their parents at the Guantánamo naval base to join our fight. Two of them never heard a shot in the Sierra Maestra, and, exhausted by the climate and the privations, they left, taken by the journalist Bob Taber. The third participated in the battle of El Uvero but after that he also left, sick, but having fought in a battle. The boys were not politically prepared for a revolution and were simply satiating their thirst for adventure in our company. We watched them go with affection, but also with relief, especially me, for as the doctor it frequently fell on my shoulders to take care of them, because they could not stand the rigors of our life.

At the same time, the government took some journalists up in a military plane to prove to them that there was no one in the Sierra Maestra. It was a strange operation, convincing no one, but it demonstrated the methods by which Batista's government deceived public opinion, with the help of men like Conte Agüero who disguised themselves as revolutionaries and lied to the people on a daily basis.

During those trying days, a canvas hammock finally came my way. The hammock is a precious thing I had not received earlier because of strict guerrilla law stating that canvas hammocks can only be given to those who had already made their own out of sacking, in order to combat idleness. Anyone could make themselves a hammock out of sacking, by which they gained the right to the next canvas one that came along. I could not sleep in the sack hammock, however, because of my allergies: the lint affected me greatly, and I was obliged to sleep on the ground. Since I did not have a hammock of sacking, I was not entitled to one of canvas. These small, daily details were part of the individual dramas each guerrilla faced alone. But Fidel noticed, broke the rule, and awarded me a hammock. I will always remember that it was on the banks of the La Plata, in the last foothills before reaching Palma Mocha, and it was one day after we ate our first horse.

The horse was more than a luxury meal; it was also a kind of trial by fire for the men's capacity to adapt. The peasants in our group were indignant and refused to eat their ration of meat; some considered Manuel Fajardo was almost a murderer, for as a butcher in peacetime he was chosen to slaughter the first animal.

This first horse belonged to a peasant named Popa, from the other side of the La Plata. Popa should know how to read by now, after the [1961 Cuban] literacy campaign, and if he sees the magazine *Verde Olivo* he will remember that night when three sinister-looking rebels banged on the door of his hut and, unjustly mistaking him for an informer, took his old horse with large harness sores across its back. Hours later this animal was to be our meager ration and its meat would constitute an exquisite banquet for some and a test for the prejudiced stomachs of the peasants, who believed they were committing an act of cannibalism as they chewed up man's old friend.

A FAMOUS INTERVIEW

In mid-April 1957 we returned with our mountain army-in-training to the region of Palma Mocha, near Turquino peak. During that period our most valuable men for fighting in the mountains were those of peasant stock.

Guillermo García and Ciro Frías, with patrols of peasants, came and went from place to place in the Sierra Maestra, bringing news, scouting, getting food; in a word, they were the mobile forward guard of our column. We were once again in the region of Arroyo del Infierno, the site of one of our battles, and peasants who came to greet us described the tragic details of that attack: which man exactly had led the soldiers directly to our camp; who had died. In fact, the peasants, well versed in the art of the gossip, amply informed us of all the life of the region.

Fidel, who had no radio in those days, asked to borrow one from a local peasant, who agreed, and so on a large radio carried in a combatant's backpack we were able to hear the news direct from Havana. They were once again speaking with a certain truth and clarity, because of the reestablishment of the so-called [civil] guarantees.

Guillermo García, brilliantly disguised as a Batista army corporal, and two *compañeros* disguised as army soldiers, went to look for the informer who had led the army to us. They brought him back the following day "on the colonel's order." The man had been tricked, but when he saw the ragged army he knew what awaited him. With great cynicism he told us everything about his relations with the army and how he had told "that bastard Casillas" that he would be perfectly willing to take the army to where we were and capture us, for he had spied on us; they had not, however, listened to him.

On one of those days, in one of those hills, the informer was killed and his remains buried on a ridge of the Sierra Maestra. We received a message from Celia announcing she was coming with two North American journalists who wanted to interview Fidel, under the pretext of seeing the three little gringos. She also sent some money collected from sympathizers of the movement.

It was decided that Lalo Sardiñas would bring the North Americans in through the region of Estrada Palma, which he knew well as a former merchant in the region. We were dedicating our time to making contact with peasants who could serve as links and who could maintain permanent camps to use as contact centers for the whole region, which was growing in size. We located houses to use as supply centers for our troops, and set up warehouses from which we drew supplies as we needed them. These places also served as rest stops for the fast human stagecoaches that moved along the edge of the Sierra Maestra carrying messages and news.

These messengers had an extraordinary ability to cover very long distances in very little time, and we constantly found ourselves fooled by their version of "a half-hour's walk" or "just over there." For the peasants this was almost always spot on, even though their concept of time and the length of an hour had little to do with that of a city dweller.

Three days after the order was given to Lalo Sardiñas, we heard news that six people were coming up through the region of Santo Domingo: two women, two gringos—the journalists—and two others no one knew. We also received some contradictory news, however, to the effect that the Rural Guard had discovered their presence through an informer, and had surrounded a house they were staying in.

News travels with extraordinary speed in the Sierra Maestra, but it is also distorted. Camilo went out with a platoon, with the order to free the North Americans and Celia Sánchez at all costs; we knew Celia was coming with the group. They arrived, however, safe and sound. The false alarm was due to enemy troop movements provoked by an informant, which in those days was easy to find among backward peasants.

On April 23, the journalist Bob Taber and a photographer arrived at our camp. With them came *compañeras* Celia Sánchez and Haydée Santamaría and the men sent by the movement in the plains: Marcos or "Nicaragua"—Commander [Carlos] Iglesias—today governor of Las Villas and in those days in charge of armed actions in Santiago; and Marcelo Fernández, who was coordinator of the movement and today is president of the National Bank. As he knew English, he acted as interpreter.

The days went according to schedule; we tried to demonstrate our strength to the North Americans and evade their more indiscreet questions. We knew nothing about these journalists; still, they interviewed the three boys who answered their questions very well, demonstrating the new spirit they had developed in the primitive life among us, despite their difficulty in adjusting and the fact that we had little in common.

We were also joined by one of the dearest and most likable figures of our revolutionary war, "Vaquerito" [Roberto Rodríguez]. Together with another *compañero*, Vaquerito found us one day saying he had spent over a month looking for us, and that he was from Morón in Camagüey. As always in such cases, we interrogated him, and then gave him the rudiments of a political orientation, a task that frequently fell to me. Vaquerito did not have a political idea in his head, and did not seem to be anything other than a happy and healthy young man, who saw all of this as a marvelous adventure. He came barefoot and Celia lent him an extra pair of her shoes, which were leather and the kind worn in Mexico. Owing to his small stature, they were the only shoes that fit him. With the new shoes and a large straw hat, he looked like a Mexican cowboy or *vaquero*, and that is how the nickname Vaquerito was born.

As is well known, Vaquerito did not see the end of the revolutionary struggle, for as head of the "suicide squad" of Column No. 8, he died one day before Santa Clara was taken. Of his life among us, we all remember his extraordinary joyfulness, his uninterrupted joviality, and the strange and romantic way he confronted danger. Vaquerito was an amazing liar; perhaps he never had a conversation in which he did not adorn the truth so much that it was practically unrecognizable. But as a messenger, which he was in the early days, and later as a combatant or as head of the "suicide squad," Vaquerito demonstrated that for him, there was no precise border between reality and fantasy, and the same acts his agile mind invented he was able to carry out on the battlefield. His extreme bravery had become legend by the time our epic war was over, which he did not live to see.

It occurred to me once, after one of the nightly reading sessions sometime after he had joined us, to question Vaquerito. He began to tell us about his life, and we began surreptitiously calculating his age, pencils in hand. When he finished, after many witty anecdotes, we asked him how old he was. Vaquerito was a little over 20, but adding up all of his deeds and jobs, it seemed that he had started working five years before he was born.

Compañero Nicaragua brought news of more weapons in Santiago—remnants of the assault on the presidential palace. He reported there were 10 machine guns, 11 Johnson machine guns, and six short carbines. There were a few more, but plans were under way to open another front in the region of the Miranda sugar mill. Fidel opposed this idea and only allowed a few arms for the second front, giving orders that all possible weapons be brought up to reinforce ours. We continued marching, distancing ourselves from the uncomfortable company of some guards who were marauding nearby. But first we decided to climb Turquino. The ascent of our highest mountain had an almost mystical meaning for us, and anyway, we were already quite close to the peak.

The entire column climbed Turquino peak and up there we finished the interview with Bob Taber. He was preparing a film that was later televised in the United States, at a time when we were not feared so much. (One illustrative note: a peasant who joined us told us that Casillas had offered him 300 pesos and a pregnant cow if he killed Fidel. The North Americans were not the only ones wrong about the price of our highest commander.)

According to an altimeter we had, Turquino peak was 1,850 meters above sea level. I note this as an incidental point—for we never properly tested the instrument—but at sea level it worked well and this figure differs substantially from that given in official records.

Since the army was on our heels, Guillermo was sent with a group of *compañeros* as snipers. Thanks to my asthma I had no extra strength, and was obliged to walk at the end of the column; I was also relieved of the Thompson submachine gun I was carrying. About three days passed before I got it back, which were some of the most bitter days in the Sierra Maestra for me, for I was unarmed while every day there was the possibility of encounters with the enemy.

In May 1957, two of the North American boys abandoned the column with the journalist Bob Taber, who had finished his story, and they reached Guantánamo safe and sound. We continued to march slowly along the ridge of the Sierra Maestra and its slopes. We were making contacts, exploring new regions, and spreading the revolutionary flame and the legend of our *barbudos* across the Sierra Maestra. The new spirit was communicated far and wide. Peasants came to greet us without so much fear, and we also feared them less. Our relative strength had increased considerably and we felt more secure against any surprise attack by Batista's army, and closer friends with our peasants.

ON THE MARCH

The first 15 days of May [1957] were a continual march toward our objective. At the beginning of the month, we were on a hill near the ridge close to Turquino peak. We were crossing regions that later became theaters of many revolutionary victories. We passed through Santa Ana and El Hombrito; later on, at Pico Verde, we found Escudero's house, and continued until we reached the Loma del Burro. We were moving eastward, looking for weapons that were supposed to be sent from Santiago and hidden in the region of the Loma del Burro, close to Oro de Guisa. One night on this journey that lasted a couple of weeks, while going to carry out a trivial mission, I confused the paths and was lost for two days until I found everyone again in El Hombrito. I was then able to see for myself that we each carried on our backs everything necessary for individual survival: salt and oil — very important — canned food and milk, everything required for sleeping, making fire, and cooking, and the instrument I had relied on very heavily until then, a compass.

Finding myself lost, the next morning I took out the compass and, guiding myself by it, continued for a day and a half until realizing I was becoming even more lost. I approached a peasant hut and the people directed me to the rebel camp. Later we found that in such rugged territory a compass can only provide a general orientation, never a definite course; one has either to be led by guides or to know the terrain oneself, as we came to know it when later operating in that same region.

I was very moved by the warm reception that greeted me when I rejoined the column. When I arrived they had just completed a people's trial in which three informers had been tried and judged; one of them, Nápoles, was condemned to death. Camilo was the president of that trial.

In that period I was still working as a doctor and in each little village or place I set up a consultation area. It was monotonous, for I had little medicine to offer and the clinical cases in the Sierra Maestra were all more or less the same: prematurely aged and toothless women, children with distended bellies, parasites, rickets, general vitamin deficiencies—these were the stains of the Sierra Maestra. Even today they continue, but to a much smaller degree. The children of those mothers of the Sierra Maestra have gone to study at the Camilo Cienfuegos School City, they are growing up and healthy; different boys from those first undernourished inhabitants of our pioneer school city.

I remember one girl was watching the consultations I was giving to the women of the region, who came in with an almost religious attitude toward finding the sources of their sufferings. When her mother arrived, the little girl—after attentively watching several previous examinations in the hut that served as a clinic—chattered gaily, "Mamá, this doctor says the same thing to everyone!"

And it was absolutely true; my knowledge was good for little else. They all had the same clinical symptoms, and without knowing it they each told the same heartbreaking story. What would have happened if the doctor had diagnosed the strange exhaustion suffered by the young mother of several children, when she carried buckets of water from the river to the house, as being simply due to too much work on such a meager diet? Her exhaustion is inexplicable to her, since all her life the woman has carried the same buckets of water to the same place and only now does she feel tired. The people in the Sierra Maestra grow like wild flowers, untended and without care, and they wear themselves out rapidly, working without reward. We began to feel in our bones the need for a definitive change in the life of the people. The idea of agrarian reform became clear, and communion with the people ceased being theory and became a fundamental part of our being.

The guerrilla group and the peasantry began to merge into one single mass, though no one could say at what point on the long road this happened, or at what moment words became reality and we became a part of the peasant masses. I only know that for me, those consultations with the peasants of the Sierra Maestra converted my spontaneous and somewhat lyrical resolve into a different, more serene force. Those suffering and loyal inhabitants of the Sierra Maestra have never suspected the role they played as forgers of our revolutionary ideology.

It was there that Guillermo García was promoted to captain and took charge of all the peasants who joined the column. Perhaps *compañero* Guillermo does not remember the date: in my diary it is noted as May 6, 1957.

The following day, Haydée Santamaría left with precise instructions from Fidel to make necessary contacts. But a day later we heard news that Nicaragua — Commander Iglesias — had been detained; he was in charge of bringing us weapons. We were greatly disconcerted and could not imagine what we would do now in order to get the arms; nevertheless, we decided to continue walking in the same direction.

We reached a place near Pino del Agua, a small ravine with an abandoned sawmill on the very edge of the Sierra Maestra; there were also two uninhabited huts. Near a highway, one of our patrols captured an army corporal. This corporal was well known for his crimes since the era of the [1930s dictator Gerardo] Machado, and for this reason some of the troop proposed that he be executed. But Fidel refused; we simply left him guarded by the new recruits who did not yet have rifles, and he was warned that any attempt to flee would cost him his life.

The majority of us continued on our way to see if the weapons had made it to the agreed spot and, if so, to transport them. It was a long walk, though without so much weight, since our full packs had been left in the camp where the prisoner was. The walk, however, brought no results: the equipment had not arrived and naturally we attributed this to Nicaragua's arrest. We bought some food at a store, and returned to camp with a different yet welcome load.

We were returning by the same road, at a slow, tired pace, moving along the ridges of the Sierra Maestra and crossing the barren spaces carefully. Suddenly, we heard shots ahead of us. We were worried because one of our men had gone ahead to reach camp as soon as possible; he was Guillermo Domínguez, lieutenant of our troop and one of those who had arrived with the reinforcements from Santiago. We prepared for all contingencies and sent out some scouts. After a reasonable length of time, the scouts appeared, and with them a *compañero* named Fiallo, a new recruit belonging to Crescencio's group who had joined the guerrillas during our absence. He had come from our camp and explained that there was a dead body on the road, and that there had been an encounter with some enemy guards. They had retreated in the direction of Pino del Agua where there was a larger detachment still close by. We advanced cautiously and came upon the body, which I recognized.

It was Guillermo Domínguez. He was naked from the waist up and had a bullet hole in the left elbow and a bayonet wound in the upper chest, over his heart; his head was literally shattered by a bullet, apparently from his own shotgun. Some buckshot pellets remained in the lacerated flesh of our unfortunate *compañero* as testimony.

Looking at the different facts, we were able to reconstruct what had happened: the guards were probably scouting for their imprisoned friend, the corporal, when they heard Domínguez coming before us—he must have been feeling confident, after walking the same path the day before—and they had taken him prisoner. But some of Crescencio's men were coming to meet us from the other direction (all this in the heights of the Sierra Maestra). Surprising the guards from the rear, Crescencio's men had fired and the guards had retreated, murdering our *compañero* Domínguez before fleeing.

Pino del Agua is the site of a sawmill in the middle of the Sierra Maestra and the path the guards took is an old crossroad for transporting timber. We had to follow this path for 100 meters to reach our narrow path. Our *compañero* had not taken the elementary precautions, and had the bad luck to collide with the guards. His bitter fate served us as an example for the future.

THE WEAPONS ARRIVE

Near the Pino del Agua sawmill we killed the magnificent horse the imprisoned corporal had been riding. The animal was useless to us in such intricate terrain, and we were low on food.

An amusing anecdote: the man urged us to return the horse to the friend who had lent it to him, giving us his address so we could do so, all the while eating stew made from that very animal. In any case, our customary diet in the Sierra Maestra was such that we could not afford to disdain fresh meat, horse or otherwise.

That day on the radio we learned of the sentencing of our *compañeros* from the *Granma*. In addition, we learned that a magistrate had directed his particular vote against the sentence. It was Magistrate [Manuel] Urrutia, whose honorable gesture later earned him the position of provisional president of the republic. The vote of a magistrate was no more than a worthy gesture—as it clearly was at that time—but later it had more serious consequences: it led to the appointment of a bad president, incapable of understanding the revolutionary process, incapable of absorbing the profound character of a revolution not made for his backward mentality. His character and his reluctance to state his position brought a lot of conflict. This, in the days of celebration for the first July 26 after liberation, culminated in his resignation as president, in the face of unanimous rejection by the people.

On one of those days a contact from Santiago arrived, by the name of Andrés, who had precise information about the weapons: they were safe, and would be moved in the next few days. A delivery point was fixed in the region of a coastal sawmill operated by the Babún brothers. The arms would be delivered with the complicity of these citizens who felt they could do lucrative business by involving themselves in the revolution. (Subsequent developments divided the family, and three of the Babún sons have the undignified privilege of being among those *gusanos* captured at the Bay of Pigs.)

It is curious to see how in that period a whole range of people tried to make use of the revolution for their own ends, doing small favors in order to later reap rewards from the new government. The Babún brothers hoped to have a free hand in the commercial exploitation of the woods and the expulsion of the peasants, thereby increasing the size of their estates. Around that time we were joined by a North American journalist, of the same ilk as the Babún family. He was Hungarian by birth, and his name was Andrew St. George.

At first he showed only one of his faces — the less bad one — that of a Yankee journalist. But in addition, he was an FBI agent. Since I was the only person in the column who spoke French (in those days no one spoke English), I was chosen to look out for him. Honestly, he didn't seem to me as dangerous as he proved he was in our second interview, when he openly showed himself to be an agent. We were moving around Pino del Agua toward the source of the Peladero river. These were rugged areas and we all carried heavy packs. There is a tributary of the Peladero river — Indio creek — where we spent a couple of days, getting food and moving the arms we had received. We passed through a few peasant villages establishing a kind of extralegal revolutionary state, leaving sympathizers charged with informing us of anything that happened, including the movements of the enemy army. But we always lived in the woods; only occasionally, at night, when we unexpectedly came across a group of houses, did some of us sleep in them. The majority always slept in the protection of the woods, and during the day all of us were on guard, protected by a roof of trees.

Our worst enemy at that time of year was the *macagüera*, a species of horsefly so named because it lays and hatches its eggs in the Macagua tree. At a certain time of year it reproduces prolifically in the woods. The *macagüera* bites exposed areas of the body; as we scratched, given the dirt on our bodies, the bites were easily infected, occasionally causing abscesses. The uncovered parts of our legs, wrists, and necks always bore proof of the presence of "the fly."

Finally, on May 18, we received news of the weapons and also a tentative inventory. This news circulated quickly and caused great excitement in the camp, for all the men wanted better weapons; they held secret hopes of getting one, either directly or by receiving the old weapon of someone acquiring a new one. We also heard that the film Bob Taber made about the Sierra Maestra had been shown in the United States with great success. This news cheered everyone but Andrew St. George, who, in addition to being an FBI agent, had his petty journalist's pride, and felt somewhat cheated of glory. The day after learning the bad news, he left by boat from the Babún estate for Santiago de Cuba.

The same day we learned the location of our weapons, we also learned that one of our men had deserted—a dangerous predicament, since everyone at the camp knew of the arrival of the weapons. Patrols were sent to look for him, and after some days returned with the news that he had managed to take a boat to Santiago. We presumed that it was to inform the authorities, although it later emerged that the desertion was simply due to the man's physical and moral inability to endure the hardships of our life. In any case, we had to tighten our precautions. Our struggle against the lack of physical, ideological, and moral preparation among the men was daily; the results were not always encouraging. Men often asked permission to leave for the pettiest reasons, and if they were refused, the same thing would happen as in this case. It has to be remembered that desertion was punishable by death immediately upon capture.

That night the weapons arrived; for us, the most marvelous spectacle in the world: the instruments of death were on exhibition before the covetous eyes of all the combatants. Three tripod machine guns, three Madzen machine guns, nine M-1 carbines, 10 Johnson machine guns, and a total of 6,000 rounds. Although the M-1 carbines had only 45 rounds apiece, they were highly prized weapons and were distributed according to the merits earned by the fighters and their time in the Sierra Maestra. One of the M-1s was given to the present-day Commander Ramiro Valdés, and two went to the forward guard Camilo commanded. The other four were to be used to cover the tripod machine guns. One of the machine guns went to Captain Jorge Sotús's platoon, another to Almeida's, and the third to the general staff, for which I had responsibility. The tripods were distributed as follows: one for Raul, another for Guillermo García, and the third for Crescencio Pérez. In this way, I began as a full-time combatant, for until then I had been the troop's doctor, knowing only occasional combat. I had entered a new stage.

I will always remember the moment I was given the machine gun, which was old and poor, but to me it was an important acquisition. Four men were assigned to help me with the piece — four guerrillas who have subsequently followed very different paths. Two of them were the brothers Pupo and Manolo Beatón, shot by the revolution after they assassinated Commander Cristino Naranjo and later took up arms in the mountains of Oriente, where a peasant captured them. Another was a boy of 15 who was almost always to carry the hugely heavy equipment for the machine gun. His name was Joel Iglesias, and today is the president of the Association of Rebel Youth and a commander in the Rebel Army. The fourth man, today a captain in our Rebel Army, had the name of [Alejandro] Oñate, but we affectionately labeled him "Cantinflas."

The arrival of the weapons did not mean an end to the troop's epic work to gain greater fighting and political strength. A few days later, on May 23, Fidel ordered new discharges, among them an entire squadron, and our force was reduced to 127 men, the majority of them armed, about 80 of them well armed.

From the squadron that was dismissed along with its leader, one man alone remained, Crucito [José de la Cruz], who later became one of our dearest fighters. Crucito was a natural poet and he had long rhyming contests with the poet from the city, Calixto Morales. Morales came on the *Granma* and had nicknamed himself "nightingale of the plains," to which Crucito in his peasant ballads always answered with a refrain, directed in mock derision at Calixto, "You old Sierra buzzard."

This magnificent *compañero* had put the entire history of the revolution into ballads, from the moment of the departure of the *Granma*, which he would compose as he smoked his pipe at every rest stop. Since there was very little paper in the Sierra Maestra, he wrote and memorized the ballads by heart, so that none of them remained when a bullet put an end to his life in the battle of Pino del Agua.

In the region of the sawmill we had received the invaluable help of Enrique López, an old childhood friend of Fidel and Raúl, who was at that time employed by the Babúns and served as a supply contact. He also made it possible for us to move through the entire area without danger. The region was full of roads used by army trucks; on various occasions we prepared ambushes to capture some of them, but we were never able to do it. Perhaps these failures contributed to the success of the approaching operation, which was to have greater psychological impact than any other in the history of the war. I refer to the battle of El Uvero.

On May 25, we heard news that an expeditionary force led by Calixto Sánchez had arrived in the boat *Corinthia* and landed at Mayarí; a few days later we were to learn of the disastrous result of this expedition: [Carlos] Prío [Socarrás] had sent his men to their deaths without ever bothering to accompany them. Hearing of their landing, we saw the pressing need to divert the enemy forces in order to allow those men to reach some place where they could reorganize and begin their actions. All this we did out of solidarity with the other group, even though we did not even know its composition or its true goals.

There we had an interesting discussion, led principally by the author of this narrative and Fidel. I believed that we should not lose the opportunity of capturing a truck and that we should specifically devote ourselves to ambushing them on the roads where they passed by carelessly. But Fidel had already planned in his mind the El Uvero action—he thought that it would be much more important and would bring us a more resounding success if we could capture the army post at El Uvero. If we succeeded, it would have a tremendous psychological impact and would become known throughout the country. This would not be the case with the capture of a truck, which could be reported as a road accident with a few deaths or injuries, and although people might suspect the truth, the effective reality of our presence in the Sierra Maestra would never be known. This was not a total rejection of the idea of capturing a truck, given the right conditions; but that it should not become the focal point of our activities.

Today, several years after that discussion, which I was not convinced by at the time, I must recognize that Fidel's judgment was correct. It would have been much less productive for us to carry out an isolated action against one of the truck patrols. In that period, our yearning to fight always led us impatiently to adopt drastic attitudes, without seeing the more distant objectives. In any case, we began the final preparations for the battle of El Uvero.

THE BATTLE OF
EL UVERO

Having decided on the point of attack, we then had to develop the exact form it would take. We had to solve important problems, ascertaining the number of soldiers present, the number of guard posts, the type of communications they used, the access roads, the civilian population and its distribution, etc. *Compañero* [Gilberto] Cardero served us admirably in all of this. Today a commander in the Rebel Army, he is and he was, I believe, the son-in-law of the sawmill manager.

We presumed that the army had more or less exact information on our presence in the area, for we had captured two informers, both carrying army identification documents, and they confessed that Casillas had sent them to ascertain our position and our regular meeting places. The spectacle of the two men begging for mercy was truly repugnant, yet poignant as well. The rules of war in those difficult times, however, could not be ignored, and both spies were executed the following day.

That same day, May 27, [1957], the general staff met together with all the officers. Fidel announced there would be combat within the next 48 hours, and ordered us to have our men and equipment ready to move out. We were not given details at that point.

Cardero was to be the guide, for he knew the post of El Uvero perfectly: its entrances, exits, and access roads. We marched out that night, a long march of some 16 kilometers, but all downhill on roads constructed especially by the Babún Company to reach its sawmill. It took us about eight hours to walk it, however, as we were slowed down by extra precautions which we had to take, particularly as we approached the danger zone. Finally we were given the attack orders, which were very simple: we were to take the guard posts and riddle the wooden barracks with bullets.

We knew the barracks had no major defenses, save a few logs scattered in the immediate vicinity. Its strong points were the guard posts, each with three or four soldiers, strategically placed around the outside of the barracks. Overlooking this was a hill from which our general staff would direct the battle. We were to approach within a few meters of the building through the trees. Our precise instructions were not to fire on the outlying buildings, since they sheltered women and children, including the manager's wife who knew about the attack but didn't wish to leave, in order to avoid suspicion later. As we moved to take up our attack positions, our greatest concern was for the civilians.

The El Uvero barracks was located at the edge of the sea, so that to surround it we had only to attack from three sides.

One guard post commanded the coast road from Peladero; the platoons led by Jorge Sotús and Guillermo García were sent to attack it. Almeida was charged with destroying a guard post facing the mountain, more or less to the north. Fidel would be on the hill overlooking the barracks and Raúl would advance from the front with his platoon. I was assigned an intermediate post with my machine gun and assistants. Camilo and Ameijeiras were to advance from the front, between my position and Raúl's. But they miscalculated because it was dark and when the battle began they were fighting on my left instead of my right. Crescencio Pérez's platoon was to advance along the road from El Uvero to Chivirico and hold back whatever army reinforcements were sent.

We expected the battle would be quite short given the surprise element we had prepared. The minutes passed, however, and we could not position our men in the ideal manner we had foreseen. News arrived via our guides: Cardero and another man from the region named Eligio Mendoza. We could see that dawn was approaching before we would be in position to surprise the soldiers as we had planned. Jorge Sotús advised us that he was not at his assigned position but that it was too late to move again. When Fidel opened fire with his telescopic rifle, we were able to locate the barracks from the shots that answered within seconds. We were on a small elevation and I could see the barracks perfectly; but it was a substantial distance away so we advanced to find better positions.

Everyone advanced. Almeida moved toward the post defending the entrance to the little barracks near him. To my left I could see Camilo, wearing his beret with a handkerchief over the back of his neck the way caps are worn in the French Foreign Legion, but with the [July 26] Movement insignia. We advanced cautiously amid the general exchange of fire.

Our small squadron was joined by men who had been separated from their own units; a *compañero* from Pilón named

"Bomba" — Mario Leal — and Acuña joined what already constituted a small combat unit. Resistance became fierce and we
reached a flat open space where we were forced to advance
with infinite precaution, for the enemy fired accurately without
pause. From my position, hardly 50 or 60 meters from the
enemy outpost, I saw two soldiers run out of the trench in front
of us, and I fired at both of them, but they hid in the outlying
buildings that were sacred to us. We continued advancing,
although now there was nothing more than a narrow, sparse
strip of land between us and the enemy, whose bullets whistled
past dangerously close. Near me I heard a groan and then some
shouts amid the din of battle. I thought it must be a wounded
enemy soldier, and I dragged myself forward, shouting for him
to surrender. But it was *compañero* Leal, wounded in the head. I
examined him quickly and found both entrance and exit wounds
were in the parietal region. Leal was losing consciousness, and
the limbs on one side of his body — I don't remember which —
were becoming paralyzed. The only bandage I had on hand was
a piece of paper that I placed over the wounds. A short time later,
Joel Iglesias went to watch over him, while we continued our
attack. The next thing, Acuña was wounded as well. No longer
advancing, we continued to shoot at the well-placed trench in
front of us, which responded in kind. We were mustering our
courage, and making the decision to capture the warehouse —
which seemed the only way to end the resistance — when the
barracks surrendered.

This has all been told in a few minutes, but the actual battle
lasted about two hours and 45 minutes from the first shot until
we took the barracks. On my left, some of the men from the
forward guard — I believe it was Víctor Mora and three others —

took the last of the resisters prisoner. From the trench in front of us a soldier emerged holding his gun above his head. Shouts of surrender came from all sides. We advanced rapidly on the barracks, hearing one last rattle of machine-gun fire that I later found out killed Lieutenant Nano Díaz.

We reached the warehouse and took prisoner the two soldiers who had escaped my shots, as well as the post doctor and his assistant. The doctor was a quiet, gray-haired man whose subsequent fate I am unaware of; I don't know whether he joined the revolution. A curious thing happened with this man: my medical knowledge has never been that great, the number of wounded was enormous, and my vocation at that moment was not focused on health. When I brought the wounded to the military doctor, he asked me how old I was and when I had finished my training. I explained that it had been some years ago, and he said frankly, "Look, son, you'd better take charge of all this because I've just graduated and I have very little experience." Between his lack of experience and his natural fright on finding himself prisoner, he had forgotten every medical fact he ever knew. So once again I had to swap my rifle for a doctor's coat, which really involved little more than a wash of my hands.

After the battle, one of the bloodiest we experienced, we put our heads together to create a more general picture of the action than that described from my personal point of view. The battle proceeded more or less as follows: When Fidel's shot gave the signal to open fire, everyone began to advance on their given objectives. The army responded with intense fire, in many cases against the hill from where our leader directed the battle. A few minutes into the action, Julito Díaz died at Fidel's side when he was hit directly in the head by a bullet. Minutes passed and the fierce resistance continued; we were unable to press toward our goal. The most important task in the center was Almeida's: he was in charge of destroying the guard post any way possible, to open the way for his and Raúl's troops, who were attacking the barracks head on.

The men later told how the guide Eligio Mendoza had taken his rifle and thrown himself into battle. A superstitious man, he had a "saint" who protected him, and when he was told to be careful, he answered contemptuously that his saint would defend him from anything; a few minutes later he fell, hit by a bullet that literally shattered his body.

The well-entrenched enemy troops drove us back, causing several of us to fall. It was very difficult to advance through the central area; from a position along the road to Peladero, Jorge Sotús attempted to flank the position with support from someone nicknamed "El Policía" [Francisco Soto], but the latter was immediately killed by the enemy and Sotús had to dive into the sea to avoid certain death. From that moment he was out of the battle. Other members of his platoon attempted to advance, but they too were forced back. A peasant named Vega, I believe, was killed; Manals was wounded in the lung; Quike Escalona took three wounds in the arm, buttock, and hand as he tried to advance. The enemy post, well protected by a wooden palisade, had automatic and semiautomatic machine guns, devastating our small troop.

Almeida ordered a final assault to attempt by any means to reduce the enemy he faced: Cilleros, Maceo, Hermes Leyva, and Pena were wounded, as was Almeida himself in the shoulder and the left leg, and *compañero* Moll was killed. Nevertheless, this push forward overcame the guard post and a path to the barracks was opened. From the other side, Guillermo García's confident machine-gunning wiped out three of the defenders; the fourth came out running and was killed in flight. Raúl, with his platoon divided in two, advanced rapidly on the barracks. It was the action of captains García and Almeida that decided the battle; each one destroyed their assigned guard post, making the final assault possible. Also deserving special mention is Luis Crespo, who came down from the general staff position to participate in the battle.

Enemy resistance was crumbling. A white handkerchief was waved and we took the barracks. At that moment someone, probably one of our men, fired again and a burst of fire came from the barracks catching Nano Díaz in the head. Until his last moment, Nano's machine gun caused many enemy casualties. Crescencio's platoon hardly participated in the battle, because his machine gun had jammed, so he guarded the road from Chivirico, on which he detained some fleeing soldiers. The fight had lasted two hours and 45 minutes and no civilian had been wounded, despite the great number of shots fired.

When we took stock of the battle we found that on our side there were six *compañeros* dead: Moll, Nano Díaz, Vega, El Policía, Julito Díaz, and Eligio Mendoza. Leal and Cilleros were badly wounded. Others wounded, with varying degrees of seriousness, were Maceo in the shoulder, Hermes Leyva with a surface wound to the chest, Almeida in the left arm and left leg, Quike Escalona in the right arm and hand, Manals in the lung, Pena in the knee, and Manuel Acuña in the right arm. In all, 15 *compañeros* had been put out of action. The enemy had 19 wounded, 14 dead, another 14 prisoners, and six escapees, which made a total of 53 men, under the command of a second lieutenant who had flown the white flag after being wounded.

Considering that we were about 80 men and they were 53, a total of 133 men, and that 38 of these—more than a quarter—were put out of action in a little over two and a half hours of fighting, it's possible to understand what kind of battle it was. It was an assault by men who had advanced bare-chested against an enemy protected by very poor defenses. It should be recognized that on both sides great courage was shown. For us this victory also marked our coming of age. From this battle on, our morale grew tremendously, our decisiveness and our hopes for triumph also grew. And although the months that followed were difficult, we already possessed the secret of victory. The action at El Uvero sealed the fate of all the small barracks situated far from major clusters of enemy forces, and they were all dismantled soon after.

One of the first shots of the battle hit the telephone lines, cutting communication with Santiago. Only a couple of light planes flew over the battlefield, but the air force sent no reconnaissance planes until hours later, when we were already high in the mountains. We have been told that, apart from the 14 dead soldiers, three of the five parrots the guards had in the barracks were killed. One has only to picture this small bird to get an idea of what befell the wooden building.

My return to the medical profession was quite emotional. The first patient I attended, the most gravely wounded, was *compañero* Cilleros. A bullet had split open his right arm and, after piercing a lung, had apparently embedded itself in his spine, paralyzing both legs. His condition was critical, and I was only able to give him a sedative and bind his chest tightly so he could breathe more easily. We tried to save him in the only way possible: we took the 14 prisoners with us and left the two wounded guerrillas, Leal and Cilleros, with the enemy, on the doctor's word of honor that they would be cared for. When I told this to Cilleros, mouthing the usual words of comfort, he answered with a sad smile that, more than any words could have, expressed his conviction that it was all over. We knew this as well, and I was tempted at that moment to place a farewell kiss on his forehead. Yet, coming from me, more than anyone else, such an act would have signified a death sentence for our *compañero*, and duty told me that I must not make his last minutes more bitter with the confirmation of something he already knew. I said good-bye, as sweetly as possible and with enormous pain, to the two fighters who remained in the hands of the enemy. They proclaimed that they would prefer to die among their *compañeros*; but we also had the duty to fight to the end for their lives. So there they remained, brothers now with 19 wounded Batista soldiers who had also been cared for with our full capability. Our two *compañeros* were decently treated by the enemy army, but Cilleros did not reach Santiago. Leal survived his wound, was imprisoned on the Isle of Pines for the rest of the war, and today bears the indelible marks of that important episode in our revolutionary war.

In one of Babún's trucks we hauled the largest possible quantity of every kind of equipment, especially medical. We left last, heading toward our mountain hideout, which we reached in time to care for the wounded and take leave of the dead, who were buried at a bend in the road. We realized there would now be an intense pursuit and decided that those men who could walk should distance themselves quickly, leaving the wounded behind in my care. Enrique López was to furnish me with transport, a hiding place, some assistants to help move the wounded, and the necessary contacts through which we could receive medicines and properly treat the men.

We were awake until morning, each describing the twists and turns of battle. Almost no one slept, or only just, as we heard from each man their personal experiences or those they had witnessed. Out of statistical curiosity I took note of all the enemy soldiers supposedly killed during the battle. There were more enemy corpses than there had been enemy soldiers; fantasy adorned each man's feats. This and other similar episodes taught us that all facts needed validating by several people; being over cautious, we even demanded physical proof, such as items taken from a fallen soldier, before we accepted an enemy casualty. Preoccupation with the truth was always a central theme in the reports of the Rebel Army, and we attempted to imbue our men with a profound respect for truth and a feeling of how necessary it was to place truth above any transitory advantage.

In the morning, we watched the departure of the victorious troop, sadly bidding us farewell. My assistants Joel Iglesias and Oñate stayed with me, as well as a guide named Sinecio Torres, and Vilo Acuña — today a commander in the Rebel Army — who stayed to be with his wounded uncle.

CARING FOR THE WOUNDED

From dawn on the day after the battle of El Uvero, planes circled above. Our farewells to the departing column were over, and we dedicated ourselves to erasing the signs of our entry into the woods. We were only some 100 meters from a truck access road and we waited for Enrique López, who was coming to help us make it to our hideout.

Almeida and Pena could not walk; neither could Quike Escalona. I recommended Manals not walk either because of the wound in his lung. Manuel Acuña, Hermes Leyva, and Maceo could all walk on their own. To defend, nurse, and transport them, there were Vilo Acuña, the guide Sinecio Torres, Joel Iglesias, Alejandro Oñate, and myself. We were well into the morning when a messenger came to tell us that Enrique López could not help us because his daughter was ill and he had to leave for Santiago. He also said he was sending us some volunteers to help, but we are still waiting for them today.

The situation was difficult. Quike Escalona's wounds were infected and I could not determine the gravity of Manals's injuries. We explored the nearby roads without encountering enemy soldiers, and decided to move the wounded to a peasant hut three or four kilometers away. The owner had abandoned it, leaving behind a good number of chickens.

On the first day, two workers from the sawmill helped us with the grueling work of carrying the wounded in hammocks. At dawn on the following day, after eating well and downing a large ration of chicken, we quickly left, for we had stayed there a whole day after the attack, practically in the same place, close to roads by which enemy soldiers could arrive. We were at the end of one of those roads constructed by the Babún Company to reach deeper into the woods. With our few available men we started on a short but very difficult trek down to Indio creek. We then climbed a narrow path to a small shack where a peasant named Israel lived with his wife and brother-in-law. Moving our wounded *compañeros* through such rugged terrain was grueling work, but we did it, and the two peasants even gave us their own double bed for the wounded to sleep in.

Near our first camp we had hidden some of the weapons that were in poor condition, along with a great variety of equipment — war booty — for the weight of the wounded increased with each step. Evidence of our presence always remained in the peasant huts, and because we had time, we decided to return to our previous camp and erase all traces, since our security depended on it. At the same time Sinecio, the guide, left to find some people he knew in the region of Peladero.

After a short time, Acuña and Joel Iglesias told me they had heard strange voices on the other slope. We honestly believed the hour had come when we would be forced to fight under the most difficult circumstances. It was our obligation to defend to the death the precious cargo of wounded men we had been entrusted with. We advanced, trying to ensure the encounter would take place as far as possible from the hut; some bare footprints on the path, which seemed very strange to us, indicated that the intruders had passed along the same track. Approaching warily, we heard a conversation between several people, speaking without fear; loading my Thompson machine gun and counting on the help of Vilo and Joel, I advanced and surprised the speakers. They turned out to be the prisoners from El Uvero whom Fidel had freed and were simply looking for a way out of the woods. Some of them were barefoot. An old corporal, almost unconscious, expressed in an asthmatic voice his admiration for us and our knowledge of the woods. They had no guide, only a safe-conduct pass signed by Fidel. Taking advantage of the impression our surprise appearance had made on them, we warned them never to enter the woods again, not for any reason.

As city men, they were not accustomed to the hardships of the mountains, and did not know how to cope with them. We entered the clearing with the hut where we had eaten the chickens, and showed them the way to the coast. We also reminded them one last time that from the woods inward the area belonged to us and that our patrol—for we looked like a simple patrol—would immediately notify the forces of that region of any foreign presence. Despite all this, we felt it prudent to move on as soon as possible.

We spent that night in the hospitable little hut, but at dawn we moved into the woods, first asking the owners of the house to find some hens for the wounded. We spent the whole day waiting for the couple, but they did not return. Some time later we learned that they had been taken prisoner in the little house and that furthermore, the next day, the enemy soldiers had used them as guides and had passed by our camp of the day before.

We kept a vigilant watch and no one could have surprised us, but the outcome of a battle in such conditions was not difficult to foresee. Nearing nightfall, Sinecio arrived with three volunteers: an old man named Feliciano, and two men who later became members of the Rebel Army. These were [Teodoro] Banderas, killed in the battle of El Jigüe with the rank of lieutenant, and Israel Pardo, the oldest of a large family of fighters, who today holds the rank of captain. These *compañeros* helped us to quickly move the wounded to a hut on the other side of the danger zone, while Sinecio and I waited practically until nightfall for the peasant couple bringing food; they couldn't come of course because they were already prisoners. Suspecting a betrayal, we decided to leave the new house early the next day. Our frugal meal consisted of some root vegetables picked near the hut.

The following day, six months after the landing of the *Granma*, we began our march early. These treks were tiring, and incredibly short for anyone accustomed to long marches in the mountains. We could carry only one wounded *compañero* at a time, and we had to carry them in hammocks hanging from strong branches that literally ruined the shoulders of the carriers. Carriers had to relieve each other every 10 or 15 minutes, so that we needed six or eight to carry each wounded man. I accompanied Almeida, who was half dragging himself along. We walked very slowly, almost from tree to tree, until Israel found a shortcut through the woods and the carriers came back for Almeida.

Afterward, a tremendous downpour made it difficult for us to reach Pardo's house, but we finally got there close to nightfall. The short distance of four kilometers had been covered in 12 hours, in other words at three hours per kilometer.

We were fortunate to have Sinecio Torres with our small group, as he knew the roads, and the locals, and he helped us in everything. He was the one who two days later arranged for Manals to go to Santiago for treatment; we were also preparing to send Quike Escalona whose wounds were infected. Contradictory news was arriving in those days, sometimes we heard that Celia Sánchez was in prison, other times that she had been killed. Rumors also circulated that an army patrol had taken Hermes Caldero, another *compañero*, prisoner. We did not know whether or not to believe these often hair-raising news items. Celia, for example, was our only known and secure contact. Her arrest would mean complete isolation for us. Fortunately, news about Celia was not true, although Hermes Caldero had been captured, but miraculously he stayed alive in the dungeons of the dictatorship.

On the banks of the Peladero river lived the overseer of a large land estate, David [Gómez] was his name, and he cooperated greatly with us. Once David killed a cow for us and we simply had to go out and get it. The animal had been slaughtered on the riverbank and cut into pieces; we had to move the meat by night. I sent the first group with Israel Pardo in front, and then the second led by Banderas. Banderas was quite undisciplined and did not follow the order. He let the others carry the full weight of the carcass, and it took all night to move it. A small troop was now being formed under my command, since Almeida was wounded. Conscious of my responsibility, I notified Banderas that unless he changed his attitude he was no longer a combatant, but merely a sympathizer. He really did change then; he was never the model of a fighter when it came to discipline, but he was one of those enterprising and broad-minded men, simple and ingenuous, who opened his eyes to reality through the shock of the revolution. He had been cultivating his small, isolated parcel of land in the woods, and he had a true passion for trees and agriculture. He lived in a small shack with two little pigs, each with its name, and a little dog. One day he showed me a portrait of his two sons who lived with his ex-wife in Santiago. He explained to me that some day, when the revolution triumphed, he would be able to go some place where he could really grow something, not like this inhospitable piece of land almost hanging from the mountaintop.

I spoke to him of cooperatives, though he did not understand my point very well. He wanted to work the land on his own, by his own efforts; nevertheless, little by little I managed to convince him that it was better to work among others, that machinery would increase his productivity. Banderas would today have undoubtedly been a vanguard fighter in the area of agricultural production. In the Sierra Maestra he taught himself to read and write and was preparing for the future. He was an enlightened peasant who knew the value of contributing his own efforts to writing a page of history.

I had a long conversation with the overseer David, who asked me for a list of all the important things we needed; he was going to Santiago and would pick them up there. He was a typical overseer, loyal to his boss, contemptuous of the peasants, racist. When the army, however, learned of his relations with us and took him prisoner and tortured him barbarously, his first concern on returning was to convince us, who had thought him dead, that he did not talk. I do not know if David is in Cuba today, or if he followed his old bosses whose land was confiscated by the revolution. Although he was a man who felt the need for a change, who understood how urgent change was, he never imagined that it would also reach him and his world. The revolution has been built on the sincere efforts of many ordinary people. Our mission is to develop what is good and noble in each person, to convert every person into a revolutionary, from the Davids who did not understand well, to the Banderases, who died without seeing the dawn. Blind and unrewarded sacrifices also made the revolution. Those of us who today see its achievements have the responsibility to remember those who fell along the way, and to work for a future where there will be fewer stragglers.

RETURN JOURNEY

We spent the whole month of June 1957 nursing our *compañeros* wounded in the battle of El Uvero, and organizing our small troop, which would return to Fidel's column.

Contact with the outside world was made through the overseer David, whose advice and opportune information, as well as the food he brought us, greatly alleviated our situation. In those first days we did not have the invaluable help of Pancho Tamayo, the same man who was murdered at the hands of the Beatón brothers in the post-war years. Pancho Tamayo, an old peasant from the area, later got in touch with us and also served as a point of contact.

Sinecio began showing signs that he was losing revolutionary morale; he got drunk on movement money and committed drunken indiscretions. He also neglected to carry out the orders he received and, after one of his binges, he brought us 11 raw unarmed recruits, disobeying an express order. We generally tried to prevent unarmed men from enlisting, but Sinecio was not the only one to ignore this. New people were joining the young guerrilla force by every means and under all conditions, and the peasants, knowing where we were, often brought us new *compañeros* who wished to enlist. No fewer than 40 people passed through our little column, but desertions were constant —

sometimes with our consent, other times against our will — so the troop never had more than 25 or 30 effective members.

My asthma was somewhat aggravated and the lack of medicine meant I was almost as immobile as the wounded. I was able to relieve the illness somewhat by smoking dried *clarín* flowers, a local remedy, until medicine arrived from civilization. This helped me to restore my health in preparation for our leaving, but day after day, our departure was delayed. Finally, we organized a patrol to search for all the weapons we had left behind as unusable after the attack on El Uvero, in order to add them to the guerrilla arsenal.

In our position, all those old weapons, including a .30-caliber machine gun without its sight, were potential treasures, with all their various defects, and we invested an entire night looking for them. We finally fixed our departure date for June 24. Our army: five recuperating wounded, five assistants, 10 new recruits from Bayamo, four new recruits from the vicinity, and two others who just showed up on their own — a total of 26. The march was organized with Vilo Acuña as head of the forward guard; next, what could be called the general staff, which I led since Almeida with his wounded thigh had enough work just walking; and two other small squadrons led by Maceo and Peña.

Peña was a lieutenant at that time. Maceo and Vilo were combatants, and Almeida, as captain, held the highest rank. We did not leave on June 24 because of some small inconveniences. First it was announced that one of the guides was arriving with a new recruit, and we had to wait for them. Then we heard that the guide was coming with a new supply of medicine and food. Old Tamayo came and went constantly, bringing news and some supplies of canned food and clothing. At one point we had to find a cave to leave some of our supplies, because our contacts in Santiago had finally come through and David brought us an important shipment which was impossible to transport, given that we were marching with convalescents and raw recruits.

On June 26, I debuted as dentist, although in the Sierra Maestra I was given the more modest title of "tooth-puller." My first victim was Israel Pardo, today a captain in the army, who came out of it pretty well. The second was Joel Iglesias, who would have needed a stick of dynamite to remove the canine tooth; in fact, he saw out the end of the war with the tooth still in place since my efforts to extract it had been fruitless. Besides the meagerness of my skill, we had no anesthetic, so I frequently used "psychological anesthesia" — a few harsh epithets when my patients complained too much about the work going on in their mouths.

Even the thought of marching caused some of the indecisive men to leave us, but new ones replaced them. Tamayo brought us a new group of four men. Among them was Félix Mendoza, who came with a rifle. He explained that an army troop had surprised him and his *compañero*, and while the other man was arrested, he threw himself over a rocky outcrop and ran, without harm, from the enemy. We later learned that the "army" was a patrol led by Lalo Sardiñas, who had not captured the *compañero* but had taken him to Fidel's troop. We were also joined by Evelio Saborit, today a commander in the Rebel Army.

With the arrival of Félix Mendoza and his group, we were now 36 men, but the following day three left, then others joined us and we numbered 35. When the march started, however, our number once again diminished. We were climbing the slopes of

Peladero, making very little progress each day.

The radio informed us of a panorama of violence throughout the island. On July 1 we heard news of the death of Josué País, Frank's brother, along with other *compañeros*, killed in the on-going battle being waged in Santiago. Despite the short marches, our troops felt demoralized and some of the new recruits asked whether they could leave in order to "carry out more useful missions in the city." On the way down the La Botella hill we passed the house of Benito Mora, who entertained us in his humble abode that clung to the steep rocks of that part of the Sierra Maestra.

Shortly before arriving at Mora's, I called the little troop together, telling the men that dangerous moments were approaching, that the army was close, that probably we would have to pass many days without food, walking almost without a break. I urged whoever did not feel capable of it to say so now; some were frank enough to speak their fears, and they left; another, named Chicho [Fernández], swore in the name of a small group that they would all follow us until death. He spoke with such conviction and extraordinary decisiveness that we were truly surprised when, after passing Benito Mora's house and camping beside a small creek for the night, this same group communicated its desire to leave the guerrilla force. We agreed, jokingly baptizing the place "death creek," for Chicho's tremendous determination and that of his friends had lasted only until that point. That name of that streak of water stuck until we left the Sierra Maestra.

We were left with 28 men, but on leaving the next day, we were joined by two new recruits: ex-soldiers who came to fight for freedom in the Sierra Maestra. They were Gilberto Capote and Nicolás. Arístides Guerra brought them, another of the local contacts who was later an invaluable asset to our column, and whom we called "Chow King." During the whole war, Chow King did us innumerable services—and many times these were more dangerous than fighting against the enemy—such as moving mule teams from Bayamo to our area of operations.

As we made or short marches, we tried to familiarize the new recruits with their weapons. We had the two ex-soldiers teach them something about handling a rifle, how to load and unload, dry run shooting, etc. Bad luck had it that no sooner had the lessons begun, than one of the instructors fired a shot; we had to remove him from the job, and eyed him suspiciously, although the consternation on his face was such that he would have needed a lot of acting talent to simulate it. The two ex-soldiers could not endure the march and left again with Arístides, but Gilberto Capote returned to us later, dying heroically in Pino del Agua with the rank of lieutenant.

We left where we had camped: Polo Torres's house at La Mesa, which later became one of our operations centers. We were led now by a peasant named Tuto Almeida. Our mission was to reach La Nevada and after make it to Fidel's camp by crossing the north face of Turquino. We were walking in that direction when, in the distance, we saw two peasants who tried to flee on seeing us. We ran after them and they turned out to be two Afro-Cuban girls with the last name of Moya. They were Adventists, and, even though their beliefs meant they were against violence of any kind, they gave us their full support at that time and for the duration of the war.

We ate magnificently and regained some strength, but when we passed through Mar Verde (in order to reach Nevada), we discovered there were army troops throughout the whole region. After brief deliberation, our little general staff and the guides decided we should fall back and cross directly over Turquino peak, a rougher route but less dangerous in the circumstances.

We caught some disquieting news on our small transistor radio; they said that heavy battles were being fought in the region of Estrada Palma, and that Raúl was badly wounded. (Today, with the time that has passed, I cannot actually say whether we heard this on our radio or from "*radio bemba*" [the grapevine].) We did not know whether to believe the news; prior experience had taught us to mistrust all such reports. But we tried to quicken our pace in order to reach Fidel as soon as possible. We marched through the night, spending part of it in the house of a lone peasant, called Vizcaíno because of his [Basque] origins. He lived in the Turquino foothills, completely alone in a small hut, and his only friends were some Marxist books, which he guarded carefully in a small hole beneath a stone away from his hut. He proudly displayed his militant Marxism, which few people in the zone knew about. Vizcaíno showed us which path to follow and we continued our slow march.

Sinecio was getting farther and farther from his own district, and for a simple soul like him—now a little out of his depth—this situation brought only anguish. One fine day, during a rest stop, while a new recruit named Cuervo was on guard with his Remington rifle given to him for his good nature, Sinecio Torres joined him at the post, also carrying a rifle. When I heard of this, about half an hour later, I went to find them, because I had little confidence in Sinecio and rifles were rather precious. But both of them had already deserted. Banderas and Israel Pardo went after them, aware that the fugitives were armed with heavy weapons while they had only revolvers. They did not find the deserters on that occasion.

It was very difficult to maintain troop morale, without weapons, without direct contact with the leader of the revolution. We were practically feeling our way, inexperienced and surrounded by enemies who loomed like giants in our imaginations and in the tales of the peasants. The reluctance of the recruits from the plains, and their unfamiliarity with the thousand difficulties on the steep paths, provoked an ongoing crisis in the spirit of our guerrilla band. There was an attempted desertion led by an individual named "El Mexicano," who had reached the rank of captain and today is in Miami, a traitor to the revolution.

I found out about it when *compañero* Hermes Leyva, a cousin of Joel Iglesias, denounced them. I called a meeting to confront the problem. El Mexicano swore on all his ancestors that even though he had thought of leaving, he had no intention of deserting the struggle; he had meant to form a small guerrilla band to assault and kill informers, for there was so little action in our forces. In reality, he wanted to kill informers for their money — typical banditry. In a subsequent battle, at El Hombrito, Hermes was our only casualty, and we were always left with the suspicion that El Mexicano could have been the principal author of the event, since Hermes had denounced him earlier. No one, however, could ever prove this.

El Mexicano remained in the column, giving his word as a man and a revolutionary, etc., that he would not leave or attempt to leave, or incite anyone else to do so. After short, arduous marches, we reached the region of Palma Mocha, on the western slope of Turquino, near Las Cuevas. The peasants received us very well and we established direct contact through my new profession as "tooth-puller," which I exercised with great enthusiasm.

We ate and gained strength to continue rapidly to the familiar regions of Palma Mocha and Arroyo del Infierno, arriving on June 15. There, Emilio Carrera, a local peasant, informed us that Lalo Sardiñas had set up an ambush nearby. He was concerned because in the case of an attack on an enemy patrol, his house would be endangered.

On June 16, our small new column met the platoon from Fidel's column, led by Lalo Sardiñas. Lalo told us why he had felt it necessary to join the revolution. As a merchant, he used to bring us supplies from the city; but he had been ambushed once and had to kill someone, which virtually forced him to become a guerrilla. Lalo had received instructions to wait for the forward guard of Sánchez Mosquera's enemy column to arrive. We learned that once again the obstinate Sánchez Mosquera had penetrated the region of the Palma Mocha river and that Fidel's column had almost closed in on him, but they managed to elude Fidel by crossing Turquino on forced marches, reaching the other side of the mountain.

We already had some news of the proximity of the troops; a few days earlier, on reaching a peasant hut, we saw the trenches soldiers had occupied until the previous day. We did not suspect that what seemed to be proof of a sustained offensive against us was in reality a sign of the retreat of the repressive column, marking a qualitative change in operations in the Sierra Maestra. We now had sufficient strength to surround the enemy and oblige it, under threat of annihilation, to withdraw.

The enemy understood this lesson very well and made only

sporadic incursions into the Sierra Maestra. But one of the most tenacious, aggressive, and bloodthirsty enemy officers was Sánchez Mosquera, who rose from a simple lieutenant in 1957 to colonel, a rank awarded him after the final defeat of the army's general offensive, in June the following year. His career path was meteoric, and lucrative, in that he robbed the peasants mercilessly each time he and his troops penetrated the labyrinth of the Sierra Maestra.

A BETRAYAL IN
THE MAKING

It was a pleasure to look at our troop again. Close to 200 men, with more discipline, much better morale, and some new weapons among us. The qualitative change I have already mentioned was now quite evident in the Sierra Maestra. There was a genuinely liberated territory, and measures of precaution were not as necessary. There was a certain amount of freedom to converse throughout the night while resting in our hammocks, and we were allowed to visit the villages of the people in the Sierra Maestra, establishing better relationships with them. The welcome given us by our old *compañeros* gave us great joy.

Felipe Pazos and Raúl Chibás were the stars of those days, although they were two totally different personalities. Raúl Chibás lived solely off the reputation of his brother [Eduardo] — who had been a real symbol of an era in Cuba — but he had none of his brother's virtues; he was neither articulate, nor wise, nor even intelligent. Only his complete mediocrity allowed him to be a unique and symbolic figure in the Orthodox Party. He spoke very little and wanted to leave the Sierra Maestra at once.

Felipe Pazos had his own personality. He had the standing of a great economist and a reputation for honesty, won by not stealing from the public treasury while he was president of the National Bank under [Carlos] Prío Socarrás's regime—a regime marked by gross larceny and embezzlement. A magnificent merit, one might think, to remain unpolluted throughout those years. A merit, perhaps, for a functionary to pursue his administrative career, indifferent to the country's grave problems. But how can one be a revolutionary without daily condemning the inconceivable abuses of the period? Felipe Pazos skilfully managed to keep his mouth shut, and following Batista's coup he left the position of president of the National Bank, adorned with his great reputation for honesty, intelligence, and talent as an economist. Smugly, he thought he would come to the Sierra Maestra and take control. This miniature Machiavelli thought he was destined to control the country's future. It is possible that he had already contemplated the idea of betraying the movement; perhaps this came later. But his conduct was never entirely honest.

Basing himself on the joint declaration [the Sierra Manifesto] that I am about to analyze, Pazos appointed himself representative of the July 26 Movement in Miami, and was going to be designated provisional president of the republic. In this way, Prío was assured that he had a man he could trust in the leadership of the provisional government.

We had little time to talk in those days, but Fidel told me about his efforts to make the document truly militant, to lay the basis for a declaration of principles. A difficult task when faced with those two stone-age minds immune to the call of the people's struggle.

Fundamentally, the manifesto issued "the slogan of a great civic revolutionary front comprising all opposition political parties, all civic institutions, and all revolutionary forces."

It made a series of proposals: the "formation of a civic revolutionary front in a common front of struggle"; the appointment of "an individual to head the provisional government"; an explicit declaration that the front would neither call for nor accept intervention by another nation in Cuba's internal affairs; and that it "would not accept any sort of military junta as a provisional government of the republic." The document expressed the determination to remove the army from politics entirely and guarantee the nonpolitical nature of the armed forces. It declared that elections would be held within one year.

The program, which was to serve as a basis for a provisional government, proclaimed freedom for all political prisoners, civilian and military; an absolute guarantee of freedom of the press and radio, with all individual and political rights to be guaranteed by the constitution; the appointment of provisional mayors in all municipalities, after consultation with the civic institutions of the locality; the suppression of all forms of government corruption, and the adoption of measures designed to enhance the efficiency of all state bodies; the establishment of a civil service; the democratization of trade union politics, promoting free elections in all trade unions and industry-wide union federations; the immediate launching of an all-out drive against illiteracy and for public education, stressing the rights and duties of the citizen in relation to society and the homeland; "putting in place the foundations for an agrarian reform designed to distribute unused land, and transform into owners all the sugarcane growers who rent land, and all the sharecroppers, tenant farmers, and squatters who work small plots of land owned either by the state or private persons, after payment of compensation to former owners"; the adoption of a healthy fiscal policy to safeguard our currency's stability and aimed at investing the nation's credit in productive works; and the acceleration of the industrialization process and creation of new jobs.

In addition, there were two points of special emphasis:

First: the need to appoint, from this point forward, a person who will preside over the provisional government of the republic, to show the entire world that the Cuban people can unite behind a call for freedom, and to support that person who — for their impartiality, integrity, capability, and decency — could personify such a stand. There are more than enough able people in Cuba to preside over the republic.

(Naturally, Felipe Pazos at least, one of the signatories, knew in his heart of hearts that there were not more than enough men, there was only one, and he was it.)

Second: that this person shall be appointed by all the civic, and therefore apolitical, institutions, whose support would free the provisional president from commitments to any party, ensuring absolutely clean and impartial elections.

The document also stated, "It is not necessary to come to the Sierra Maestra for discussions. We can have representatives in Havana, Mexico, or wherever else is necessary."

Fidel had pressed for more explicit statements regarding the agrarian reform, but it was very difficult to break the monolithic front of the two cavemen. "Putting in place the foundations for an agrarian reform designed to distribute unused land" — this was precisely the kind of policy the *Diario de la Marina* might agree with. And to make it worse: "after payment of compensation to former owners."

The revolution did fulfill some of the commitments as originally stated. We must emphasize that the enemy [Pazos et al.] broke the tacit pact expressed in the manifesto when they refused to acknowledge the authority of the *Sierra* and made an attempt to shackle the future revolutionary government.

We were not satisfied with the agreement, but it was necessary; and at that moment it was progressive. It could not last beyond the moment when it would represent a brake on the revolution's development; but we were ready to comply with it. By their treachery, the enemy helped us to break uncomfortable bonds and show the people these individuals' true intentions.

We knew the program was a minimum, that it limited our efforts, but we also had to recognize that it was impossible to impose our will from the Sierra Maestra. For a long period, we would have to depend upon a whole range of "friends" who were trying to utilize our military strength and the great trust that the people already felt in Fidel Castro for their own macabre maneuvers. Above all, they wanted to maintain imperialist domination of Cuba, through its imported bourgeoisie closely linked with their masters to the north.

The manifesto had its positive sides: it mentioned the Sierra Maestra and stated explicitly, "Let no one be deceived by government propaganda about the situation in the Sierra Maestra. The Sierra Maestra is already an indestructible bastion of freedom, which has taken root in the hearts of our compatriots, and it is from here that we will know how to honor the faith and confidence of our people." The words, "we will know how" in reality meant that Fidel Castro knew how, for the other two were incapable of following, even as spectators, the development of the struggle in the Sierra Maestra. They left immediately. One of them, Chibás, was surprised by Batista's police and treated badly. Afterward, both of them went to the United States.

It was a well-planned coup: a group of the most distinguished representatives of the Cuban oligarchy arrived in the Sierra Maestra "in defense of freedom," signed a joint declaration with the guerrilla chief imprisoned in the wilds of the Sierra Maestra, and left with full freedom to play this trump card from Miami. They failed to take into account that the true success of political coups is dependent on an opponent's strength, in this case, the weapons were in the hands of the people. Quick action by our leader, who had full confidence in the guerrilla army, prevented the betrayal's success. Months later, when the results of the Miami Pact became known, Fidel's fiery reply paralyzed the enemy. We were accused of being divisive and of trying to impose our will from the Sierra Maestra; but they had to change their tactics and prepare a new trap: the Caracas Pact.

The Sierra Manifesto, dated July 12, 1957, was published in the newspapers of the time. For us, this declaration was nothing more than a brief pause on the road. Our fundamental task — to defeat the oppressor's army on the battlefield — had to continue. A new column was being organized then, with myself in charge, and I became a captain. There were other promotions: Ramiro Valdés became a captain and his platoon joined my column. Ciro Redondo was also promoted to captain, and was to lead a platoon. The column was made up of three platoons. The first, led by Lalo Sardiñas, made up the forward guard, and he was also second-in-command. Ramiro Valdés and Ciro Redondo led the other two platoons. Our column, named the "Evicted Peasants," was made up of close to 75 men, variously dressed and armed; nonetheless, I was very proud of them. Some nights later, I felt even prouder, even closer to the revolution, if that were possible, even more anxious to prove my military award was well deserved ...

We sent a letter of congratulations and appreciation to "Carlos," Frank País's underground name, who was living his final days. It was signed by all the officers of the guerrilla army who knew how to write (many of the Sierra Maestra peasants were not very skilled in this art but were already an important component of the guerrillas). The signatures appeared in two columns, and as we wrote down the ranks in the second one, when my turn came, Fidel simply said, "Make it commander." In this most informal way, almost in passing, I became commander of the second column of the guerrilla army, which would later become known as Column No. 4.

The letter, written in a peasant's house—though I don't remember where—was the guerrilla fighters' warm message to their brother in the city, fighting so heroically in Santiago to obtain supplies for us and alleviate the enemy's pressure.

There is a bit of vanity hiding within every one of us, and I felt like the proudest man in the world that day. The symbol of my promotion, a small star, was given to me by Celia, and came with a gift: one of the wristwatches ordered from Manzanillo. With my recently formed column, my first task was to set a trap for Sánchez Mosquera, but he was the most devious all of Batista's henchmen and had already left the area.

We had to do something to justify the semi-independent life we were to lead in what was to be our new zone, the region of El Hombrito where we were headed, so we began to plan a range of great deeds.

We had to prepare to celebrate with dignity the approaching glorious date of July 26, and Fidel gave me free rein to do whatever I could, with prudence. At the last meeting we met a new doctor who had joined the guerrilla forces: Sergio del Valle, now chief of the general staff of our revolutionary army. At that time he practiced his profession as the conditions of the Sierra Maestra allowed.

We needed to prove we were still alive, since we had received a few setbacks on the plains: weapons from the Miranda sugar mill that were to be used to open another front had been seized by the police, and several valuable leaders, among them Faustino Pérez, had been captured. Fidel had opposed dividing our forces but had ceded to the demands of the *Llano compañeros*. The correctness of Fidel's view was demonstrated, and from then on we devoted ourselves to strengthening the *Sierra* as the first step toward expanding the guerrilla army.

THE ATTACK ON BUEYCITO

Our new independence brought with it new problems. We had to establish rigid discipline, organize commands, and establish some form of general staff in order to assure success in new battles, not an easy task given the lack of discipline of the combatants.

No sooner had we formed the detachment than a beloved *compañero* left us — Lieutenant Maceo. He went to Santiago on a mission and we would never see him again, for he yielded there in battle.

We also made a few promotions: *compañero* William Rodríguez became lieutenant, as well as Raúl Castro Mercader. With this, we were trying to give shape to our small guerrilla force. One morning, we learned, regrettably, that a man had deserted with his rifle, a .22-caliber weapon, precious in the deplorable conditions of that period. The deserter was known as Chino Wong, from the forward guard, and he had most probably returned to his own district in the foothills of the Sierra Maestra. Two men were sent after him, but we lost hope in that mission when Israel Pardo and Banderas returned after a fruitless search for earlier deserters. Israel, with his knowledge of the terrain and his great physical resilience, was assigned to carry out special functions at my side.

We began to elaborate a highly ambitious plan, which consisted first of attacking Estrada Palma by night and then capturing the small garrisons in the nearby villages of Yara and Veguitas, returning to the mountains by the same route. In this way, counting on the element of surprise, we could take three barracks in one assault. We had some firing practice, using bullets sparingly, and found that all our weapons were good, except for the very old and very dirty Madzen machine gun. In a short note to Fidel we outlined our plan and asked for his approval or rejection. We did not receive an answer, but over the radio on July 27 we learned of the attack on Estrada Palma by 200 men led, according to the official report, by Raúl Castro.

The magazine *Bohemia*, in its only uncensored issue published during the period, ran an article describing the damage inflicted by our troops at Estrada Palma, where the old barracks was burned down. It also mentioned Fidel Castro, Celia Sánchez, and an entire pleiad of revolutionaries who had come down from the mountains. Truth was mixed with myth, as happens in these cases, and the journalists could not untangle the two. In reality, the attack was launched not by 200 men but by many fewer, and it was led by Commander Guillermo García (then captain). There had been no real combat because Colonel Barrera had retreated shortly before, logically fearing that there would be heavy attacks on July 26 and unsure, perhaps, of his position. The Estrada Palma operation was basically a simple expedition. The following day army troops gave chase to our guerrillas and, through organizational weakness, one of our men who had fallen asleep somewhere near San Lorenzo was captured, as I remember it. After hearing this news, we decided to rapidly try to attack another barracks in the days immediately following July 26 and to continue maintaining an atmosphere appropriate to insurrection.

Marching toward the Sierra Maestra, near a place called La Jeringa, one of the two men who had gone to look for the deserter caught up with us. He told us that his *compañero* for the mission had told him he was a close friend of Chino Wong and could not betray him. Then he invited him to desert and indicated that he himself would not be returning to the guerrillas. The *compañero* ordered him to halt, but the deserter continued walking, and the *compañero* shot and killed him.

I gathered the entire troop together on the hill facing the spot where this grim event had played out. I explained to our men what they were going to see and what it meant, why desertion was punishable by death, and why anyone who betrayed the revolution must be condemned. We passed single file, in total silence, before the body of the man who had tried to abandon his post. Many of the men had never seen death before and were perhaps moved more by personal feelings for the dead man and by political weakness natural at that period, than by disloyalty to the revolution. Times were hard and we used this man as an example. It is not worth giving the man's name here; we will say only that the dead man was a young, humble peasant from the vicinity.

We passed through some familiar territory. On July 30, Lalo Sardiñas made contact with an old friend, a merchant in the mining region named Armando Oliver. We made an appointment in a house near the California zone and there we met with him and Jorge Abich. We spoke of our intention to attack Minas and Bueycito. It was a risky step to put this secret in the hands of other people, but Lalo Sardiñas knew and trusted these *compañeros*.

Armando told us that on Sundays Casillas passed through the area; according to the inveterate habits of the soldiers, he had a sweetheart there. We were anxious to attack quickly before our presence became known, strike a lucky blow, and capture the infamous soldier. We agreed that we would launch the attack on the following night, July 31. Armando Oliver would take charge of getting us trucks, guides who knew the zone, and a miner who could blow up the bridges linking the Bueycito highway with that of Manzanillo–Bayamo. At 2 p.m. on the following day, we set out. We spent a couple of hours getting to the crest of the Sierra Maestra, where we hid all our packs and continued with only our field equipment. We had to march a long time and quite often passed houses, in one of which a party was going on. We called all the party goers together and "read them the riot act," making it clear we would hold them responsible if our presence were discovered. We hurried on. The danger of these encounters was of course not very great, for there was no telephone or any other means of communication in the Sierra Maestra in those days, and an informer would have had to run to arrive before us.

We reached the house of *compañero* Santiestéban, who placed a pickup truck at our disposal; we also had two other trucks Armando Oliver had sent us. With the entire troop riding in the trucks—Lalo Sardiñas in the first, Ramirito and I in the second, and Ciro with his platoon in the third—we reached the village of Minas in just on three hours. In Minas the army had relaxed its vigilance, so the main task was to make sure no one moved toward Bueycito; the rear guard remained here, under the command of Lieutenant Vilo Acuña, today a commander in our Rebel Army, and we continued with the rest of the men to the outskirts of Bueycito.

At the entrance to the village, we stopped a coal truck and sent it on ahead with one of our men to see if there were army guards on watch, because sometimes at the entrance to Bueycito an army post inspected things coming from the Sierra Maestra. But there was no one; all the guards were sleeping happily.

Our plan was simple, though a bit pretentious: Lalo Sardiñas would attack the west side of the barracks, Ramiro and his platoon would surround it completely, Ciro with the machine gun belonging to the general staff squadron would be ready to attack from the front. Armando Oliver would arrive casually by car, suddenly illuminating the guards with his headlights. At that moment, Ramirito's men would invade the barracks and take everyone prisoner; at the same time precautions had to be taken to capture all the guards sleeping in their houses. Lieutenant Noda's squadron—Noda died later in the attack at Pino del Agua—was charged with detaining all vehicles on the highway until shooting began, and William was sent to blow up the bridge connecting Bueycito with the central highway, to slow down the enemy forces.

The plan never materialized: it was too difficult for inexperienced men unfamiliar with the terrain. Ramiro lost some of his men during the night and arrived somewhat late, and the car did not arrive, and at one point some dogs barked loudly while our troops were getting into position.

As I was walking along the main street of the village, a man came out of a house. I shouted, "Stop! Who is it?" The man, thinking I was a soldier, identified himself, "The Rural Guard!"

When I aimed my gun at him he ran back into the house, slamming the door, and I heard the sound of falling tables and chairs and breaking glass as he ran through the house. There was, I suppose, a tacit agreement between the two of us: I could not shoot, since the important thing was to take the barracks, and he did not shout a warning to his companions.

We advanced cautiously, and were putting the last men in position when the barracks guard moved forward, alerted by the barking dogs and probably by the noise of my encounter with the Rural Guard. We came face to face with each other, only a few meters apart. I had my Thompson cocked and he had his Garand. Israel Pardo was with me. I shouted, "Stop!" and the man with the Garand at the ready went to move. That was sufficient: I pulled the trigger with the aim of shooting him in the chest, but the gun failed and I was left defenseless. Israel Pardo tried to shoot, but his defective little .22 rifle did not discharge either. I don't really know how Israel came out of this alive. I only remember that, beneath a shower of bullets from the soldier's Garand, I ran at a speed I have never again matched, and flying through the air, turned the corner to land in the next cross street, where I fixed my Thompson.

The soldier, however, had unwittingly given the signal to attack, as his was the first shot to ring out. On hearing shots from all sides, the intimidated soldier hid behind a column, where we found him at the end of the battle that lasted only minutes. While Israel went to make contact, the gun battle stopped and we received notice of their surrender. When Ramirito's men heard the first shots, they moved in and attacked the barracks from the rear, firing through a wooden door.

There were 12 guards in the barracks, six of whom were wounded. We suffered one loss: *compañero* Pedro Rivera, a recent recruit, was shot in the chest. Three of our men had light wounds. We set fire to the barracks — after removing everything that might be useful to us — and left in the trucks, taking with us as prisoners the post sergeant and an informer named Orán.

Villagers along the way offered us cold beer and refreshments, for dawn had broken. The small wooden bridge near the central highway had been blown up. After the last truck passed, we blew up another small wooden bridge over a stream. The miner who did it, brought to us by Oliver, became a new member of the troop and he was a valuable acquisition; his name was Cristino Naranjo. He later became a commander and was murdered in the days following the triumph of the revolution.

We continued on and reached Minas, where we stopped to hold a small meeting. As part of the comedy, one of the Abich family, shopkeepers in the area, begged us in the name of the people to free the sergeant and the informer. We explained that we held them prisoner to guarantee with their lives that there would be no reprisals in the village, but he was so insistent that we agreed. So the two prisoners were released and the people's safety assured. Before leaving for the Sierra Maestra we buried our *compañero* in the town cemetery. A few reconnaissance planes flew high over us and, just to be safe, we stopped in a store and attended to the three wounded men. One had a light wound in the shoulder but it had torn the flesh, so treatment was somewhat difficult. One had a light wound in the hand from a small-caliber weapon. The third had a bump on his head: when the mules in the barracks, frightened or wounded by the shooting, had begun to kick wildly, they had apparently dislodged some plaster that had fallen on his head.

At Altos de California we left the trucks and distributed

the new weapons. Although my participation in the battle had been minimal and nothing heroic — the few shots fired in my direction were aimed at my back — I took a Browning machine gun, the jewel of the barracks, leaving the old Thompson and its dangerous bullets, which never fired at the right moment. The best arms were distributed to the best fighters, and we dismissed those who had acted poorly, including "the wet ones," a group of men who had fallen into the river as they were fleeing the first shots. Among those who performed well were Captain Ramiro Valdés, who led the attack, and Lieutenant Raúl Castro Mercader, who together with his men played a decisive role in the small battle.

When we reached the hills again, we learned that a state of emergency had been declared and censorship reestablished. We also heard of the great loss suffered by the revolution: Frank País had been murdered in the streets of Santiago. With his death, one of the purest and most glorious lives of the Cuban Revolution ended, and the people of Santiago, Havana, and all Cuba took to the streets in the spontaneous August strike. The government's semi-censorship became total censorship, and we entered a new period characterized by the silence of the pseudo-oppositionist chatterboxes, and by savage murders committed by Batista's thugs throughout Cuba, which spread the war to the entire country.

In Frank País we lost one of our most valiant fighters, but the reaction to his assassination showed that new forces were joining the struggle and the fighting spirit of the people was growing.

THE BATTLE OF
EL HOMBRITO

The column was only one month old and we were already tiring of our sedentary life in the Sierra Maestra. We were in the valley of El Hombrito [the little man], so named because looking toward the Sierra Maestra from the plains one could see a pair of gigantic slabs of rock one on top of the other, on the peak, resembling the figure of a small man.

Our force was still very green and we had to prepare the men before they faced really difficult situations. But the exigencies of our revolutionary war obliged us to be ready for combat at all times. We were obliged to attack any enemy columns invading that part of the Sierra Maestra, which by then was becoming known as the Liberated Territory of Cuba.

On August 29, [1957], or better said, the night of August 29, a peasant informed us that a large troop was preparing to ascend the Sierra Maestra along the road to El Hombrito, which ends at the valley or continues to Altos de Conrado to cross the mountains. We had been cured of falling for false information, and I took the man hostage and ordered him to tell the truth, threatening him with terrible punishment if he lied. But he swore and reswore that he was telling the truth and that the soldiers were already at Julio Zapatero's farm a couple of kilometers from the Sierra Maestra.

We moved into position by night. Lalo Sardiñas's platoon was to occupy the eastern flank in a small grove of dry, low-altitude ferns, and open fire on the column when it stopped. Ramiro Valdés, leading those men with less firepower, was to cover the western flank in order to carry out "acoustic violence" to spread the alarm. Although lightly armed, their position was less dangerous because the guards would have to cross a deep ravine to reach them.

The path by which the enemy would be coming bordered the side of the hill where Lalo was concealed. Ciro would attack them from the side. With a small column of the best-armed shooters, I would open hostilities with the first shot. The best squadron was led by Lieutenant Raúl Mercader, of Ramiro's platoon; they were to be used as shock troops to gather the fruits of victory. The plan was very simple: when the enemy reached a small bend in the path, turning almost 90 degrees around a boulder, I was to let 10 or 12 soldiers pass and then shoot the last one, in order to separate those men from the rest. Then the others would be annihilated rapidly by my men, Raúl Mercader's squadron would advance, the weapons of the dead would be taken, and we would retreat at once, protected by the fire of the rear guard led by Lieutenant Vilo Acuña.

At dawn, in a coffee grove — the position assigned to Ramiro Valdés — we were looking toward Julio Zapatero's house below us on the mountain slope. As the sun rose, we saw soldiers going in and out in early morning routines. After a while some of them put on their helmets, verifying our hostage's information. All of our men were ready in their combat positions.

I went to my post and we watched the first men of the column climbing laboriously. The wait was interminable and my fingers played on the trigger of my new weapon, the Browning machine gun, ready to enter action against the enemy for the first time. Finally, word came that they were approaching, and we heard their unworried voices and their raucous shouts. The first one passed, the second, the third, and I calculated that they were so spread out we wouldn't have enough time for the dozen to pass as planned. When I counted the sixth I heard a shout from ahead, and one of the soldiers raised his head in surprise. I opened fire immediately and the sixth man fell. Then the gun battle spread and at the second burst from my machine gun the six men disappeared from the path.

I ordered Raúl Mercader's squadron to attack, and some volunteers also moved in; the enemy was receiving fire from both flanks. Lieutenant Orestes of the forward guard, Raúl Mercader himself, Alfonso Zayas, Alcibíades Bermúdez, and Rodolfo Vázquez, among others, advanced, and from behind a large boulder they fired on the enemy column, which was of company strength and under the direction of Major Merob Sosa. Rodolfo Vázquez took the weapon of the soldier I had wounded. To our regret he turned out to be a medic and carried only the .45 revolver of the Rural Guard with 10 or 12 bullets. The other five men had escaped, scrambling off to the right of the path and retreating along a nearby riverbed. After a while we began to hear the first bazooka shots, fired by the enemy troops, now somewhat recovered from their shock at our surprise attack.

The Maxim machine gun was the only weapon of any weight we had, apart from my machine gun, but it had not yet been fired and Julio Pérez, who was assigned to it, failed to get it to work. On Ramiro Valdés's flank, Israel Pardo and Joel Iglesias had advanced on the enemy with their almost infantile weapons; shotguns fired from both sides made an infernal racket and increased the enemy's confusion. I ordered the two lateral platoons to retreat, and when they began to move, we also began our retreat, leaving the rear guard in charge of maintaining fire until all of Lalo Sardiñas's platoon had passed, as we anticipated a second line of resistance.

A little later, Vilo Acuña returned, having accomplished his mission, announcing the death of Hermes Leyva, cousin of Joel Iglesias. In the course of our withdrawal we came across a platoon sent by Fidel, whom I had notified of the imminent clash with superior enemy forces. Captain Ignacio Pérez led the group. We retreated some thousand meters from the battlefield and established a new ambush for the soldiers. They arrived at the small plateau where the battle had taken place and, before our very eyes, they burned Hermes Leyva's body, exercising their vengeance. In our impotent anger, we were limited to firing our rifles from a distance, which they answered with bazookas.

It was then that I learned that the soldier who had provoked my hasty shot with his shout had yelled, "This is a picnic," probably referring to the fact that he was reaching the peak of the hill. This battle proved to us how ill-prepared for combat our troop was, unable to fire accurately at a moving enemy line from close range—there could not have been more than 10 or 20 meters between the head of the enemy's column and our positions. Notwithstanding, it was a great triumph for us, as we had stopped Merob Sosa's column, which retreated at nightfall, and we had won a small victory over them. We had the miniscule recompense of winning one small weapon, but we lost a valiant fighter. All this we had accomplished with a handful of weapons against an entire company, 140 men at least, all of them well armed for modern warfare, who had used bazookas and perhaps even mortars against our positions, although their shots had been as wild and crazy as ours.

After this battle there were some promotions: Alfonso Zayas was named lieutenant for his brave conduct in combat, along with others I can't remember. That night, or the following day, after the soldiers had retreated, we had a conversation with Fidel in which he related euphorically how they had attacked Batista's forces in the region of Las Cuevas. I also learned of the deaths of some brave *compañeros* in that battle: Juventino Alarcón, from Manzanillo, one of the first to join the guerrilla band; Pastor [Palomares]; Yayo Castillo; and [Rigoberto] Oliva, son of a lieutenant of the Batista's army, a great fighter and great young man, as all of them were.

The battle won by Fidel was much more important than our own, since it involved not an ambush but an attack on a defended garrison. Although they did not destroy the enemy forces, they caused many casualties, and the soldiers retreated from that position the next day. One of the heroes of the day was "El Negro Pilón" [Félix Lugones], the brave fighter who recounted how he arrived one day at a peasant hut to see "a heap of strange tubes with boxes next to them," which turned out to be bazookas abandoned by the enemy. But none of us—and much less Félix (Pilón)—was familiar with this weapon except by name. Suffering from a leg wound, he left them there and withdrew from the hut. That is how we lost the opportunity of acquiring these weapons, so effective in attacks on small enemy fortifications.

There was another repercussion of our battle; one or two days later we heard that an army communiqué had spoken of five or six dead; later we learned that, in addition to our *compañero* whose body they had abused, we also had to mourn four or five murdered peasants. The sinister Merob Sosa had assumed they were responsible for the ambush because they had not reported our troop's presence in the area to the army. I remember their names: Abigaíl, Calixto, Pablito Lebón (of Haitian descent), and Gonzalo González, all of them completely or partially innocent of complicity with us. They knew of our presence and sympathized with our cause, as did all the peasantry, but they had been totally unaware of the maneuver we were preparing. Conscious of the methods employed by the chiefs of Batista's army, we concealed our intentions from the peasants; if one of them happened to pass through an area where an ambush was being prepared, we held them until it was over. The unfortunate peasants were murdered in their huts, which were then set on fire.

This battle showed us how easy it was, in certain conditions, to attack columns on the march. Furthermore, we became convinced of the tactical correctness of always aiming at the head of the approaching troops, in an attempt to kill the first one or the first few. The enemy troops would then refuse to advance, immobilizing the enemy force. Little by little, this tactic crystallized and finally it became so systematic that the enemy stopped entering the Sierra Maestra, and, scandalously, soldiers even refused to march in the forward guard. Yet there had still not been enough battles for this tactic to be perfected.

Now reunited with Fidel, we were able to talk about our small deeds, which were nonetheless impressive because of the greatly disproportionate forces between our poorly armed combatants and the exceptionally well-armed forces of repression.

This battle more or less marked the moment of the withdrawal of Batista's troops from the Sierra Maestra. Thereafter, they only entered on rare occasions, in daring feats by Sánchez Mosquera, the bravest, most murderous, and one of the most thieving of all of Batista's military chiefs.

EL PATOJO

A few days ago, a cable brought the news of the death of some Guatemalan patriots, among them Julio Roberto Cáceres Valle.

In this difficult profession of a revolutionary, in the midst of class wars convulsing the entire continent, death is a frequent accident. But the death of a friend, a *compañero* during difficult hours, someone who has shared dreams of better times, is always painful for the friend receiving the news, and Julio Roberto was a great friend. He was short and frail; for that reason we called him "El Patojo," Guatemalan slang meaning "Shorty" or "Kid."

El Patojo had witnessed the birth of our revolution while in Mexico and had volunteered to join us. Fidel, however, did not want to bring any more foreigners into the struggle for national liberation in which I had the honor to participate.

A few days after the revolution triumphed, El Patojo sold his few belongings and, with only a small suitcase, appeared in Cuba. He worked in various branches of public administration, and he was the first head of personnel of the Department of Industrialization of the National Institute of Agrarian Reform (INRA). But he was never happy with his work. El Patojo was looking for something different; he was seeking the liberation of his own country. The revolution had changed him profoundly, as it had all of us. The bewildered young man who had left Guatemala without fully understanding the defeat had now become a fully conscious revolutionary.

The first time we met we were on a train, fleeing Guatemala, a couple of months after the [1954] fall of [Jacobo] Árbenz. We were going to Tapachula, from where we could reach Mexico City. El Patojo was several years younger than I, but we immediately formed a lasting friendship. Together we made the trip from Chiapas to Mexico City; together we faced the same problems — we were both penniless, defeated, and forced to earn a living in an indifferent if not hostile environment. El Patojo had no money and I only a few pesos; I bought a camera and, together, we undertook the illegal job of taking pictures of people in city parks. Our partner was a Mexican who had a small darkroom where we developed the film. We got to know all of Mexico City, walking from one end to another, delivering the atrocious photographs we had taken. We battled with all kinds of clients, trying to convince them that the little boy in the photo really was very cute and it really was a great bargain to pay a Mexican peso for such a marvel. This is how we ate for several months. Little by little the contingencies of revolutionary life separated us. I have already said that Fidel did not want to bring him to Cuba, not because of any shortcomings of his, but to avoid turning our army into a mosaic of nationalities.

El Patojo had been a journalist, had studied physics at the University of Mexico, had left his studies and then returned to them, without ever getting very far. He earned his living in various places, at various jobs, and never asked for anything. I still do not know whether that sensitive and serious young man was overly timid, or too proud to recognize his weaknesses and personal problems to approach a friend for help. El Patojo was an introvert, highly intelligent, broadly cultured, sensitive. He matured steadily and in his last moments was ready to put his great sensibilities at the service of his people. He belonged to the Guatemalan Labor Party and had disciplined himself in that life; he was developing into a fine revolutionary cadre. By then, little remained of his earlier hypersensitivity. Revolution purifies people, improves and develops them, just as the experienced farmer corrects the deficiencies of crops and strengthens their good qualities.

After he came to Cuba we almost always lived in the same house, as was fitting for two old friends. But we no longer maintained our earlier intimacy in this new life, and I only suspected El Patojo's intentions when I sometimes saw him earnestly studying one of the native Indian languages of his country. One day he told me he was leaving, that the time had come for him to do his duty.

El Patojo had no military training; he simply felt that duty called him. He was going to his country to fight, gun in hand, to somehow reproduce our guerrilla struggle. It was then that we had one of our few long talks. I limited myself to recommending strongly these three things: constant movement, constant wariness, and eternal vigilance. Movement—never stay put; never spend two nights in the same place; never stop moving from one place to another. Wariness—at the beginning, be wary even of your own shadow, friendly peasants, informants, guides, contacts; mistrust everything until you hold a liberated zone. Vigilance—constant guard duty; constant reconnaissance; establishment of a camp in a safe place and, above all, never sleep beneath a roof, never sleep in a house where you can be surrounded. This was the synthesis of our guerrilla experience; it was the only thing — along with a warm handshake — which I could give to my friend. Could I advise him not to do it? With what right? We had undertaken something at a time when it was believed impossible, and now he saw that it had succeeded.

El Patojo left and in time came the news of his death. At first we hoped there had been a confusion of names, that there had been some mistake, but unfortunately his body was identified by his own mother; there could be no doubt he was dead. And not only El Patojo, but a group of *compañeros* with him, all of them as brave, as selfless, as intelligent perhaps as he, but not known to us personally.

Once more there is the bitter taste of defeat and the unanswered question: Why did he not learn from the experience of others? Why did those men not heed more carefully the simple advice we had given them? There is an urgent investigation into how it came about, how El Patojo died. We still do not know exactly what happened, but we do know that the region was poorly chosen, that the men were not physically prepared, that they were not sufficiently wary and, of course, that they were not sufficiently vigilant. The repressive army took them by surprise, killed a few, dispersed the rest, then returned to pursue them, virtually annihilating them. They took some prisoners; others, like El Patojo, died in battle. After being dispersed, the guerrillas were probably hunted down as we had been after Alegría de Pío.

Once again youthful blood has fertilized the fields of the Americas in order to make freedom possible. Another battle has been lost; we must make time to weep for our fallen *compañeros* while we sharpen our machetes. From the valuable and tragic experience of the cherished dead, we must firmly resolve not to repeat their errors, to avenge the death of each one of them with many victories, and to achieve definitive liberation.

When El Patojo left Cuba, he left nothing behind, and he did not leave any messages; he had few clothes or personal belongings to worry about. Old mutual friends in Mexico, however, brought me some poems he had written in a notebook and left there. They are the last verses of a revolutionary; they are, in addition, a love song to the revolution, to the homeland, and to a woman. To that woman El Patojo knew and loved in Cuba, this final verse is addressed, this injunction:

> Take this, it is only my heart
> Hold it in your hand
> And when the dawn arrives,
> Open your hand
> And let the sun warm it ...

El Patojo's heart has remained among us, in the hands of his beloved and in the loving hands of an entire people, waiting to be warmed beneath the sun of a new day which will surely dawn for Guatemala and for all the Americas. Today, in the Ministry of Industry where he left many friends, there is a small school of statistics named "Julio Roberto Cáceres Valle" in his memory. Later, when Guatemala is free, his beloved name will surely be given to a school, a factory, a hospital, to any place where people fight and work to build a new society.

Part**2** Further Writings on the Cuban Revolutionary War

A REVOLUTION BEGINS

The history of the military takeover on March 10, 1952 — the bloodless coup led by Fulgencio Batista — does not, of course, begin on the day of that barracks revolt. Its antecedents must be sought far back in Cuban history: further back than the intervention of US Ambassador Sumner Welles in 1933; further back still than the Platt Amendment in 1901; much further back than the landing of the hero Narciso López, direct envoy of the US annexationists. We have to go back to John Quincy Adams's times, who, at the beginning of the 19th century, announced his country's policy regarding Cuba: that like an apple torn from Spain, Cuba would fall into the hands of Uncle Sam. These are all links in a long chain of continental aggression that has not been aimed solely at Cuba.

This tide, this ebb and flow of the imperial wave, is marked by the fall of democratic governments and the rise of new ones in the face of uncontainable pressure from the multitudes. History exhibits similar characteristics in all of Latin America: dictatorial governments representing a small minority come to power through coups d'état; democratic governments with a broad popular base arise laboriously and, frequently, even before coming to power, are already compromised by concessions they have had to make beforehand to survive. Although in this sense the Cuban Revolution marks an exception in all the Americas, it is necessary to point out the antecedents of this whole process. It was because of this process that the author of these lines, tossed here and there by the waves of social movements convulsing the Americas, had the opportunity to meet another Latin American exile: Fidel Castro.

I met him on one of those cold Mexican nights, and I remember that our first discussion was about international politics. Within a few hours — by dawn — I was one of the future expeditionaries. But I would like to clarify how and why it was in Mexico that I met Cuba's current head of state.

It happened in 1954, during a low-point for democratic governments, when the last Latin American revolutionary democracy still standing — that of Jacobo Árbenz — succumbed to cold, premeditated aggression, conducted by the United States behind the smokescreen of its continental propaganda. The visible head of that aggression was US Secretary of State John Foster Dulles, who by a strange coincidence was also the lawyer for and a stockholder in the United Fruit Company, the main imperialist enterprise in Guatemala.

I had departed from Guatemala defeated, united with all Guatemalans by the pain, hoping, searching for a way to rebuild the anguished country's future.

And Fidel came to Mexico looking for neutral ground in which to prepare his forces for the big effort. An internal split had already occurred after the assault on the Moncada military garrison in Santiago de Cuba. All the weak at heart had split away, those who for one reason or another joined political parties or revolutionary groups which demanded less sacrifice. New recruits were already joining the freshly formed ranks of what was called the July 26 Movement, named after the date of the 1953 attack on the Moncada garrison. For those in charge of training these people—under necessarily clandestine conditions in Mexico—an extremely difficult task was beginning. They were fighting against the Mexican government, agents of the FBI, and also those of Batista—three forces that in one way or another joined together, for whom money and buying people off were integral tools. In addition, we had to struggle against [Rafael] Trujillo's spies and against the poor selection of the human material—especially in Miami. And after overcoming all these difficulties we had to accomplish something extremely important: we had to depart ... and then ... arrive, and all the rest, which, at the time, seemed easy to us. Today we can measure how much it all cost in effort, sacrifice, and lives.

Aided by a small, intimate team, Fidel Castro gave himself, all his energy, and his extraordinary work spirit entirely to the task of organizing the armed fighters who were to leave for Cuba. He almost never gave classes on military tactics, since time for him was in short supply. The rest of us were able to learn quite a bit from Commander Alberto Bayo. Listening to those first classes, my almost immediate impression was that victory was, in fact, possible. It had seemed doubtful when I first enrolled with the rebel commander, to whom I was linked from the beginning by a leaning toward romantic adventure and the notion that it would be well worth dying on a foreign beach for such pure ideals.

Several months passed in this way. Our marksmanship began to improve, and the best shooters emerged. We found a ranch in Mexico where—under Commander Bayo's direction and with myself as head of personnel—the final preparations were made, aiming to leave in March 1956. Around that time, however, two

Mexican police units—both on Batista's payroll—were hunting Fidel Castro, and one of them had the good fortune, in financial terms, to capture him; but they made the absurd error, also financial, of not killing him after taking him prisoner. Within a few days many of his followers were captured. Our ranch on the outskirts of Mexico City also fell into police hands, and we all went to jail.

This all postponed the beginning of the last part of the first stage.

Some of us were imprisoned for 57 days, which we counted off one by one, with the perennial threat of extradition hanging over our heads (as Commander Calixto García and I can attest). But at no time did we lose our personal confidence in Fidel Castro. And Fidel did some things we could almost say compromised his revolutionary discipline for the sake of friendship. I remember explaining my specific case to him: a foreigner, in Mexico illegally, with a whole series of charges against me. I told him that by no means should the revolution be held up on my account; that he could leave me behind; that I understood the situation and would try to fight wherever I was sent; and that the only effort on my behalf should be to have me sent to a nearby country and not to Argentina. I also remember Fidel's sharp reply: "I will not abandon you." And he didn't, and precious time and money had to be diverted to get us out of the Mexican jail. Fidel's personal commitment toward people he holds in esteem is the key to the fanatical loyalty he inspires. Adherence to principles, and adherence to the individual, combine to make the Rebel Army an indivisible fist.

The days passed as we worked clandestinely, hiding ourselves where we could, shunning public appearances to the extent possible, hardly going out into the streets. After several months, we discovered there was a traitor in our ranks, whose name we did not know, and that he had sold a shipment of arms. We also learned that he had sold the yacht and a transmitter, although he had not yet drawn up the "legal contract" of the sale. That first instalment served to show the Cuban authorities that the traitor, in fact, knew our internal workings; but it also saved us, since it showed us the same thing.

From that moment on, our preparations were necessarily feverish. The *Granma* was put into shape at an extraordinary speed. We piled up as many provisions as we could get — very few, in fact — along with uniforms, rifles, equipment, and two antitank guns with hardly any ammunition. Finally, on November 25, 1956, at 2 a.m., we set out to make Fidel's words — mocked by the official press — real: "In 1956 we will be free or we will be martyrs."

We left the port of Tuxpan with our lights out, an infernal heap of men and all types of equipment. We had very bad weather, yet although sea travel was prohibited, the estuary remained calm. We entered the Gulf of Mexico and shortly after turned on the lights. We made a frantic search for antihistamines to combat seasickness, and could not find them. We sang the Cuban national anthem and the July 26 hymn for a total of perhaps five minutes, and then the whole boat assumed a ridiculous, tragic appearance: men clutching their stomachs, anguish written in their faces, some with their heads in buckets, others lying immobile on the deck in strange positions, their clothes covered in vomit. With the exception of two or three sailors, and four or five others, the rest of the 82 crew members were seasick. But after the fourth or fifth day, the general panorama improved slightly. We discovered that what we thought was a leak in the boat was actually an open plumbing faucet. We had already thrown anything superfluous overboard in order to lighten the ballast.

The route we had chosen involved making a wide turn south of Cuba, bordering Jamaica and the Grand Cayman Islands, and landing someplace close to the village of Niquero in Oriente province. We were progressing quite slowly. On November 30 we heard over the radio news of the uprising in Santiago de Cuba, started by our great Frank País, to coincide with the expedition's arrival. The following day, December 1, at night, we set the bow on a straight line toward Cuba, desperately seeking the Cape Cruz lighthouse as we ran out of water, food, and fuel.

At 2 a.m., on a black, stormy night, the situation was disturbing. The lookouts paced back and forth, searching for the ray of light that refused to appear on the horizon. [Roberto] Roque, an ex-navy lieutenant, once again climbed on to the small upper bridge, looking for light from the cape. Losing his footing, he fell into the water. Shortly after continuing on our way, we saw the light; but the labored advance of our boat made the final hours of the trip interminable. It was already daylight when we reached Cuba at a place known as Belic on Las Coloradas beach.

A coast-guard boat spotted us and radioed the discovery to Batista's army. We had just disembarked and entered the swamp, in great haste and carrying only vital supplies, when enemy planes attacked us. Walking through the mangroves, we naturally could not be seen or pursued by the planes, but the dictatorship's army was already on our trail. It took us several hours to get out of the swamp, where we had ended up due to the inexperience and irresponsibility of a *compañero* who said he knew the way. We wound up on solid ground, lost, walking in circles.

We were an army of shadows, ghosts, walking as if to the beat of some dark, psychic mechanism. The crossing had been seven days of constant hunger and seasickness, followed by three more days — terrible days — on land. Exactly 10 days after the departure from Mexico, in the early hours of December 5, after a night march interrupted by fainting, exhaustion, and rest for the troops, we reached a point known — paradoxically — by the name of Alegría de Pío [joy of the pious]. It was a small grove of trees, bordering a sugarcane field on one side and open to some valleys on the other, with dense woods starting farther back. The place was ill-suited for camp, but we stopped anyway to rest for a day and resume our march the following night.

ADRIFT

The day after the surprise attack at Alegría de Pío, we were walking through trees where red earth alternated with "dog-tooth" rocks. Recoiling from the cracks of solitary shots, from all directions, we never managed to find a real road. Chao, a veteran of the Spanish Civil War, pointed out that moving as we were was a surefire way to fall into an enemy ambush. He suggested we find an appropriate place to wait for nightfall, and continue our journey then.

We were virtually without water and a mishap had befallen our only milk container. Benítez, to whom it had been entrusted, had slipped it into his uniform pocket upside down, so the little holes made in it to drink through were facing down. When we went to drink our ration—a vitamin tube of condensed milk with a sip of water—we saw with dismay that it had spilled all over Benítez's pocket and uniform.

We managed to establish ourselves in a kind of cave that had a wide view to one side, but unfortunately it was impossible to cut off any enemy advance from the other. Since, however, we were more concerned with not being seen than with defending ourselves, we resolved to stay there all day. All five of us made an express promise to fight to the death. Those who made this pledge: Ramiro Valdés, Juan Almeida, Chao, Benítez, and the author of this account. All five survived the terrible experience of the defeat [at Alegría de Pío], and the subsequent battles.

When night came, we set out again. I figured out which was the North Star, remembering what I knew of astronomy, and for two days we guided ourselves eastward by it, heading toward the Sierra Maestra. A long time later, I learned that the star we used to find our way was not the North Star, it was simply good luck that had us moving in approximately the right direction. At dawn we arrived at some cliffs near the coast.

We could see the sea some 50 meters below us, and the tempting sight of a pool of water, which appeared to us to be fresh water. That night, a swarm of crabs crawled around us and, driven by hunger, we killed a few, but since we could not build a fire we swallowed their jelly-like parts raw, provoking a horrible thirst.

After a lot of searching, we discovered a reasonable path by which we could descend to the water. But in the confusion of climbing back and forth, we lost sight of the pool we had seen from above, and could only mitigate our thirst at some little puddles of rain water gathered in holes in the "dog-tooth" rocks. We used the tiny asthma inhaler pump to extract the water; only a few drops for each of us.

We marched on, demoralized, in no particular direction. From time to time, a plane passed over the sea. Walking across the coastal rocks was exhausting, and some suggested that we move along the cliffs. But that held a serious drawback: the enemy could see us. So we stayed in the shade of some bushes, waiting for the sun to go down. At nightfall we found a small beach and bathed.

I tried to repeat a trick I had once read about in some novel or popular science magazine, where it was explained that fresh water mixed with a third of seawater produced very good drinking water. I experimented, using what remained in a canteen, but the result was pathetic: a briny potion that earned me the criticism of my *compañeros*. Somewhat refreshed by the swim, we resumed our march. It was night and, if I remember correctly, there was quite a good moon. Almeida and I, marching in the lead, suddenly noticed that in one of the little huts fishermen put up at the sea's edge to protect themselves from bad weather, there were shadows of sleeping men. We believed they were soldiers, but we were already too close to retrace our steps, and instead advanced quickly. Almeida was about to demand that they surrender, when we had a happy surprise—they were three expeditionaries from the *Granma*: Camilo Cienfuegos, Pancho González, and Pablo Hurtado. At once we began to exchange experiences, news, and opinions about the little each of us knew concerning other *compañeros* and the battle. Camilo's group offered us sugarcane stalks, which they had pulled up before fleeing. Their sweet juice somewhat appeased our stomachs. They were chewing avidly on crabs. They had found a way to quench their thirst by drawing water from the little holes in the rocks with hollowed-out sticks.

We trekked on together—eight of us now the number of surviving combatants of the remnant *Granma* army—and we had no information about whether there were other survivors. Logic had it that there should be other groups like ours, but we had no idea where to find them. All we knew was that by continuing with the sea to our right we were heading east, that is, toward the Sierra Maestra, where we were to take refuge. It did not escape us that in the case of an encounter with the enemy, trapped as we were between the rocky cliffs and the sea, we would have no chance to flee. I don't remember whether we marched along the coast for one day or two, I only know that we ate a few of the little prickly pears growing along the shore—one or two each to stave off hunger. We were also tortured by thirst, and had to ration every last drop of water.

One dawn, desperately tired, we arrived at the sea shore. We stopped there to doze, waiting for enough light to see how to continue—it seemed the cliffs we faced were too steep.

As soon as it was light enough, we began to explore. Before our eyes appeared a big house of palm wood, which seemed to belong to some fairly prosperous peasant. My immediate instinct was to not get too close to this sort of house, since presumably its inhabitants would be hostile to us; indeed, the army might even be occupying the house. Benítez did not share my opinion, and in the end we approached the house.

I stayed outside while he climbed over a barbed-wire fence; someone else was with us but I don't remember who. Suddenly, I noticed in the dim light the clear silhouette of a uniformed man, an M-1 rifle in his hands. I thought our last moments had come, at least for Benítez, whom I could not warn since he was closer to the man. Benítez made it nearly to the soldier's side, then wheeled around and returned to me, saying ingenuously that he had come back because he had seen "a man with a shotgun" and that it had not seemed wise to ask him any questions.

Benítez and the rest of us felt as if we had been born again, but our odyssey did not end there. After a discreet inspection of the area, we realized it was necessary to scale the cliffs, which were not so steep there. In fact, we were approaching the zone called Ojo de Buey [eye of the ox], thus named because of a small river flowing down to the sea, cutting right through the cliff.

Daylight surprised us before the end of our climb, and we only had time to find a cave, from which the entire quiet horizon could be observed. Then we saw some men come ashore from a navy skiff—we counted about 30 of them—and others embarked, in what appeared to be a relief operation. We learned later that these were Laurent's men, that fearful murderer of the navy, who had accomplished his mission to execute a group of our *compañeros*, and was relieving his men.

Before Benítez's astounded eyes, the "men with the shotguns" appeared, in all their tragic reality. The situation was not good. If we were discovered, we had not the slightest chance of escape; we would have no alternative but to fight it out to the end.

We passed the day without a mouthful, rigorously rationing our water in the eyepiece of a pair of field glasses so that each received exactly the same amount.

At night we resumed our march, trying to put as much distance between ourselves and the area where we had spent some of the most anguished days of the war, between hunger and thirst, our sense of defeat, and the imminence of palpable, unavoidable danger, making us feel like cornered rats.

After some wandering, we came upon the river that empties into the sea, or one of its tributaries. Throwing ourselves to the ground, we drank avidly and at length, like horses, until our empty stomachs refused to absorb another drop. We filled our canteens and kept going. At dawn we reached the top of a small hill with some trees. The group spread out in order to hide or resist more effectively. We spent the entire day watching small, low-flying planes equipped with loudspeakers emitting noises that would have been incomprehensible except that Almeida and Benítez, veterans of Moncada, understood they were calling for our surrender. From time to time, we heard unidentifiable shouts from the woods.

That night, our wanderings led us near a house where a band could be heard playing. Once more, we had differences of opinion. Ramiro, Almeida, and I were of the firm opinion that we must absolutely avoid showing ourselves at a dance or any such festive occasion, because the peasants would announce our presence immediately—out of nothing more than normal indiscretion. Benítez and Camilo felt that we had to enter, at any price, so that we could eat. Finally, Ramiro and I were assigned the task of going to the house, finding out any news, and procuring food. As we approached, the music stopped suddenly and we distinctly heard a man's voice saying something like, "Now, let us toast our fellow soldiers, whose exploits have been so brilliant," etc. That was enough for us to turn around as quickly and stealthily as possible, and we reported to our *compañeros* exactly which men were celebrating at the party.

We took up our march, but the men increasingly refused to walk. That night, or perhaps the following, almost all the *compañeros* were resistant to continuing. We had no choice but to knock at the door of a peasant near the road, at Puercas Gordas, nine days after the surprise attack at Alegría de Pío.

We were warmly received, and the little hut became the scene of endless feasting. We ate for hours and hours, until dawn surprised us and it was not possible to leave. During the morning, peasants arrived who had learned of our presence. Filled with curiosity and friendly concern, they came to meet us, offer us food, or bring us gifts.

But then the little house sheltering us transformed into a kind of hell. First, Almeida was struck down by diarrhea; then, in a flash, eight thankless intestines gave proof of their ingratitude, poisoning our small refuge. Some of the men began to vomit. Pablo Hurtado — exhausted by days of marching, seasickness, and accumulated thirst and hunger — could no longer stand up.

We determined to leave that night. The peasants told us they had heard news that Fidel was alive. They said they could take us to some places he might be, with Crescencio Pérez, but that we would have to leave our weapons and uniforms behind. Almeida and I kept our Two Star Thompson machine guns; the eight rifles and all the cartridges stayed in the peasant's hut for safekeeping. We planned to make it to the Sierra Maestra in stages, stopping over with peasants; we therefore divided into two groups, one of three men, one of four.

Our group, if I don't remember incorrectly, comprised Pancho González, Ramiro Valdés, Almeida, and myself. In the other were Camilo, Benítez, and Chao. Pablo Hurtado was so sick he stayed at the house.

We had scarcely left when the owner gave in to the temptation of passing on the news to a friend, asking his advice concerning the best way to hide our arms. The latter convinced him he could sell them. They had dealings with a third person and it was he who denounced us to the army. So, a few hours after our departure from the first hospitable Cuban hearth, there was an enemy raid; they took Pablo Hurtado prisoner and seized our weapons.

We were staying in the house of an Adventist named Argelio Rosabal, known by everyone as "Pastor." This *compañero*, hearing the ill-fated news, quickly contacted another peasant who knew the zone thoroughly and was a rebel sympathizer. That same night we left for another, safer shelter. The peasant whom we met on that occasion was Guillermo García: today he is the commander of the western army and a member of the national leadership of our party.

Subsequently, we stayed in several peasant homes, those of Carlos Más, who later joined our ranks, Perucho [Carrillo], and other *compañeros* whose names I don't remember. One morning at daybreak, after crossing the road to Pilón and marching without any guide at all, we reached the farm of Mongo Pérez — Crescencio's brother. There we found all the surviving expeditionaries who were free: Fidel Castro, Universo Sánchez, Faustino Pérez, Raúl Castro, Ciro Redondo, Efigenio Ameijeiras, René Rodríguez, and Armando Rodríguez. A few days later, we were joined by Morán, Crespo, Julito Díaz, Calixto García, Calixto Morales, and Bermúdez.

Our small troop was without uniforms and without weapons — the two Thompsons were all we had salvaged from the disaster. Fidel reproached us bitterly.

Throughout the campaign, and even today, I remember his admonition, "You have not paid for the error you committed, because the price you pay for abandoning your weapons in such circumstances is your life. Your only hope of survival, in the event of a head-on encounter with the army, was your guns. To abandon them was criminal, and stupid."

PINO DEL AGUA

After meeting with Fidel on August 29, [1957], we marched for several days, together sometimes and sometimes separated by some distance, but with the aim of reaching the Pino del Agua sawmill together. We had information that there were no enemy troops at Pino del Agua, or at the most, only a small garrison.

Fidel's plan was as follows: if there were a small garrison, to take it; if not, to make our presence known, and then he would continue with his troops toward the region of Chivirico, while we lay in wait for Batista's army. They always came immediately in such cases, to make a show of strength and diminish the revolutionary effect of our presence on the peasants.

In the days leading up to the battle of Pino del Agua, during the march from Dos Brazos del Guayabo to the place of battle, several events transpired, whose principal actors were to play a role in the subsequent history of the revolution.

One of those was the desertion of two local peasants: Manolo and Pupo Beatón. They had joined the guerrilla ranks shortly before the battle of El Uvero, and fought there; today they were abandoning our camp. Later, these two individuals were reincorporated into the guerrilla forces, and Fidel pardoned their treachery, but they never rose above being seminomadic bandits. For some personal reason, Manolo killed Cristino Naranjo after the triumph of the revolution. Later, he succeeded in escaping his confines in La Cabaña fortress and organized a small guerrilla band in the very place in the Sierra Maestra where he had fought alongside us. There he committed more misdeeds, such as murdering Pancho Tamayo, a brave *compañero* who had joined us during the first days of the revolution. Eventually, a group of peasants captured Manolo and his brother Pupo; both of them were shot in Santiago.

A painful accident also happened: A *compañero* named Roberto Rodríguez was disarmed for insubordination. He was very undisciplined and the squadron lieutenant took his weapon, exercising a disciplinary right. Roberto Rodríguez got hold of the revolver of a *compañero* and committed suicide. A small argument took place, because I was opposed to granting him military honors, whereas the men considered him one of the fallen. I argued that committing suicide in conditions such us ours was a criminal act, independent of the good qualities of the *compañero*. After a few insubordinate stirrings, we finally held a wake for him, without granting him honors.

One or two days earlier, he had told me part of his story, and it became clear he was excessively sensitive. He was making great efforts to adapt to the hard life of the guerrilla, and, furthermore, to guerrilla discipline, all of which clashed with his physical weakness and instinctive rebelliousness.

Two days later, we sent a small detachment to Minas de Bueycito to make a show of strength there, since it was September 4. The little group was commanded by Captain Ciro Redondo, who came back with a prisoner, Leonardo Baró. This same Baró was to play an important role in the ranks of the counterrevolution. He remained our prisoner for a good while, until one day he told me the miserable story of his mother's illness, which I believed. I tried in passing to convince him to make a political stand. I proposed that he take a bus, see his mother in Havana, and then demand asylum in an embassy, proclaiming his unwillingness to fight against us any more and denouncing Batista's regime. He objected, saying he could not denounce the regime his brothers were fighting for, and we agreed that he should limit himself, in requesting asylum, to declaring that he didn't want to fight any more.

We sent him off with four *compañeros*. They had rigorous orders not to allow him to see anyone on the way, since he knew many of the peasants who had visited us at our camp. The four *compañeros* were also told to make the trip on foot, as far as the outskirts of Bayamo, where they could leave him and return by another route.

These men did not follow their orders. They allowed themselves to be seen by many people; they even held a meeting at which Baró was celebrated as a liberated prisoner and a supposed sympathizer. Then they traveled to Bayamo by jeep. On the way they were intercepted by Batista's troops and the four *compañeros* were murdered. We never knew for sure if Baró participated in this crime. We do know that he immediately installed himself at Minas de Bueycito, put himself under the orders of the assassin Sánchez Mosquera, and began to identify, among those who came to do their market shopping, the peasants who had been in contact with our guerrilla group. My error cost the people of Cuba countless victims.

Several days after the triumph of the revolution, Baró was captured and executed.

Soon after the incident, we went down to San Pablo de Yao, where we were welcomed with open arms. We occupied it peacefully for several hours (there were no enemy troops), and began to make contacts, meeting many people from the area. We loaded as much merchandise as possible into trucks provided for us by the same merchants who sold us supplies on credit (during that period we paid with bonds). It was on that occasion that we met our great *compañera* Lidia Doce, who was later charged with the column's various contact tasks, until her death in Havana.

The task of transporting the goods from Yao was hard, as the road climbing from San Pablo de Yao to Pico Verde, past the Cristina mine, is very steep, and only trucks with four-wheel drive and not much weight can make the climb. Ours broke down en route, and the supplies had to be carried up between mules and men.

We also witnessed in those days a range of partings, for different motives. A *compañero*, a good fighter, was expelled from the guerrilla for drunkenness during the expedition to Yao, while he was on guard, and therefore endangering the entire column. Another, Jorge Sotús, left his position as squadron leader and went to Miami with a letter of recommendation from Fidel. In reality, Sotús had never adapted himself to the Sierra Maestra, and his men disliked him because of his despotic nature. His career had many ups and downs. In Miami his attitude was a vacillating one, if not traitorous. He rejoined the ranks of our army, was pardoned, and his past errors forgiven. During Hubert Matos's time he betrayed us and was sentenced to 20 years' imprisonment. With the complicity of a jailer, he fled to Miami. He had finished the preparations for a pirate incursion into Cuban territory, when he died, apparently electrocuted in an accident.

Among the other *compañeros* who left us at that time was Marcelo Fernández, coordinator of the July 26 Movement in the cities. He returned to work in his area of responsibility after a long stay with us in the Sierra Maestra.

After these incidents, we resumed our march toward Pino del Agua, arriving there on September 10. Pino del Agua is a hamlet built around a sawmill on a ridge of the Sierra Maestra. During that period it was managed by a Spaniard, and had a number of workers, but not one soldier. We occupied the hamlet that night, and Fidel let his itinerary become known to local residents, calculating that the news would filter through to the army.

We conducted a small diversionary maneuver, and while Fidel's column continued its march toward Santiago, in full view of all, we detoured during the night and laid an ambush for the enemy. In charge of our provisions—assuming the enemy did not take too long to arrive—was, as always, old Tamayo, who lived in the region at a place called Cuevas de Peladero.

We distributed the troops in such a way that all roads would be under surveillance. We extended our surveillance to the road from Yao to Pico Verde, some leagues before Pino del Agua, and to another more direct trail that climbed into the Sierra Maestra, not passable by trucks. The Pico Verde group was very small— the best shots—and was charged with raising the alarm in case that were necessary. It was a good road to withdraw along, and we planned to use it after the action. Efigenio Ameijeiras was in charge of guarding one of the rear access roads, which also came from the region of Pico Verde. Lalo Sardiñas and his platoon remained in the Zapato zone, guarding several sawmill roads that extend to the banks of the Peladero river. It was an excessive precaution, since the enemy would have to march a long time through the Sierra Maestra to reach these roads, and it was not their custom to march through the mountains in columns. Ciro Redondo and his platoon were in charge of defending the access road from Siberia — that is the region between El Uvero and Pino del Agua, and the road chosen for Ciro on the edge of the Sierra Maestra connected two sawmills.

Our forces were distributed along the road that climbs to Guisa, on a rocky outcrop in the woods, to surprise the trucks and concentrate our firepower on their most probable route. The position allowed us to observe the trucks from a great distance. The plan was simple: to open fire on them from both sides, immobilizing the first truck at a bend in the road, and firing on all the others in order to halt them. We thought we could take three or four vehicles if the surprise tactic worked. The platoon assigned to the action had the best arms, and was reinforced with some of Captain Raúl Castro Mercader's people.

We spent approximately seven days in ambush, waiting patiently, without any troops arriving. On the seventh day, when I was at the small command post where food was made for the troops in waiting, I was informed that the enemy was approaching. Since the climbs are very pronounced, before seeing anything we could hear the humming of the trucks as they clambered up the slope.

Our forces prepared for battle. In the key position, we placed the men under Captain Ignacio Pérez's command, whose job was to stop the first truck. Others who were to fire on the other vehicles were along the flanks. Twenty minutes before the battle, a torrential downpour fell—normal in the Sierra Maestra—soaking us to the bone. Meanwhile, the enemy soldiers were advancing, more concerned with the rain than with the possibility of an attack. The *compañero* charged with opening hostilities fired his Thompson machine gun; effectively, he opened the battle, but under the circumstances hit no one. The gunfire spread and the soldiers in the first truck, more frightened and surprised than hurt by our attack, leaped on to the road and disappeared behind some boulders, after killing one of our great fighters and the poet of our column, whom we called "Crucito," José de la Cruz.

The battle developed somewhat strangely. An enemy soldier took refuge under the truck at the bend in the road, and would not show his head to anyone. A minute or two later, I arrived at the scene. Many of our people were retreating, obeying a false order—a frequent accident in the midst of combat. Arquímedes Fonseca was wounded in the hand while retrieving a submachine gun abandoned by its gunner. I had to give orders for everyone to return to their combat posts, and asked Lalo Sardiñas and Efigenio Ameijeiras to concentrate their forces with ours.

A fighter named Tatín was on the road. As I climbed down to the road he said to me defiantly, "There he is, under the truck, let's go, let's go, let's see who's a man!" I summoned up my courage, deeply offended by his implication that I was reluctant. When we tried to approach the anonymous enemy fighter, however, who was firing on us with his machine gun from beneath the truck, we had to acknowledge that the price for displaying our manliness was too great. Neither my challenger nor I passed the test.

There were five army trucks transporting one company. The

squadron led by Antonio López carried out its orders not to allow anyone to pass after the opening of hostilities precisely. Nevertheless, a group of soldiers, resisting energetically, impeded our advance. Lalo and Efigenio arrived with their reinforcements; they advanced on the trucks and eliminated all resistance. Some of the soldiers fled in disarray down the road, others fled in the two trucks they had managed to save, abandoning all the other equipment and ammunition.

Through Gilberto Cardero, we received information concerning their forces and some of their plans. This *compañero* had been taken prisoner during an incursion by our forces into another region. He was captive for a certain time, and the enemy had brought him along with the idea that he could poison Fidel by emptying the contents of a vial into Fidel's food. When he heard the shots, Cardero threw himself from the truck, like all the soldiers; but instead of fleeing the gunfire, he reported to us at once, and rejoined our ranks, narrating his odyssey.

After taking the first truck, we found two dead and one wounded soldier, who in his agony was still going through the motions of battle as he lay dying. One of our fighters finished him off without giving the man an opportunity to surrender—which being semi-conscious he was unable to do. The combatant responsible for this mindless act of violence had seen his family decimated by Batista's army. I reproached him fiercely for the act, unaware that another wounded soldier, concealed and motionless under some tarpaulins in the truck, could hear me. Emboldened by my words and the apology of the *compañero*, the enemy soldier made his presence known and begged us not to kill him. He had taken a shot in the leg—it was fractured—and he remained at the side of the road while the battle continued around the other trucks. Every time a fighter passed near him he would shout, "Don't kill me! Don't kill me! Che says not to kill prisoners!" When the battle was over, we transported him to the sawmill and gave him first aid.

As for the other trucks, we had inflicted only a few casualties, but a good number of weapons remained in our possession. The outcome of the battle: one Browning machine gun; five Garands; one tripod machine gun and its ammunition; and another Garand, which was whisked away by Efigenio Ameijeiras. Efigenio, who belonged to Fidel's column, judged his platoon's participation in the battle to have been decisive; consequently, he felt they had a right to some of the captured weapons. But Fidel had placed these troops under my orders, precisely so they would help us capture weapons. Ignoring their protestations, I divided the trophies among the men of my column, except for the rifle that had already been appropriated.

The Browning went to Antonio López, lieutenant of one of the squadrons that had performed the best. The Garands went to Lieutenant Joel Iglesias, Virelles (a member of the *Corinthia* expedition who had joined our troops), Oñate, and two others whose names I don't remember. We set about burning the three captured trucks, since they were unsalvageable, and to cause even greater losses to the enemy.

While we were assembling our troops, some planes passed overhead, advised of our attack; but we opened fire on them and they left.

Mingolo, one of the Pardo brothers, had been sent to warn Fidel of the approaching guards, if I remember correctly, but we decided to send another messenger to tell him the results of our battle (accompanied by Cardero, to recount his adventure). We sent word to Ciro to withdraw from his position since the battle was over; Mongo Martínez carried that message.

After a few minutes we heard gunfire. A group of our marksmen had discovered a soldier advancing surreptitiously. They shouted to him to halt; when he tried to resist, they fired at him. The man fled, abandoning his gun. They brought us a Springfield as evidence of their triumph. It worried us that there were still dispersed soldiers in the region, but we added the gun to our tally.

Two or three days later, Mongo Martínez returned. He told us that some enemy soldiers had taken him by surprise, firing on him with rifles, and that he was forced to flee because he was wounded. His face was literally covered in the powder burns of gunshot wounds. His was the Springfield that our *compañeros* had seized from the enemy. The result had been that this wounded *compañero*, believing the soldiers to be very near, had taken a crossroad and got lost in the woods, without letting Ciro Redondo know about our battle or the order to withdraw. The next day, Ciro, who had heard echoes of the battle, sent a messenger to us, and the order was conveyed to him.

While the B-26s were flying low over the sawmill in search of victims, we were calmly having our breakfast. Installed throughout the building, we drank hot chocolate brought to us by the landlord of the house; she was not exactly cheered by the sight of the B-26s passing and repassing, almost grazing the roof. The planes finally left and we, utterly relaxed, were about to leave when we saw on the road from Siberia (the same one Ciro had been watching a few hours earlier) four trucks, full of soldiers. It might have been possible to set a similar trap, but it was already too late; a good number of our men had fallen back to safer positions. We fired twice in the air, our signal of retreat, and left quietly.

This battle had important repercussions, as news of it spread throughout Cuba. The enemy toll was three dead and one wounded, in addition to one prisoner captured by Efigenio's platoon the next day, during a final combing of the zone: Corporal Alejandro, whom we took with us and who stayed until the end of the war as our cook. Crucito was buried at the site of our battle. Our entire troop was grief-stricken, having lost in him a great *compañero* and a peasant bard. Crucito used to conduct fierce poetic duels with Calixto Morales, whom he called the "old Sierra buzzard," as opposed to himself, the "nightingale of the Maestra."

Those who distinguished themselves in this battle are: Efigenio Ameijeiras, Captain Lalo Sardiñas, Captain Víctor Mora, Lieutenant Antonio López and his squadron, Dermidio Escalona, and Arquímedes Fonseca, to whom the tripod machine gun was entrusted. He would be using it after the bullet wound in his hand healed. On our side we had one dead, one slightly wounded, some contusions, some scratches, and Monguito's powder burns.

We left Pino del Agua along various roads, with plans to regroup in the Pico Verde region. There we would reorganize ourselves and wait for *compañero* Fidel's arrival, who had already learned of the clash.

Analysis of the battle showed that, although it was a political and military victory, our shortcomings were enormous. The surprise factor should have been fully exploited, to wipe out the occupants of the first three trucks. Furthermore, after the shooting had started, a false order to retreat had been circulated, leading the men to lose control and fighting spirit. A lack of decisiveness was evident in seizing the vehicles, which were defended by a small number of soldiers. Later we spent the night at the sawmill, exposing ourselves unnecessarily. And the final withdrawal was carried out with great disorder. All this proved the imperative necessity of improving combat preparation and discipline among our troop, a task we devoted ourselves to in the days to come.

AN UNPLEASANT
EPISODE

After the battle of Pino del Agua, we set about improving the organizational structure of our guerrilla force — strengthened at that point by several of Fidel's units — to increase our usefulness and effectiveness in combat.

Lieutenant López, who had distinguished himself at Pino del Agua, and his squadron, whose members were all very responsible, were chosen to staff a disciplinary commission. Its tasks would be surveillance and overseeing established norms of vigilance, general discipline, camp cleaning, and revolutionary morality. But its life was ephemeral, and it was dissolved in tragic circumstances a few days after its creation.

About this time, near the La Botella hill, in a little camp we regularly used as a way station, we brought to justice an earlier deserter, named Cuervo, who two months earlier had fled with his rifle. What became of his gun we never found out; we were, however, well informed of his activities. Under the pretext of fighting for the revolutionary cause and executing informers, he was simply victimizing an entire section of the Sierra Maestra population, perhaps in collusion with the army.

The trial process was speedy, in view of his desertion, and progressed to his physical elimination. The execution of antisocial individuals, who took advantage of the prevailing atmosphere in the area to commit crimes was, unfortunately, not infrequent in the Sierra Maestra.

We learned that Fidel had completed his tour of the Sonador region, after going to Chivirico, and was returning through our zone. We decided to march toward Peladero, trying to connect with him as fast as we could.

There was a merchant in the coastal region, Juan Balansa, whose ties with the dictatorship and the big landowners were known, but he had never shown any active hostility toward our guerrillas. Juan Balansa had a mule, famous in the region for its stamina, and as a kind of war tax, we took it.

With the mule we made it to a region named Pinalito, near the Peladero river. We had to descend steep cliffs to reach its banks. We had to choose between sacrificing the mule and carting its meat down in pieces; abandoning it in hostile territory; or trying to get the animal to continue as far as possible. We decided to try, since carrying the meat would have been difficult.

The surefooted mule descended without hesitation through parts we ourselves had to slide down, clinging to vines or hanging on to rocky outcrops, where even our little mascot—a puppy— had to be picked up and carried in the arms of combatants. The mule put on an extraordinarily acrobatic display.

He repeated his exploits by crossing the Peladero river at a point full of boulders, by a sequence of hair-raising leaps from rock to rock. This is what saved his life. Later, he was mine to ride, my first regular mount, until the day he fell into the hands of Sánchez Mosquera, during one of our numerous clashes in the Sierra Maestra.

It was on the banks of the Peladero that the unpleasant incident occurred that provoked the abolition of the disciplinary commission. The commission's work was facing resistance from several *compañeros* who disliked the idea of establishing disciplinary norms, obliging the commission to take drastic measures.

One of the rear guard squadrons played a tasteless practical joke on the members of the commission. According to the jokers, there was a very serious problem requiring the commission to come immediately. It turned out to be manure left to bait the *compañeros*. Following the incident, various members of the group were arrested. Among them was Humberto Rodríguez, of sad repute due to his penchant for playing executioner whenever we found ourselves faced with the painful duty of executing a delinquent. After the revolution triumphed, Rodríguez, with another rebel soldier as his accomplice, murdered a prisoner; they subsequently escaped La Cabaña prison.

Two or three *compañeros* were imprisoned along with Humberto. In the conditions of the guerrilla forces, prison did not mean much. But when the crime was serious enough, the prisoner guilty of a lack of discipline was deprived of food for a day or two, a punishment that did strike home.

Two days after the incident, when the principal participants were still prisoners, news arrived that Fidel was close by, in the region called El Zapato, where I went to welcome and talk with him. We hadn't been together for more than 10 minutes when Ramiro Valdés arrived with the news that Lalo Sardiñas, in an impulsive act of punishment toward an undisciplined *compañero*, had held his pistol to the man's head as if to shoot him. The gun went off unintentionally and the *compañero* was killed on the spot. There were the beginnings of a riot among the troops. I went back to camp immediately and put Lalo under guard.

The atmosphere was hostile and combatants were demanding a summary trial and execution.

We began to take statements and look for evidence. Opinions were divided; some men were convinced it was premeditated murder, others said it was an accident. Independent of these opinions, inflicting corporal punishment on a *compañero* was forbidden in the guerrilla forces, and this was not Lalo Sardiñas's first offense.

The situation was difficult. The *compañero* Lalo Sardiñas had always been a very brave fighter, a strict supporter of discipline, a man with a great spirit of sacrifice. Those who were fiercely demanding the death penalty were far from the best of the group.

The declarations of the witnesses continued until nightfall. Fidel came to the camp, and was strongly opposed to the death penalty, but he did not judge it prudent to make a decision of this nature without consulting each of the fighters. The next stage of the trial called for Fidel and me to defend the accused, who was observing the deliberations concerning his fate impassively, without showing the slightest trace of fear. After the many impulsive demands for his death, it was my turn to speak and ask that the problem be examined carefully. I tried to explain that the death of our *compañero* had to be ascribed to our conditions of struggle, to the very fact that we were at war, and that, in the end, it was the dictator Batista who was guilty. My words, however, were not convincing to this hostile audience.

It was well into the night; we had lit several pine torches and some candles to continue the discussion. Fidel then spoke, for a full hour, explaining why, in his opinion, Lalo Sardiñas should not be executed. He enumerated our faults, our lack of discipline, the other errors we committed daily, the weaknesses these caused; and he explained that in the end this reprehensible act had been committed in defense of the concept of discipline and that we should always keep that fact in mind. His voice, as he stood within the woods illuminated by the torches, took on a moving tone, and many of our men changed their minds after hearing their leader's opinion.

His enormous powers of persuasion were put to the test that night.

Fidel's eloquence, however, could not put an end to all opposition. We concluded that two alternative punishments should be put to the vote: immediate death by shooting, or demotion and the punishment this would entail. Owing to enflamed passions, many forces were at work in this vote, in which a man's life was at stake. We had to suspend proceedings because some were voting twice, and excited argument was fast distorting the terms of the solution. Once more the alternatives open to the voters were explained and everybody was asked to make their choice clear.

I was put in charge of tallying the votes in a little notebook. Lalo was dear to many among us; we recognized his error but wanted his life spared, for he was a valuable cadre of the revolution. I recall that Oniria [Gutiérrez], a young woman who joined our column — then not much older than a girl — asked in an anguished voice if as a combatant of the column she could vote. She was permitted to do so and after all had cast their votes, we began to count the ballots.

I recorded the results of this strange vote on little squares of paper, similar to those used in medical laboratories. It was extremely close. After the last hesitations, opinion among the

146 guerrillas who voted was divided among 76 who wanted another type of punishment and 70 who asked for the death penalty. Lalo was saved.

But that wasn't the end of it. The next day, a group of men opposed to the decision of the majority announced their decision to leave the guerrilla movement. This group included many elements of very poor quality, but there were also some brave men among them. Paradoxically, Lieutenant Antonio López, head of the disciplinary commission, and various members of his squadron, were dissatisfied and left the Rebel Army. I remember several names: someone called Curro, and Pardo Jiménez (who took part in the struggle even though he was the nephew of a Batista minister). I don't know what became of them, but at the same time, the three Cañizares brothers also left. Their fate was less than glorious: one of them died at the Bay of Pigs and another was taken prisoner there, after the attempted invasion by the mercenaries. These men, who had not respected the majority and who abandoned the struggle, subsequently put themselves at the service of the enemy, and it was as traitors that they returned to fight on our soil.

Our revolutionary war was already beginning to acquire new characteristics. The consciousness of the leaders and the combatants was growing. We were beginning to feel in our flesh and blood the need for an agrarian reform and for profound, essential changes in the social structure that were vital to cleanse the country. But this deepening consciousness among the best and the majority of our fighters provoked clashes with those elements who had come to the struggle out of nothing but a hunger for adventure, or in the hope of winning not only glory but economic advantage.

Some other malcontents also withdrew, whose names I don't remember, except the one that comes to mind: Roberto, who subsequently spun out an long tale full of lies, and to his ridicule Conte Agüero published it in *Bohemia*. Lalo Sardiñas was demoted and sentenced to win his rehabilitation by fighting the enemy as a simple soldier in a small platoon. One of our lieutenants, Joaquín de la Rosa, Lalo's uncle, decided to accompany him. As a replacement for Captain Sardiñas, Fidel gave me one of his best fighters: Camilo Cienfuegos, who became a captain in our column's forward guard.

We had to set out immediately to neutralize a group of bandits who, utilizing the name of our revolution, were committing crimes in both the region where we had begun our struggle and in Caracas and El Lomón. Camilo's first mission in our column was to advance rapidly and take all those elements prisoner, whom we would then put on trial.

THE STRUGGLE
AGAINST BANDITRY

Conditions in the Sierra Maestra were now permitting us to live freely across quite a vast territory. The army hardly ever occupied any of it, and in many places, they had never bothered even to set foot. But we had not organized a system of government strong or rigorous enough to impede the free action of groups of men who, under the pretext of revolutionary activity, dedicated themselves to looting, banditry, and a host of other offenses.

Political conditions in the Sierra Maestra were also still quite precarious. The political development of its inhabitants was still superficial, and the presence of a threatening enemy army made it difficult for us to overcome these weaknesses.

Once again, the enemy was closing in. Signs indicated that they intended to advance on the Sierra Maestra, creating nervousness among people in the district. The least resolute among them were already looking for a way to save themselves from the dreaded invasion of Batista's assassins. Sánchez Mosquera was camped in the village of Minas de Bueycito and a new invasion was becoming evident.

As for us, during those days of October 1957, we were in the valley of El Hombrito laying the groundwork for a liberated territory, and creating the first rudiments of industrial activity seen in the Sierra Maestra: a bakery. In the same region as El Hombrito was an encampment serving as a sort of halfway house for the guerrilla forces. Groups of young people wanting to join us were placed under the authority of trusted peasants.

The leader of the group, Arístidio, had belonged to our column until a few days before the battle of El Uvero; but the battle took place without him, because he had fallen and fractured a rib. He later showed little interest to continue fighting as a guerrilla.

Arístidio was a typical example of a peasant who joined the ranks of the revolution without having any clear understanding of its significance. In his own analysis of the situation, he found there were more advantages in waiting to see which way the wind would blow. He sold his revolver for a few pesos and began to repeat to anyone who would listen that he was not crazy enough to allow himself to be quietly caught at home, after the guerrillas left, and that he was going to make contact with the army. Various versions of Arístidio's declarations were brought to my attention. These were difficult moments for the revolution. In my capacity as head of the region, I called for a very summary investigation, and the peasant Arístidio was executed.

Today, we might ask ourselves whether he was really guilty enough to deserve death, and if it might not have been possible to save that life for the constructive phase of the revolution. War is difficult and harsh and when the aggression of the enemy is on the rise it is not possible to tolerate even the suspicion of treason. Months earlier, when the guerrilla movement was much weaker, it might have been possible to save his life, or months later, when we were far stronger. But Arístidio had the bad luck that his weakness as a revolutionary combatant coincided precisely with a point at which we were strong enough to drastically punish an act like his, but not strong enough to sanction him in another way, since we had no jail or any other type of confinement.

Leaving the region for a time, our forces set out toward Los Cocos along the Magdalena river. We were to join with Fidel there and capture a gang that, under the command of Chino Chang, was ravaging the Caracas region. Camilo, who had gone ahead with the forward guard, had already taken a number of prisoners before we arrived, and we stayed there about 10 days.

It was there in a peasant hut that Chino Chang was tried and condemned to death. He was the leader of a gang that had murdered some peasants and tortured others, usurping the name and possessions of the revolution while sowing terror in the district. Together with Chang, a peasant was condemned to death who had raped an adolescent girl, at the same time boasting of his authority as a messenger for the Rebel Army. We also put on trial a good number of the gang, consisting of youths from the cities and peasants seduced by the prospect of a carefree life without having to submit to any rules, which was promised to them by Chang.

Most were acquitted, but with three of them, we decided to stage a symbolic lesson.

First we executed Chang and the peasant guilty of rape. They were tied to a tree in the woods, both calm. The peasant died without a blindfold, facing the guns, shouting, "Long Live the Revolution!" Chang faced death with complete serenity but asked for the last rites to be administered by Father [Guillermo]

Sardiñas, who at that moment was away from our camp. Since we were unable to grant this request, Chang said he wanted it known he had asked for a priest, as if this public testimony would serve as an extenuating circumstance in the hereafter.

Later we carried out the symbolic execution of three boys of the gang, who had been most involved in Chang's outrages, but whom Fidel felt should be given a chance. The three were blindfolded and subjected to the distress of a simulated firing squad. After shots were fired into the air, the boys found that they were still very much alive. One of them, in a spontaneous demonstration of joy, gave me a noisy kiss, as if I were his father.

The CIA agent Andrew St. George witnessed these events. His reportage, published in *Look* magazine, won a prize in the United States for the most sensational story of the year.

In retrospect, this method, practiced for the first time in the Sierra Maestra, might seem barbaric. At the time, however, no other form of punishment for those men was possible. True, they did not quite deserve death, but they had on their records a number of serious offenses. All three joined the Rebel Army; I later heard reports of the brilliant performance of two of them during the entire insurrectionary period. The third spent a long time in my column, and whenever the combatants' conversation touched on various feats of the war, if some *compañero* questioned any of his stories, he always said emphatically, "It's true, I've never been afraid of death, as Che is my witness."

Two or three days later, we captured another group. Their execution was especially painful. Among them was a peasant named Dionisio and his brother-in-law Juan Lebrigio, two among the very first to aid our guerrilla troop. Dionisio, who had helped unmask the traitor Eutimio Guerra, and who had assisted us in one of the most difficult moments of our revolution, had later grossly abused our confidence, as had his brother-in-law. They had appropriated, for their own use, all the provisions sent to us by the urban organizations and had established several camps to slaughter the cattle arbitrarily. Once on this path, they descended as far as committing murder.

At that time in the Sierra Maestra, a man's wealth was measured essentially by the number of women he had. Dionisio, faithful to custom and taking himself for a potentate, had, thanks to the powers conferred on him by the revolution, taken over three houses, and in each of them he kept a woman and an abundant supply of food. In the course of his trial, Fidel reproached him for his treachery and his immorality in maintaining three women on the people's money, but Dionisio maintained, with peasant ingenuousness, that it was not three, but two, since one of them was already his (which was true).

Together with them, we also executed two spies sent by Masferrer, who had been caught red-handed and confessed, as well as a boy named Echeverría, who had been assigned to special missions in the movement. Echeverría belonged to a family of Rebel Army combatants—one of the brothers had arrived on the *Granma*—but this boy, after having formed a little troop while waiting for our arrival, succumbed to who-knows-what temptation and began to organize armed attacks in guerrilla territory.

The Echeverría case was poignant. Recognizing his errors he did not, however, want to die by execution. He begged us to let him die in the next battle, swearing he would seek death there, and that he did not want to bring dishonor to his family. Condemned to death by the trial, Echeverría (who we had nicknamed "squinty") wrote a long, moving letter to his mother, explaining the justice of his punishment and advising her to remain loyal to the revolution.

The last of the executed was a colorful character called "El Maestro," who was my sole companion during some difficult hours when I had wandered aimlessly through these mountains, sick. He soon left the guerrillas, using some illness as a pretext, and dedicated himself to an immoral life. His exploits culminated in an attempt to pass himself off as me, and in the guise of a doctor attempt to rape a young peasant girl who had sought medical treatment from him.

They all died proclaiming their commitment to the revolution, except for Masferrer's two spies. I was not present at the scene, but I'm told that when Father Sardiñas, present this time, approached one of the condemned in order to offer the last rites, the man answered, "Look, father, see if anyone else needs you, because the truth is I don't really believe in any of that stuff."

With men like these, the revolution was being made. Rebels, at the beginning, against any injustice, they soon became solitary rebels accustomed to satisfying their own needs, with no conception of a struggle to change the social order. Whenever the revolution relaxed its vigilance on their acts for even a minute, they fell into errors that, with astonishing ease, led them into crime.

Dionisio and Juanito Lebrigio were no worse than other occasional delinquents whom the revolution spared, and who can be found today in the ranks of our army. But that moment demanded a strong hand. We were obliged to inflict exemplary punishment to curb violations of discipline and to eliminate the seeds of anarchy which sprang up in areas lacking a stable government.

Echeverría, taking it one step further, could have become a hero of the revolution, a distinguished fighter like his two brothers — officers of the Rebel Army. But he had the bad luck to commit an offense in that particular time, and he had to pay with his life. I hesitated to name him in these pages, but his attitude in the face of death was so dignified, so revolutionary, he recognized so clearly the justice of his punishment, that his end, it seemed to us, did not denigrate him. Rather, it served as an example, tragic as it was, but valuable, in that it helped others to understand the need to keep our revolution pure, uncontaminated by acts of banditry that were the heritage of Batista's men.

During these trials, a case was argued for the first time by a lawyer who had taken refuge in the Sierra Maestra after various disputes with *Llano* leaders of the July 26 Movement. He became minister of agriculture after the revolution, until the very moment the Agrarian Reform Law was signed (by others, since he did not wish to commit himself to it): his name was [Humberto] Sorí Marín.

When we had performed the painful duty of establishing peace and moral order throughout the territory under the administration of the Rebel Army, we headed back toward our zone of El Hombrito with the column divided into three platoons. The forward guard was led by Camilo Cienfuegos and had as lieutenants Orestes [Guerra], today a commander, Boldo, Leyva, and Noda. The second platoon was led by Captain Raúl Castro Mercader, whose lieutenants were Alfonso Zayas, Orlando Pupo, and Paco Cabrera. Ramiro Valdés commanded our little general staff, with Joel Iglesias as his lieutenant. Joel, not yet 16, was in command of men over 30, whom he addressed respectfully as *usted* when giving them orders; they addressed him as *tú*, but obeyed his orders with discipline. The rear guard was led by Ciro Redondo, whose lieutenants were Vilo Acuña, Félix Reyes, William Rodríguez, and Carlos Más.

Toward the end of October 1957 we reestablished ourselves at El Hombrito. We then began efforts to establish a region firmly defended by our army. With the aid of two students recently arrived from Havana—one studying engineering and the other veterinary science—we began to lay plans for a miniature hydroelectric station, which we planned to construct at the El Hombrito river. We also began production of our *Mambí* newspaper [early independence fighters]. We had brought up from the city an old mimeograph machine on which we printed the first issues of *El Cubano Libre*, whose editors and printers were the students Geonel Rodríguez and Ricardito Medina.

We began to organize our life at this sedentary stage, thanks to the open generosity of the residents of El Hombrito, particularly our good friend, "Old Lady Chana," as we called her. We then proceeded to build a bakery in an old, abandoned peasant hut, so that enemy aircraft would not detect any new construction. We also had an immense July 26 flag made, bearing the inscription "Happy 1958!" We raised it on the highest plateau of El Hombrito, so that it would be seen from afar, as far away as Minas de Bueycito. Meanwhile, we traveled through the region, establishing a real authority. At the same time, we were preparing for an imminent invasion from Sánchez Mosquera, fortifying the access roads to El Hombrito he was most likely to use.

THE MURDERED PUPPY

For all the harshness of conditions in the Sierra Maestra, the day was superb. We were hiking through Agua Revés, one of the steepest and most labyrinthine valleys in the Turquino basin, patiently following Sánchez Mosquera's troops. The relentless killer had left a trail of burned-out farms, sadness, and despair throughout the entire region. But his trail led him, by necessity, to ascend along one of the two or three points of the Sierra Maestra where we knew Camilo would be: either the Nevada ridge, or the area we called the "ridge of the crippled," now known as the "ridge of the dead."

Camilo had left hurriedly with about a dozen men, part of his forward guard; this small number had to be divided up in three different places to stop a column of over 100 soldiers. My mission was to attack Sánchez Mosquera from behind and surround him. Our fundamental aim was encirclement; we therefore followed him patiently, over a considerable distance, past the painful trail of burning peasant houses, set alight by the enemy's rear guard. The enemy troops were far away, but we could hear their shouts. We didn't know how many there were in all. Our column advanced with difficulty along the slopes, while the enemy advanced through the center of a narrow valley.

Everything would have been perfect had it not been for our

new mascot, a little hunting dog only a few weeks old. Despite repeated attempts by Félix [Mendoza] to scare the animal back to our center of operations—a house where the cooks were staying—the puppy continued to trail behind the column. In that part of the Sierra Maestra it is extremely difficult to move along the slopes because there are no paths. We made it through a difficult spot where the "tomb"—old, dead trees—was covered by new growth, though the going was extremely laborious. We jumped over the tree trunks and bushes trying not to lose contact with our guides.

In these conditions the small column marched in silence, hardly a broken branch disturbing the usual murmurings of the mountain. But suddenly, this code of silence was broken by the disconsolate, nervous barking of the pup. He was falling behind and was desperately barking for his owners to come and get him out of his trouble. Somebody went and picked up the little animal and we continued, but as we were resting in a creek bed with a lookout keeping an eye on enemy movements, the dog started up again with its hysterical howling. Comforting words no longer had any effect; the animal, afraid we would leave it behind, howled desperately.

I remember my emphatic order, "Félix, that dog must stop its howling once and for all. You're in charge; strangle it. There will be no more barking." Félix regarded me with eyes that said nothing. In the middle of our exhausted ranks, as if marking the center of a circle, stood Félix and the dog. Very slowly he took out a rope, placed it around the animal's neck, and began to pull. The affectionate movements of the dog's tail suddenly became convulsive, before gradually dying out, accompanied by a steady moan that escaped from its throat, despite the firm

Fidel Castro and Che Guevara in the Sierra Maestra.

triste pero aleccionadora: Sergio Acuña, el desertor de días atrás, fue a la casa de unos parientes, allí se puso a relatar a sus primas sus hazañas como guerrillero, lo escuchó un tal Pedro Herrera, lo delató a la guardia, vino ~~el famoso~~ _el_ cabo Rosselló* (ya ajusticiado por el pueblo), lo torturó, le dio cuatro tiros y, al parecer, lo colgó. Esto enseñaba a la tropa el valor de la cohesión y la inutilidad de intentar huir individualmente del destino colectivo; pero, además, nos colocaba ante la necesidad de cambiar de lugar pues, presumiblemente, el muchacho hablaría antes de ser asesinado y él conocía la casa de Florentino, donde estábamos. Hubo un hecho curioso en aquel momento, que sólo después atando cabos, hizo la luz en nuestro entendimiento: Eutimio Guerra, había manifestado que en un sueño se había enterado de la muerte de Sergio Acuña, y, todavía más, dijo que el cabo Rosselló lo había muerto. Esto suscitó una larga discusión filosófica de si era posible la predicción de los acontecimientos por medio de los sueños o no. Era parte de mi tarea diaria hacer explicaciones de tipo cultural o político a la tropa ~~y explicaba claramente~~ que eso no era posible, que podía deberse a alguna casualidad muy grande, que todos pensábamos que era posible ese desenlace para Sergio Acuña, que Rosselló era el hombre que estaba asolando la zona, etc. ~~; además,~~ Universo Sánchez dio la clave diciendo que Eutimio era un «paquetero», que alguien se lo había dicho, pues éste había salido el día antes y había traído cincuenta latas de leche y una linterna militar. Uno de los que más insistían en la teoría de la iluminación era un guajiro analfabeto de 45 años a quien ya me he referido: Julio Zenón Acosta. Fue mi primer alumno en la Sierra; ~~estaba~~ haciendo esfuerzos por alfabetizar**la** y, en los lugares donde nos deteníamos, le iba enseñando las primeras letras; estábamos en la etapa de identificar la A y la O, la E y la I. Con mucho empeño, sin considerar los años pasados sino lo que quedaba por hacer, Julio Zenón se había dado a la tarea ~~de alfabetizarse~~. Quizás su ejemplo en este año pudiera servir a muchos

por lo que se trate de explicar

— 31 —

* No hay certeza de la veracidad de ~~esta~~ _la_ noticia sobre la identidad del asesino.

Pages of the original _Reminiscences of the Cuban Revolutionary War_, corrected by Che.

conocía algo la región. Se había propuesto la división en dos patrullas para aligerar la marcha y dejar menos rastro, pero Almeida y yo nos opusimos para conservar la integridad de aquel grupo. Reconocimos el lugar, llamado Limones y, después de algunos titubeos, pues algunos compañeros querían alejarse, Almeida, jefe del grupo en razón de su grado de capitán, ordenó seguir hasta el Lomón, que era el lugar de reunión dado por Fidel. Algunos compañeros argumentaban que el Lomón era un lugar conocido por Eutimio y, por tanto, que allí estaría el ejército. Ya no nos cabía, por supuesto, la menor duda de que Eutimio era el traidor, pero la decisión de Almeida fue cumplir la orden de Fidel.

Tras tres días de separación, el 12 de febrero, nos reunimos con Fidel cerca del Lomón, en un lugar denominado «Derecha de la Caridad». Allí ya se tuvo la confirmación de que el traidor era Eutimio Guerra y se nos hizo toda la historia; ella empezaba cuando después de La Plata fuera apresado por Casillas y, en vez de matarlo, le ofreciera una cantidad por la vida de Fidel; nos enteramos de que había sido él el que delatara nuestra posición en Caracas, y que, precisamente, él había dado la orden de atacar la Loma del Burro porque ese era nuestro itinerario (lo habíamos cambiado a última hora), y también él había organizado el ataque concentrado sobre el pequeño hueco que teníamos de refugio en el Cañón del Arroyo, del cual nos salvamos con una sola baja por la oportuna retirada que ordenara Fidel. Además, se tenía confirmación también de la muerte de Julio Acosta y de que un guardia, por lo menos, había muerto y se decía que algunos heridos. Tengo que confesar que ni el muerto ni los heridos pueden cargarse a mi fusil, porque no hice nada más que una «retirada estratégica» a toda velocidad en aquel encuentro. Ahora estábamos de nuevo reunidos, nosotros doce menos Labrada, extraviado un día antes, con el resto del grupo: Raúl, Almejeiras, Ciro Redondo, Manuel Fajardo, Echevarría, el Gallego Morán y Fidel, en total, 18 personas; era el «Ejér-

Fidel Castro in the Sierra Maestra.

Che Guevara in the Escambray mountains.

FROM LEFT TO RIGHT: Che Guevara, Fidel Castro, Calixto García, Ramiro Valdés, and Juan Almeida in the Sierra Maestra.

FROM LEFT TO RIGHT: Guillermo García, Che Guevara, Universo Sánchez, Raúl Castro, Fidel Castro, Crescencio Pérez, Jorge Sotús, and Juan Almeida in the Sierra Maestra.

Fidel Castro showing Haydée Santamaría (left) and Celia Sánchez how to use a rifle.

Che Guevara and Celia Sánchez in the Sierra Maestra.

ABOVE: Fidel Castro in the Sierra Maestra.

BELOW: Fidel Castro speaking with a peasant family in the Sierra Maestra. Celia Sánchez is to his right.

Fidel Castro, Che Guevara, and others in the Sierra Maestra.

A peasant village in the Sierra Maestra (photo taken by Che Guevara).

Guerrilla fighters and peasants gathered around the body of a murdered peasant.
Che Guevara is crouching on the right.

Journalist Jean Daniel interviewing Che Guevara.

US journalist Bob Taber interviewing Fidel Castro.

Che Guevara with Jorge Ricardo Masetti, Argentine journalist.

Che Guevara in the Escambray mountains.

Fidel Castro and Ramiro Valdés in the Sierra Maestra.

Che Guevara at "El Hombrito" in the Sierra Maestra.

Che Guevara (center) with members of Column No. 4, in front of the giant banner raised in the heights of "El Hombrito."

Che Guevara and Camilo Cienfuegos.

CHE GUEVARA
Extranjero pernicioso y Lider
Comunista expulsado de la
Argentina

CAMILO CIENFUEG
Lider Comunista

"Villaclareños"

Estos son los dos hombres que quie
llevar a nuestros jóvenes a la muerte y
truir nuestras riquezas.

Nosotros somos Cubanos y no Rusos.

¡LUCHEMOS CONTRA ELLO

JUVENTUD CIVICA CUBA

Poster accusing Che and Camilo Cienfuegos of being communists, late 1958.

The derailment of the armored train in Santa Clara, December 1958.

Che Guevara in Fomento, speaking to locals, December 1958.

ABOVE: Before the surrender of Santa Clara, Che Guevara receives a message from Aleida March.

BELOW: Che Guevara and Aleida March at the Leoncio Vidal garrison, Santa Clara.

Che Guevara with Aleida March in Las Villas, December 1958.

FROM LEFT TO RIGHT: José Argudín, Che Guevara, Aleida March, Harry Villegas, and Ramón Pardo Guerra, in downtown Santa Clara.

Roberto Rodríguez, "Vaquerito."

FROM LEFT TO RIGHT: Ramiro Valdés, Olo Pantoja, and Miguel Manals, in Santa Clara, December 1958.

Fidel Castro greets the Cuban people after the revolutionary triumph of January 1, 1959.

grip. I don't know how long it took for the end to come, but to all of us it seemed like forever. The puppy, after a last nervous shudder, stopped writhing. There it lay, sprawled out, its little head spread over the twigs.

We continued the march without even a word about the incident. Sánchez Mosquera's troops had gained some ground and shortly afterward we heard gunfire. We quickly descended the slopes, amid the difficult terrain, searching for the best path to reach the rear guard. We knew that Camilo had attacked. It took us a considerable amount of time to reach the last house before starting up the other side, moving carefully because we imagined that we might come upon the enemy any moment. The exchange of fire had been intense, but it had not lasted long and we were all tense with expectation. The last house was abandoned. There was no sign of the troops. Two scouts climbed the "ridge of the crippled" and soon returned with the news: "There is a grave up above. We dug it up and found one of the metal-heads buried." They also brought the identity papers of the victim, found in his shirt pocket. There had been a clash and one man was killed. The dead man was theirs, but that was all we knew.

We returned slowly, discouraged. Two scouting parties came upon a large number of footprints along both sides of the ridge of the Sierra Maestra, but nothing else. We made the return trip slowly, this time through the valley.

We arrived during the night at a house, also vacant. It was the Mar Verde homestead where we could rest. Soon, a pig was cooked along with some yucca, and we ate. Someone started to sing along to a guitar, since the peasant's houses had been hastily abandoned with all their belongings still inside.

I don't know whether it was the sentimental tune, or the darkness of night, or just plain exhaustion. What happened, though, is that Félix—seated on the ground to eat—dropped a bone. One of the house dogs came up meekly and took it. Félix put his hand on its head, and the dog looked at him. Félix looked back at the dog, and then he and I exchanged a guilty look. We were suddenly silent.

An imperceptible stirring came over us. There, in our presence, with its mild, mischievous and slightly reproachful gaze, observing us through the eyes of another dog, was the murdered puppy.

THE BATTLE OF MAR VERDE

Shortly before dawn, at 5 or 5:30 a.m., I woke up from a restful sleep, with my sixth sense—developed in military life—dulled that day by exhaustion and the comfort of a peasant's bed in the settlement of Mar Verde. We made breakfast in peace while awaiting news from the numerous messengers who had been sent out to make contact with the guerrilla squadrons.

The sun had barely begun to shine, when one of the few peasants remaining in the area came with strange and alarming news. He had seen soldiers looking for hens and eggs in a house no more than half a kilometer away. I sent him immediately to find out everything he could about the guards; to try and make contact with them and judge their forces. The peasant was not eager to carry out his mission in full. He returned, however, with news that a large group of soldiers was camped in the house belonging to Reyes, one or two kilometers up the Nevada mountain. It could be none other than Sánchez Mosquera.

We then had to rapidly organize the form our combat would take. Our goal was to surround them at a suitable point and then annihilate them.

First, I had to imagine his future plans. He had two possible routes: he could take the path along the Nevada, an exhausting trek through Santa Ana to reach California, and from there to Minas de Bueycito. Alternately, and what seemed most logical, because of the short trip and the possibilities it entailed for him, Sánchez Mosquera could follow the opposite route along the Turquino river, arriving at the small village of Ocujal, at the foot of the Turquino mountain.

Because of our doubts, we had to rapidly reinforce both positions, to prevent them breaking out of the encirclement. If they decided to take the high road across the Nevada, there would be no possibility for us to confront them with adequate forces, save the possibility that Camilo had followed them.

The previous day Camilo had clashed with them near Altos de Conrado, but at that moment we did not know where he was stationed.

Messengers, however, were fast arriving. Our reserve forces at El Hombrito were mobilized in the regions of Nevada and the cemetery, in order to take positions above Sánchez Mosquera and close off his route. Camilo had arrived and was in that zone. An order was sent instructing them not to let themselves be seen or engage in combat until they heard the first shots, unless the soldiers tried to leave through the area they were defending. The squadrons of lieutenants Noda and Vilo Acuña were sent to the west. Captain Raúl Castro Mercader closed the circle to the east. My small squadron, with some reinforcements, was in charge of conducting the ambush in the event they tried to descend toward the sea, which we considered likely.

In the early hours of the morning, with the circle already complete, the alarm was sounded. We could see the head of the enemy's forward guard, advancing along the main road that followed a small stream flowing into the Turquino river. The spot chosen to begin the battle, in the event they came along my side, was flanked by hilly pastureland that allowed our troops to hide on one side, but they were not to make observations or attack until the battle had begun. This was to occur on one side of the road. On the other, was a patch of trees, a mango tree at the end; that was where I was posted. It was my job to fire on the soldiers at point-blank range; Joel Iglesias and other *compañeros* were one or two meters ahead of me. The position was ideal for killing the first soldiers, but it would not permit us to continue the fight; we thought the enemy troops would retreat immediately to look for better positions, at which time we would be able to abandon the ambush.

We heard the soldiers passing almost right in front of us; in the pasture the others had seen that there were only three men, but they were unable to alert us in time. During those days my only weapon was a Luger pistol, and I felt nervous over the fate of the two or three *compañeros* who were closer to the enemy than I was. For that reason I rushed the first shot too much and missed. As happens, the firing immediately spread, and an attack was launched against the house where the bulk of Sánchez Mosquera's forces were stationed.

Then, in the midst of the ambush, an eerie silence developed. As we went to gather the dead, after the initial exchange, there was no one on the main road. Alongside the road were some trees, and a hollowed-out path through the Tibisí bushes, through which the enemy soldiers had slipped away. We immediately began a search to surround them, as no more soldiers had appeared.

While we were searching, Joel Iglesias, followed by Rodolfo Vázquez and Geonel Rodríguez, entered the same path the soldiers had taken, through the bushes. I heard his voice calling on them to surrender and guaranteeing the prisoners' lives. Suddenly a rapid burst of fire was heard, and I was informed that Joel was seriously wounded. All things considered, Joel's fate was extraordinary. Three Garand machine guns had opened fire on him at point-blank range: his rifle was hit by two bullets, and its butt was destroyed. Another shot burned his hand, another hit his cheek, two went through his arm, two through his leg, and other shots grazed him. He was covered in blood but his wounds were nevertheless relatively superficial. We retrieved him immediately and sent him in a hammock to the field hospital for medical attention.

Before concentrating on the general battle, we had to continue looking for the three soldiers. Soon Silva's voice was heard, shouting, "There they are!" and pointing out the place with a burst from his 12-gauge shotgun. We soon heard the soldiers calling out their surrender. We thus obtained three Garands with their corresponding prisoners; one of our good combatants was wounded. That was the tally, for the moment.

We sent the prisoners along the same road as our wounded man and were then able to concentrate on organizing the battle. Interrogating the prisoners, we learned that Sánchez Mosquera had between 80 and 100 men. It was impossible to know whether or not the figure was accurate, but those were the prisoners' statements. The soldiers were in a well-defended position and had automatic weapons, light arms, and abundant ammunition.

We understood that it was best to avoid frontal combat, since our prospects were doubtful, with approximately the same number of combatants but inferior weapons, and Sánchez

Mosquera was in a well-defended, entrenched position. We decided to harass them and make movement impossible, until nightfall when we would begin our attack.

A few hours later, however, news arrived that enemy reinforcements commanded by Captain Sierra were ascending the mountain from the sea. We immediately organized two patrols to stop them. One, led by William Rodríguez, was to attack them in the region of Dos Brazos del Turquino. The other patrol, commanded by Lieutenant Leyva, was to wait for reinforcements, and attack as soon as they reached the top of a mountain only two kilometers from the battle site. This was a very favorable position for us, where we could annihilate their forward guard. I personally was in charge of preparations at this spot, leaving other *compañeros* in charge of preparing the other ambushes.

The entire front was calm, and only occasionally did we fire at the zinc roof of the house the soldiers were stationed in, to keep them in check. At mid-afternoon, however, a prolonged exchange of fire was heard at the top of the position. Later I learned the sad news: Ciro Redondo had been killed trying to attack the enemy lines, and his body lost, though not his weapons, which Camilo rescued. On our side, we also heard shots announcing the arrival of the enemy troops. Moments later, intense gunfire began, and our defenses along the southern part were overwhelmed by the reinforcements that had reached Sánchez Mosquera.

We were forced to retreat. Once again, the killer was saved. We issued the relevant orders for an orderly retreat, and left, walking slowly. We reached the Guayabo stream, and later, the valley of El Hombrito, our most secure refuge.

After we arrived and heard the results of all the actions, we could piece together what had happened. According to the combatants' accounts, a number of enemy soldiers were killed, though we could not verify this news. Those defending the extreme south position, under the command of Lieutenant Leyva, said the same thing. A number of backpacks, however, being stored at our combatants' position in the southern zone, were lost. One of these fighters, named Alberto, had been sent in the morning with the prisoners; upon returning he decided to stop to sleep instead of continuing the battle. Enemy troops took him by surprise while sleeping, together with all the backpacks. Later, we learned he was murdered in the region of El Hombrito.

Our wounded were: Roberto Fajardo; Joel Pardo, from the battle the day before with Sánchez Mosquera; a combatant named Reyes, who later died with the rank of captain; Javier Pazos; and Joel Iglesias. Ciro Redondo was killed. There was a great deal of sorrow. We had not been able to take advantage of the victory against Sánchez Mosquera, and we had lost our great *compañero* Ciro Redondo.

I sent a letter to Fidel proposing his posthumous promotion, and shortly afterward the rank was conferred. News of this was published in our newspaper *El Cubano Libre.*

The battle, and Ciro Redondo's death, occurred on November 29, 1957.

Shortly before withdrawing, a bullet hit the trunk of a tree a few centimeters from my head, and Geonel Rodríguez scolded me for not ducking. Geonel reasoned later, perhaps with a tendency toward mathematical speculation learned from engineering, that he had a greater chance than I did of surviving to the end of the revolution, since he never risked his life unnecessarily. And it was true, Geonel Rodríguez—who had his baptism of fire in that battle—never risked his life unnecessarily. He was always an exemplary combatant, owing to his courage, decisiveness, and intelligence. But it was he who did not live to see the end of the revolutionary war. A few months later, he died during the army's great offensive against us.

We slept that night at Guayabo. We had to prepare conditions to prevent any surprises and to reach El Hombrito without having to fight our way there. That was our fundamental task at that moment.

ALTOS DE CONRADO

The days following the Mar Verde battle were feverish with activity. We knew very well that we did not yet have sufficient fighting strength to maintain combat continuously, to encircle the enemy effectively, or to resist frontal attacks. For this reason we redoubled our defense measures in the valley of El Hombrito. This valley is a few kilometers from Mar Verde and to get there, you have to take the road that climbs to Santa Ana and crosses the Guayabo, a little mountain stream. From Santa Ana you get to the valley of El Hombrito. You can also reach it, however, along the Guayabo river to the south, past the La Botella hill. You can also take the road from Minas del Frío.

We had to defend each of these points and establish a constant watch to avoid the enemy surprising us by advancing their troop directly through the woods.

The bulk of our excess supplies had been sent to Polo Torres's house in the La Mesa region. We had also taken our wounded there, among them Joel Iglesias, the only one unable to walk because his leg was injured.

Sánchez Mosquera's troops were stationed at Santa Ana and other enemy troops had taken the California road, headed for an unknown destination.

Four or five days after the Mar Verde confrontation, the

combat alarm sounded. Sánchez Mosquera's troops were advancing by the most logical route, directly from Santa Ana to El Hombrito. We immediately warned our men who were waiting in ambush, and they checked the mines. These first mines made by us had a rudimentary detonation system, consisting of a spring and a spike, which when released was thrust forward by the spring, striking the detonator. They had not functioned during the Mar Verde ambush, however, and this time they functioned no better.

A few moments later, noise of firing reached our command post and news arrived that as the mines were not working and the enemy had arrived in force, our fighters had retreated, not without causing some damage to the enemy. Their first victim was described as a tall, fat sergeant armed with a .45 revolver, who led a mounted column. Lieutenant Enrique Noda and another fighter, El Mexicano, fired at him with their Garands from short range, and their descriptions of the man coincided. They said other damage had been inflicted, yet the fact remained that Sánchez Mosquera's troops had beaten our defenses.

(Weeks later, a peasant by the name of Brito came to thank me for our generosity. He had been forced by the enemy to take a position at the head of the column, and he had clearly seen our men "pretend to take aim and shoot at him." This same peasant told me that they had not suffered any casualties, although there had been some at Altos de Conrado.)

The spot we occupied was so difficult to defend with our small forces that we had not bothered to dig proper trenches. We only had the old defenses, constructed to prevent access from Minas de Bueycito. Furthermore, as the enemy advanced along the road, they endangered all our ambushes, so we ordered them lifted and withdrew. Only a few families remained in the area, determined to bravely resist the atrocities of the Rural Guard, or because they had some secret contact with them.

We slowly fell back to the road leading to Altos de Conrado [Conrado's Heights], which is nothing more than a small hill rising from a ridge in the Sierra Maestra, on whose heights lived a peasant named Conrado. This *compañero* was a member of the Popular Socialist Party, who had been in contact with us from the beginning, providing many noble services. He had evacuated his family, and his house was isolated. The place was magnificent for an ambush. There were only three narrow paths leading in to it, which wound through the dense vegetation of the hills, and therefore very easy to defend. The rest of it was defended by sheer boulders and equally sheer slopes, extremely difficult to climb.

At one spot, where there was a small depression, the road widens. There, we prepared the conditions to resist Sánchez Mosquera's attacks. On the first day, we had placed two bombs, with their fuses, in the hearth of the little hut. The trap was very simple: if we withdrew, the enemy would probably stay at the house and use the fire. The two bombs lay covered completely by ashes; we assumed that the heat of a fire or a live coal would light the fuses, setting off an explosion which would surely have a number of victims. Naturally, this was a later recourse; first we would have to fight at Altos de Conrado.

We waited patiently there for three days, guards on 24-hour rotation. The nights were very cold and damp at that altitude and in that season, and in reality, we were not yet sufficiently prepared or accustomed to the hardship of spending entire nights in the open, in battle position.

We had prepared a leaflet for the soldiers, using the mimeo-graph we printed *El Cubano Libre* on, the first issue of which appeared in those days. We were going to post these on the trees along the road they would take.

On the morning of December 8, from the heights of our boulder, we heard the troop beginning its ascent; it wound along the road, getting to about 200 meters below us. We sent someone to post the leaflets; *compañero* Luis Olazábal did so. We heard the troops shouting, in a violent argument, and since I was on watch at the edge of the boulder, I clearly heard the shouted orders of someone who was apparently an officer: "By my balls, you're going in front!" The soldier, or whoever he was, refused angrily. The argument ceased and the troop began moving.

We could see the column advancing, in small groups, hidden among the trees. After observing them for a moment, I became filled with doubt about the prudence of revealing our ambush to them with our leaflets. In the end, I sent Luis again to remove them. He had only a few seconds to do it, for the first soldiers were climbing rapidly.

The battle arrangements were very simple. We assumed that when the enemy reached the open space, a single man would come into view, at some distance from his companions. That man, at least, had to fall. Camilo waited for him, hidden behind a large mastic tree; at the moment the soldier passed him, looking attentively ahead, Camilo was to fire his machine gun at less than a meter. The snipers concealed in the bushes on both flanks would then open fire. Lieutenant Ibrahim [Sotomayor] and someone else, at the edge of the road, some 10 meters from Camilo, were to cover Camilo by firing from the front, so that no one could approach his position after he killed the forward guard.

My post was some 20 meters away, off to the side behind a tree trunk that protected half of me. My gun was pointed directly at the opening to the path along which the soldiers were coming. Several of us were at first unable to look, because we were in exposed positions and risked being seen. We were supposed to wait for Camilo to open fire. I sneaked a glance, violating the order I myself had given. I could sense the tension prior to combat. I saw the first soldier appear. He looked around him suspiciously and advanced slowly. In truth, everything smelled of ambush: the little clearing's spectacular, strange landscape, and the small spring running constantly amid the exuberant woods surrounding us. The trees, some cut down, others standing and charred by fire, gave the impression of despair. I hid my head, waiting for the battle to begin. A shot rang out and firing began. Later, I learned it was not Camilo but Ibrahim who had fired, unnerved by the waiting. He had fired ahead of time and generalized gunfire instantly followed. In reality, however, no vantage point allowed us to see much. Our isolated shots, each with pretensions of being lethal, and the wasteful, lengthy bursts of fire by the soldiers, "met, but did not mingle." We recognized in each noise which army was shooting. Several minutes later (five or six), we heard overhead the first whistles of mortar shells or bazookas fired by the soldiers; but their trajectory was too long and they exploded behind our backs.

Suddenly, I felt a disagreeable sensation, a little like a burn or the tingling of numbness, a sign that I had just been shot in my left foot, which was not protected by the tree trunk. I had finished firing my rifle (I had chosen one with a telescopic sight for more precise aim); at the moment I was hit, I heard some men advancing rapidly in my direction, making a great noise as they broke through branches. My rifle was of no further use to me, since I had just discharged it; and my pistol had fallen from my hand when I threw myself to the ground. It was beneath my body, but I could not lift myself up since I was directly exposed to enemy fire. With desperate speed, I rolled over and succeeded in grabbing the pistol; at the same moment one of our men appeared, the one we called Cantinflas. On top of the anguished moments and the pain from my wound, poor Cantinflas came to tell me he was withdrawing because his rifle was jammed. I snatched the Garand roughly from his hands and examined it, while he crouched beside me. The only thing wrong was that the clip was tilted slightly. I handed it back to him, in working order, along with a razor-sharp diagnosis, "You are a dummy!" Cantinflas, whose real name was Oñate, took the rifle and rejoined the battle. Leaving the refuge of the tree trunk, he hastened to empty his Garand in a demonstration of courage. He could not complete this, however, because a bullet struck his left arm and came out through his shoulder blade, following a strange trajectory. Now two of us were wounded and stranded in the same place, and it was difficult to retreat under the firing. We had to ease ourselves over the trunks of the tomb and then walk beneath them, wounded as we were and without knowing where the rest of our group was. Little by little we did so, but Cantinflas kept fainting. In spite of the pain, I was able to move more freely and made it to the others to ask for help.

We knew that there were deaths among the enemy soldiers, but not the exact number. After rescuing the wounded (both of us), we set off toward Polo Torres's house, two or three kilo-meters below in the Sierra Maestra. After the first euphoric moments and the excitement of combat had passed, I began to feel the pain more sharply, making it difficult to walk. At last, halfway there, I mounted a horse and thus arrived at our improvised hospital. Cantinflas, meanwhile, was carried on our field stretcher—a hammock.

The gunfire had ceased, and we assumed the enemy had tak-en Altos de Conrado. We sent out guards to detain them on the banks of a little stream in a place we had christened "Pata de la Mesa" [table leg]. At the same time we organized the with-drawal of the peasants and their families. I sent a long letter to Fidel describing the events.

I sent the column, commanded by Ramiro Valdés, to join up with Fidel. There was a certain atmosphere of defeat and fear among our troop, and I wanted to stay there only with indispensable men, to ensure an agile defense. Camilo remained at the head of a small defense group.

Owing to the apparent calm, the day after the battle we sent [Raimundo] Lien, one of our best scouts, to find out what the enemy was up to. We then learned that the troop had completely withdrawn from the region. The scout went as far as Conrado's house but saw no trace of the soldiers. As proof of his search he brought us one of the bombs we had hidden in the hut.

Reviewing the weapons, we realized we were lacking a rifle, that of *compañero* Guile Pardo. He had swapped his gun for another, and in retreating had taken only the second, leaving the first at his battle position. That was one of the gravest crimes one could commit, and the order was explicit: you had to go out equipped with only a small arm to retrieve the rifle from enemy hands, or bring in another. Crestfallen, Guile left to fulfill his mission, but he returned several hours later, smiling and with his own gun in his hands. The mystery was eventually cleared up: the army had never advanced from where they had dug in to resist our attack. Each had retreated along their own side, so that not a living soul had reached the combat post. The only thing the gun suffered was a downpour.

This was, for a good while, the farthest penetration made by the army into the Sierra Maestra. In this particular zone, it never made it beyond this point. A trail of burned-out huts, typical of Sánchez Mosquera's passing, was all that remained of El Hombrito and other areas. Our bakery had been conscientiously destroyed. In the midst of the smoking ruins we found nothing but some cats and a pig; they had escaped the destructive fury of the invaders only to fall into our gullets. A day or two after the battle, Machadito [José Ramón Machado], today the minister of public health, operated on me with a razor, extracting an M-1 rifle bullet. From then on, my recovery was rapid.

Sánchez Mosquera had carried off everything he could, from sacks of coffee to furniture, which his soldiers had to carry. We had the impression that it would be a long time before he repeated his incursion into the Sierra Maestra. It then became necessary to prepare the political conditions of the region and to begin once more to organize our basic industrial center, which would no longer be at El Hombrito but farther back, in the same zone as La Mesa.

ONE YEAR OF ARMED STRUGGLE

By the beginning of 1958 we had completed more than a year of fighting. A brief account of our military, organizational, and political situation at that point is necessary, as is a description of how we were progressing.

Regarding our military situation, let us concisely recall that our troop had disembarked on December 2, 1956, at Las Coloradas beach. Three days later, on December 5, we were surprised and beaten at Alegría de Pío. By the end of the month, we had regrouped to begin small-scale actions, appropriate to our strength, at La Plata, a small barracks on the banks of the river of the same name, on the southern coast of Oriente.

The fundamental characteristic of our troop, during the whole period between disembarking, the immediate defeat at Alegría de Pío, and the battle of El Uvero, was that it was one single guerrilla group, led by Fidel Castro, and constantly mobile (we could call this the nomadic phase).

Between December 2, [1956], and May 28, [1957], the date of the battle of El Uvero, we slowly established links with the city. During this period, these relations were characterized by lack of understanding on the part of the urban leadership [of the July 26 Movement] of our importance as the vanguard of the revolution and of Fidel's stature as its leader.

Then, two distinct opinions began to crystallize regarding tactics to be followed. They corresponded to two distinct concepts of strategy, which were thereafter known as the *Sierra* and the *Llano*. Our discussions and our internal conflicts were quite sharp. Nevertheless, the fundamental concerns of this phase were survival and the establishment of a guerrilla base.

The reactions of the peasants have already been analyzed many times. Immediately after the Alegría de Pío disaster, we felt their warm camaraderie and spontaneous support for our defeated troop. After the regrouping and the first clashes, and the simultaneous repression by Batista's army, terror spread among the peasants and a coldness toward our forces appeared. The fundamental problem was that if they saw us, they had to denounce us. If the army learned of our presence through other sources, they were lost. Denouncing us went against their conscience and, in any case, put them in danger, since revolutionary justice was swift.

In spite of a terrorized, or at least neutralized and insecure peasantry, which chose to avoid this serious dilemma by leaving the Sierra Maestra, our army was increasingly entrenching itself. We were taking possession of the terrain and achieving absolute control of a zone of the Sierra Maestra extending beyond Turquino peak in the east and toward Caracas peak in the west. Little by little, as the peasants saw the length of the struggle and that the guerrillas were invincible, they began to respond more rationally, joining our army as fighters. From then on, they not only filled our ranks, they also grouped themselves around us and the guerrilla army became strongly entrenched in the countryside, especially since the peasants usually had relatives throughout the entire zone. We called this "dressing the guerrillas in palm leaves."

The column was strengthened not only through the support of the peasants and individual volunteers, but also by forces sent from the national committee [of the July 26 Movement] and the Oriente provincial committee, which had considerable autonomy. In the period between the disembarkation and El Uvero, a column arrived consisting of some 50 men divided into five fighting platoons, each with a weapon, although these were all different and only 30 were good quality. The battles of La Plata and Arroyo del Infierno took place before this group joined us. We had been taken by surprise in Altos de Espinosa, losing one of our men there; the same thing almost happened in the Gaviro region, after a traitor, whose mission was to kill Fidel, led the army to us three times.

The bitter experiences of these surprises and our arduous life in the mountains were tempering us as veterans. The new troop received its baptism of fire in the battle of El Uvero. This action was of great importance because it marked the point at which we carried out a frontal attack in broad daylight against a well-defended post. It was one of the bloodiest episodes of the war, taking into account the length of the battle and the number of participants. As a consequence of this clash, the enemy was dislodged from the coastal zones of the Sierra Maestra.

After El Uvero, our smaller column—of the wounded under my care and other individual combatants who had joined us—rejoined the principal column. I was named chief of Column No. 2, later called Column No. 4, which operated east of Turquino. It is worth noting that the column led personally by Fidel operated primarily to the west of Turquino peak, and ours on the other side, as far as we could extend ourselves. There was a certain tactical independence of command, but we were under Fidel's orders and kept in touch with him every week or two by messenger.

The division of forces coincided with the July 26 anniversary, and while the troops of "José Martí" Column No. 1 attacked Estrada Palma in a series of actions, we marched rapidly toward the settlement of Bueycito, which we attacked and took in our column's first battle. Between that time and the first days of January 1958, the consolidation of rebel territory was achieved. In order to penetrate this territory, the army had to concentrate its forces and advance in strong columns; their preparations were extensive and results limited, since they lacked mobility. Various enemy columns were encircled and others decimated, or at least halted. Our knowledge of the area and our maneuverability increased, and we entered a sedentary period, one of fixed encampments. In the first attack on Pino del Agua we used subtler methods, fooling the enemy completely, since we were by then familiar with their habits, which were as Fidel anticipated: a few days after he let himself be seen in the area, the punitive expedition would arrive … my troops would ambush it, and meanwhile, Fidel would pop up elsewhere.

At the end of the year, the enemy troops retreated once more from the Sierra Maestra, and we remained in control of the territory between Caracas peak and Pino del Agua, on the west and east. To the south was the sea, and the army occupied the small villages on the slopes of the Sierra Maestra to the north.

Our area of operations was broadly extended when Pino del Agua was attacked for the second time by our entire troop under the personal command of Fidel. Two new columns were formed, the "Frank País" Column No. 6, commanded by Raúl, and Almeida's column. Both had come out of Column No. 1, commanded by Fidel, which was a steady source of these offshoots, created to establish our forces in distant territories.

This was a period of consolidation for our army, lasting until the second battle of Pino del Agua on February 16, 1958. It was characterized by deadlock: we had insufficient forces to attack the enemy's fortified and relatively easily defended positions, while they did not advance on us.

In our camp, we had suffered the deaths of the *Granma* martyrs, each of them sharply felt, but especially Ñico López and Juan Manuel Márquez. Other fighters, who for their bravery and moral qualities had acquired great prestige among the troops, also lost their lives during this first year. Among them we can mention Nano and Julio Díaz—not brothers—both of whom died in the battle of El Uvero; Ciro Redondo, who died in the battle of Mar Verde; and Captain Soto, who died in the battle of San Lorenzo. In the cities, among the many martyrs of our struggle, we have to mention the greatest loss to the revolution up to that time: Frank País, who died in Santiago de Cuba.

To the list of military feats in the Sierra Maestra, must be added the work carried out by the *Llano* forces in the cities. In each of the nation's principal towns, groups were fighting against Batista's regime, but the two focal points of the struggle were Havana and Santiago.

Comprehensive communication between the *Llano* and the *Sierra* was always lacking, due to two fundamental factors: the geographical isolation of the Sierra Maestra, and all types of tactical and strategic differences between the two groups. This situation arose from differing social and political conceptions.

The Sierra Maestra was isolated because of geographical conditions and because the army's cordon was sometimes extremely difficult to break through.

In this brief sketch of the country's struggle over the course of a year, we must mention the activities — generally fruitless and culminating in unfortunate results — of other groups of fighters.

On March 13, 1957, the Revolutionary Directorate attacked the presidential palace in an attempt to bring Batista to justice. A fine handful of fighters fell in that action, headed by the president of the Federation of University Students — a great fighter and a symbol of our youth, "Manzanita" Echeverría.

A few months later, in May, a landing was attempted. It had probably already been betrayed before setting out from Miami, since it was financed by the traitor Prío. It resulted in a massacre of almost all its participants. This was the *Corinthia* expedition, led by Calixto Sánchez, who was killed together with his *compañeros*, by Cowley, the assassin from northern Oriente, who was later brought to justice by members of our movement.

Fighting groups were established in the Escambray, some of them led by the July 26 Movement and others by the Revolutionary Directorate. The latter groups were originally led by a member of the Revolutionary Directorate who later betrayed them and then the revolution itself — Gutiérrez Menoyo, today in exile. The combatants loyal to the Revolutionary Directorate formed a separate column that was later directed by Commander Chomón; those who remained set up the Second National Front of Escambray.

Small cells were formed in the Cristal and Baracoa mountains, which at times were half guerrilla, half cattle-rustler;

Raúl cleaned them up when he invaded with Column No. 6. Another incident in the armed struggle of that period was the uprising at the Cienfuegos naval base on September 5, 1957, led by Lieutenant San Román, who was assassinated when the coup failed. The base was not supposed to rebel alone, but this was not a spontaneous action. It was part of a large underground movement among the armed forces, led by a group of so-called pure military men (those untainted by the dictatorship's crimes), which—today it is obvious—was penetrated by Yankee imperialism. For some obscure motive, the uprising was postponed to a later date, but the Cienfuegos naval base did not receive the order in time. Unable to stop the uprising, they decided to go through with it. At first they gained control but they committed the tragic error of not marching for the Escambray mountains—only a few minutes away from Cienfuegos—at the moment when they controlled the entire city and had the means to form a solid front in the mountains.

National and local leaders of the July 26 Movement participated. So did the people; at least they shared in the enthusiasm that led to the revolt, and some of them took up arms. This may have created a moral obligation on the part of the uprising's leaders, tying them even closer to the conquered city; but the course of events developed as in every uprising of its type, which history has seen and will see again.

Obviously, the underestimation of the guerrilla struggle by academy-oriented military men played an important role, as did their lack of faith in the guerrilla movement as an expression of the people's struggle. The conspirators, probably assuming that without the aid of their comrades-in-arms they were lost, decided to fight to the death within the narrow boundaries of a city, their backs to the sea, until they were virtually annihilated by the superior forces of the enemy, which had easily mobilized its troops and converged on Cienfuegos. The July 26 Movement, participating as an unarmed ally, could not have changed the scenario, even if its leaders had seen the end result clearly, which they did not. The lesson for the future is that he who has the strength dictates the strategy.

The large-scale killing of civilians, repeated failures, murders committed by the dictatorship in distinct points of the struggle, indicate that guerrilla action on favorable terrain is the best expression of popular struggle against a despotic, still-strong government, that it is the least painful for the children of the people. After the guerrilla force was established, we could count our losses on our fingers — *compañeros* of outstanding courage and resolve in battle, to be sure. In the cities, however, not only the resolute died, but so did many among their followers who were not totally committed revolutionaries, or who were innocent of any involvement at all. They were more vulnerable in the face of repressive action.

By the end of this first year of struggle, a general uprising throughout the country was on the horizon. Acts of sabotage — ranging from the well planned and technically executed, to the trivial, hot-headed terrorist acts carried out on individual impulse — left a tragic toll of innocent deaths and sacrifices among the best fighters, without any real advantage to the people's cause.

We were consolidating our military situation and the territory we occupied was extensive. We were in a state of armed truce with Batista; his men did not go up into the Sierra Maestra and we hardly ever went down. They made their encirclement as effective as they could, but our troops still managed to evade them.

By the end of the year, in organizational terms, our guerrilla army had developed sufficiently to have an elementary infrastructure regarding provisions, certain minimal industrial services, hospitals, and communications services.

The problems of each guerrilla fighter were very simple. To subsist as an individual, they needed small amounts of food and certain indispensable items like clothes and medicine. To subsist as a guerrilla, that is, as part of an armed force in struggle, they needed arms and ammunition. For their political development, they needed information. To assure these minimal necessities is precisely why a communications and information apparatus was required.

In the beginning, the small guerrilla units, some 20 men, would eat a meager ration of Sierra Maestra vegetables, chicken soup in the case of a banquet, and sometimes the peasants provided a pig, for which they were paid religiously. As the guerrilla force grew and groups of new "pre-guerrillas" were trained, more provisions were needed. The Sierra Maestra peasants did not have cattle and theirs was generally a subsistence diet. They depended on the sale of their coffee to buy any processed items they needed, such as salt, which did not exist in the Sierra Maestra. As an initial measure, we arranged with certain peasants that they should plant specific crops—beans, corn, rice, etc.—which we guaranteed to purchase. At the same time, we agreed on terms with some merchants in nearby towns for the supply of foodstuffs and equipment. Mule teams were organized, belonging to the guerrilla forces.

As for medicines, we obtained them in the cities, not always in the quantity or quality we needed; but at least we were able to maintain some kind of functioning apparatus for their acquisition.

It was difficult to bring arms up from the plains. To the natural difficulties of geographical isolation were added the requirements of the city forces themselves, and their reluctance to deliver arms to the guerrillas. Fidel was constantly involved in sharp discussions in an effort to secure the arrival of equipment. The only substantial shipment made to us during that first year of struggle, except for what the combatants brought with them, was the remainder of the arms used in the attack on the presidential palace. These were transported with the cooperation of a big landowner and timber merchant of the zone, a man named Babún whom I have already mentioned.

Our ammunition was limited in quantity and lacking the necessary variety. It was impossible, however, for us to manufacture it ourselves or even to recharge cartridges in this first period, except for .38 bullets, which our gunsmith would recharge with a little gunpowder, and some of the .30-06 bullets to use in the single-shot guns, since they caused the semiautomatics to jam and impeded their proper functioning.

In respect of organizing the life of the camps and communications, certain sanitary regulations were established, and in this period the first hospitals were organized. One was set up in the zone under my command, in an inaccessible place that offered relative security to the wounded, since it was invisible from the air. But it was in the heart of a dense woods, and dampness made it unhealthy for the wounded and sick. This hospital was organized by *compañero* Sergio del Valle. The Drs. Martínez Páez, Vallejo, and Piti Fajardo organized similar hospitals in Fidel's column, but these were only improved during the second year of the struggle.

The troop's equipment needs, such as cartridge boxes, belts, backpacks, and shoes were covered by a small leather-goods workshop set up in our zone. I took the first army cap we turned out to Fidel, bursting with pride. Later, I became the butt of everyone's joke; they claimed it was the cap of a *guagüero* [bus driver], a word unknown to me until then. The only one who showed me any mercy was one of Batista's councillors from Manzanillo, who was visiting the camp to arrange to join our forces and who took it with him as a souvenir.

Our most important industrial installation was a forge and armory, where defective arms were repaired and bombs, mines, and the famous M-26s [small bombs] were made. At first, the mines were made of tin cans and we filled them with material from the unexploded bombs frequently dropped by enemy planes. These mines were very defective. Furthermore, their firing pins, for striking the detonator, frequently missed. Later, a *compañero* had the idea of using the whole bomb in major attacks, removing the detonator and replacing it with a loaded shotgun; we pulled the trigger from a distance using a cord, and it exploded. Afterward, we perfected the system, making special fuses of metal alloy and electric detonators. These gave better results. Although we began this development, Fidel gave it real impetus; later, in his new operations center, Raúl created stronger industries than ours were during the first year of the war.

To please the smokers among us, we set up a cigar factory; the cigars we made were terrible but, lacking better, they tasted glorious.

The butcher shop of our army was supplied with cattle confiscated from informers and big landowners. We shared equitably, one part for the peasant population and one part for our troop.

As for disseminating our ideas, first we started a small newspaper, *El Cubano Libre*, in memory of those heroes of the jungle [the *Mambís*]. Three or four issues came out under our supervision; it was later edited by Luis Orlando Rodríguez, and subsequently Carlos Franqui gave it new impetus. We had a mimeograph machine brought up to us from the plains, on which the paper was printed.

By the end of the first year and the beginning of the second, we had a small radio transmitter. The first regular broadcasts [of Radio Rebelde] were made in February 1958. Our only listeners were Palencho, a peasant who lived on the hill facing the station, and Fidel, who was visiting our camp in preparation for the attack on Pino del Agua. He listened to it on our own receiver. Little by little the technical quality of the broadcasts improved. Then it was taken over by Column No. 1 and by the end of the campaign, in December 1958, had become one of the highest "rating" Cuban stations.

All these small advances, including our equipment—such as a winch and some generators, laboriously carried up to the Sierra Maestra to have electric light—were due to our own connections. To confront our difficulties we had to begin creating our own network of communications and information. In this respect, Lidia Doce played an important part in my column, Clodomira [Acosta] in Fidel's.

Help came not only from people in neighboring villages; even the urban bourgeoisie contributed equipment to the guerrilla struggle. Our lines of communication reached as far as the towns of Contramaestre, Palma, Bueycito, Minas de Bueycito, Estrada Palma, Yara, Bayamo, Manzanillo, and Guisa; these places served as relay stations. Goods were then carried by mules along hidden trails in the Sierra Maestra up to our positions. At times, those among us who were in training but not yet armed, went down to the nearest towns, such as Yao or Minas, with some of our armed men, or they would go to well-stocked stores in the district. They carried supplies up to our refuge on their backs. The only item we never—or almost never—lacked in the Sierra Maestra was coffee. At times we lacked salt, one of the most important foods for survival, whose virtues we became aware of only when it was scarce.

When we began to broadcast from our own transmitter, the undeniable existence of our troops and their determination to fight became known throughout the republic. Our links began to become more extensive and complex, even reaching Havana and Camagüey to the west, where we had important supply centers, and Santiago in the east.

Our information service developed in such a way that peasants in the zone immediately notified us of the presence not only of the army, but of any stranger. We could easily detain such a person to investigate their activities. Many army agents and informers, infiltrating the zone to scrutinize our lives and actions, were eliminated in this way.

We began to establish a legal service, but as of then no Sierra Maestra law had been promulgated.

Such was our organizational situation at the beginning of the last year of the war.

As for the political struggle, it was very complicated and

contradictory. Batista's dictatorship was supported by a congress elected through so many frauds that it could count on a comfortable majority to do its bidding.

Certain dissident opinions — when there was no censorship — were allowed expression, but officials and official spokespeople had powerful voices, and the networks transmitted their calls for national unity throughout the island. Otto Meruelo's hysterical voice alternated with the pompous buffooneries of Pardo Llada and Conte Agüero. The latter, repeating in writing what he had broadcast, called on "brother Fidel" to accept coexistence with Batista's regime.

Opposition groups were varied and diverse, though as a common denominator most had the wish to take power (read public funds) for themselves. This brought in its wake a sordid internal struggle to win that victory. Batista's agents infiltrated all the groups and, at key moments, denounced any significant activities to the government. Although gangsterism and opportunism characterized these groups, they also had their martyrs, some of national repute. In effect, Cuban society was in such total disarray that brave and honest people were sacrificing their lives to maintain the comfortable existence of such personages as Prío Socarrás.

The Revolutionary Directorate took the path of insurrectional struggle, but their movement was independent of ours and they had their own line. The Popular Socialist Party (PSP) joined us in certain concrete activities, but mutual distrust hampered joint action and, fundamentally, the workers party did not clearly understand the role of the guerrilla force, or Fidel's personal role in our revolutionary struggle.

During a friendly discussion, I once made an observation to

a PSP leader, which he later repeated to others as an accurate characterization of that period, "You are capable of creating cadres who can endure the most terrible tortures in jail, without uttering a word, but you can't create cadres who can take out a machine gun nest." As I saw it from my guerrilla vantage point, this was the consequence of a strategic conception: a determination to struggle against imperialism and the abuses of the exploiting classes, together with an inability to envision the possibility of taking power. Later, some of their people — of guerrilla spirit — were to join us, but by then the end of the armed struggle was near; its influence on them was slight.

Within our own movement there were two quite clearly defined tendencies, which we have already referred to as the *Sierra* and the *Llano*. Differences over strategic concepts separated us. The *Sierra* was already confident of being able to carry out the guerrilla struggle, to spread it to other places and, from the countryside, to encircle the cities held by the dictatorship, and by strangulation and attrition, destroy the entire apparatus of the regime.

The *Llano* took an ostensibly more revolutionary position, that of armed struggle in all towns, culminating in a general strike which would topple Batista and allow the prompt taking of power.

This position was only apparently more revolutionary, because in that period the political development of the *Llano compañeros* was not complete and their conception of a general strike was too narrow. A general strike called the following year without warning, in secrecy, without prior political preparation or mass action, would lead to the defeat of April 9, [1958].

These two tendencies were represented in the national committee of the movement, which changed as the struggle developed. In the preparatory stage, until Fidel left for Mexico, the national committee consisted of Fidel, Raúl, Faustino Pérez, Pedro Miret, Ñico López, Armando Hart, Pepe Suárez, Pedro Aguilera, Luis Bonito, Jesús Montané, Melba Hernández, and Haydée Santamaría—if my information is not incorrect and considering my personal participation at that time was very limited and documentation is scarce. Later, for reasons of incompatibility, Pepe Suárez, Pedro Aguilera, and Luis Bonito withdrew. While we were preparing for the struggle [in Mexico], the following people joined the committee: Mario Hidalgo, Aldo Santamaría, Carlos Franqui, Gustavo Arcos, and Frank País.

Of all the *compañeros* named, Fidel and Raúl alone went to the Sierra Maestra and remained there during the first year. Faustino Pérez, a *Granma* expeditionary, was put in charge of actions in the city. Pedro Miret was jailed a few hours before we were to leave Mexico. He remained there until the following year, when he arrived in Cuba with an arms shipment. Ñico López died only a few days after the landing. Armando Hart was jailed at the end of that year (or early the next). Jesús Montané was jailed after the landing, as was Mario Hidalgo. Melba Hernández and Haydée Santamaría worked in the cities. Aldo Santamaría and Carlos Franqui joined the struggle in the Sierra Maestra the following year. Gustavo Arcos remained in Mexico, in charge of political liaison and supplies. Frank País, assigned to head up actions in Santiago, was killed in July 1957.

Later, the following people joined the leadership body within the *Sierra*: Celia Sánchez, who stayed with us throughout 1958; Vilma Espín, who was working in Santiago and finished the war with Raúl Castro's column; Marcelo Fernández, coordinator of the movement, who replaced Faustino after the April 9 strike and stayed with us only a few weeks, since his work was in the towns; René Ramos Latour, assigned to organizing the *Llano* militia, came up to the Sierra Maestra after the April 9 failure and during the second year of the struggle died heroically as a commander; David Salvador, in charge of the labor movement, on which he left the imprint of his opportunist and divisive actions—he was later to betray the revolution and is now in prison. Some of the *Sierra* fighters, such as [Juan] Almeida, were to join the national leadership some time later.

As can be seen, during this stage the *Llano compañeros* constituted the majority. Their political backgrounds, which had not really been influenced by the revolutionary process, led them to favor a certain type of "civil" action, and to a kind of resistance to the caudillo they saw in Fidel and to the "militarist" faction represented by us in the Sierra Maestra. The differences were already apparent, but they were not yet strong enough to provoke the turbulent discussions that characterized the second year of the war.

It is important to point out that those fighting the dictatorship in the *Sierra* and the *Llano* were able to sustain opinions on tactics that were at times diametrically opposed, without this leading to abandoning the insurrectional struggle. Their revolutionary spirit continued to deepen until the moment when—victory in hand, followed by our first experiences in the struggle against imperialism—they all came together [in 1961] in a strong, party-like organization, led indisputably by Fidel. This group then joined with the Revolutionary Directorate and the Popular Socialist Party to form the United Party of the Socialist Revolution (PURS) [in 1963]. In the face of external pressure from outside our movement and attempts to divide or infiltrate it, we always presented a common front. Even those *compañeros* who in the period we are describing viewed the picture of the

Cuban Revolution with imperfect perspective, were wary of opportunists.

When Felipe Pazos, invoking the name of the July 26 Movement, sought to appropriate for himself, and for the most corrupt oligarchic interests of Cuba, the positions offered by the Miami Pact, including the position of provisional president, the entire movement united solidly against this stand, and supported the letter Fidel Castro sent to the organizations involved in the struggle against Batista. We reproduce this historic document here in its entirety. It is dated December 14, 1957, and was copied out by Celia Sánchez, since conditions of that period made it impossible to print.

Letter by Fidel Castro on the Miami Pact

Cuba
December 14, 1957

To the leaders of:
The Cuban Revolutionary Party
The Orthodox Party
The Authentic Organization
The Federation of University Students
The Revolutionary Directorate
The National Workers Front

It is my moral, patriotic, and even historic duty to address this letter to you. The events and circumstances that have recently troubled us—and that, furthermore, have been the most disturbing and difficult events since our arrival in Cuba—make the drafting of this statement indispensable.

The day of Wednesday, November 20, was the same day our forces sustained three battles during six consecutive hours, signifying the sacrifices and efforts our men have made, without aid from other organizations. It was also the very day we received in our zone of operations surprising news and a document containing the public and secret terms of a so-called unity pact signed in Miami, it appears, by the July 26 Movement and the organizations I address above. The arrival of these papers—and note the fateful irony in this, since what we actually needed was arms—coincides with the strongest offensive launched by the dictatorship against us.

In conditions of struggle such as ours, communications are difficult. In spite of the difficulties, it has been necessary to convene, out in the field, the leaders of our organization to discuss this matter, in which not only the prestige but the historic justification of the July 26 Movement is at stake.

For those who struggle against an enemy incomparably superior in numbers and weapons; for those who have fought for a whole year supported only by dignity and the conviction that their cherished cause is worth dying for; for those who have been bitterly isolated by the neglect of their *compañeros*, who systematically, not to say criminally, refused all aid, even when they had the means; for those *compañeros* who have personally witnessed daily sacrifice in its purest and most selfless form, and who have frequently suffered the pain of seeing the best among them fall, this news wounds us to the quick and provokes our indignation. At the moment, in which one asks with anguish who will be the next victim in the next, inevitable holocaust; in this dark hour, when we cannot even see the day of triumph we struggle for so steadfastly, with no other hope or solace than that we do not sacrifice ourselves in vain, we hear of this deliberately broadcast news of a pact, committing the movement to a future course without consulting its leaders and fighters, which propriety, not to say simple courtesy, demands.

Acting improperly always brings the worst consequences. Those who consider themselves capable of overthrowing a dictatorship—and of the more difficult work of reorganizing a country after revolutionary overturn—would do well not to forget this.

The July 26 Movement never appointed a delegation or granted anyone the authority to participate in the negotiations in question. The movement would not have been opposed to such a step, however, if it had been consulted, and it would have given concrete instructions to its representatives on a matter so important to the present and future activities of our organization. Instead, our information concerning relations with these various groups was limited to a report by Lester Rodríguez—whom we had commissioned exclusively to settle certain military problems with them. He told us the following:

> On the subject of Prío and of the directorate, I can report to you that I have had several conferences with them, for the exclusive purpose of coordinating military plans right up to the formation of a provisional government that is guaranteed and respected by the three groups. Of course, I pointed out that firstly, it was necessary to accept the principles of the Sierra Manifesto, specifying that this government should be formed in accord with the will of the political forces of the country. First hitch.
>
> During the general strike, we had an emergency meeting. I proposed that considering the circumstances, we utilize all the forces at hand, in an effort to resolve Cuba's problem definitively. Prío answered that he did not have enough forces to enter such an enterprise with assurance of victory, and that it would be madness to go along with my proposal. I responded that when everything was ready to weigh anchor, he should advise me, so that we could speak of the possibility of pacts then; and that he should be so kind, in the meantime, to let me—and those I represent as part of the July 26 Movement—work with complete independence. My firm opinion is that there is no way to come to an understanding with these gentlemen and that it is even better to refrain from trying to do so in the future. At the moment Cuba most needed it, they denied having the material they had never stopped accumulating and with which they are flooded.

This report speaks for itself, and confirms our suspicions; we rebels could not expect any outside aid.

We recognize that the organizations you represent have considered it advisable to discuss the terms of unity with certain members of our movement. It is inconceivable that you should publicize these as settled agreements, without having advised the national leaders of the movement and without their consent—even less so, considering these agreements changed the institutional foundations we set out in the Sierra Manifesto. This is a pact for publicity purposes, and usurps the name of our organization.

The situation is paradoxical to say the least: at the very moment the national leadership—with its underground headquarters somewhere on the island—is preparing to oppose outright the terms that have been publicly and privately put forward as the basis for an agreement, this leadership learns through underground circulars and the foreign press that these very terms have been proclaimed from the rooftops and constitute the basis for agreement. It found itself presented with a public fait accompli: it was compelled either to deny it, with all the confusion and injury to morale this would entail, or to accept it, without ever actually expressing its opinion. Of course, as might be expected, a copy of the document only reached us in the Sierra Maestra several days after it had been published.

Faced with this dilemma, and before making a public denial of the agreement, the national leadership reasserted the need to return to the principles of the Sierra Manifesto. Meanwhile, it held a meeting in rebel territory, in which the views of each member of the leadership were expressed and analyzed. As a result, a unanimous resolution was adopted, which forms the basis for this letter.

It goes without saying that any unity pact must be well received by national and international public opinion. Among other reasons, because foreigners are ignorant of the real situation of the political and revolutionary forces that oppose Batista; and in Cuba, because the word unity possessed great prestige in the days when the relationship of forces was really very different from what it is today; and finally, because it is always best to unite all efforts, from the most enthusiastic to the lukewarm.

What is important for the revolution is not unity in itself, but the groundwork of this unity, the form it assumes, and the patriotic intentions that animate it.

To decide in favor of this unity, whose terms—ratified by people not qualified to do so—we have not discussed, and to proclaim unity without further ado from the comfortable refuge of a foreign city, is a fraud against the country, a fraud against the world. It causes the movement to have to challenge a public opinion deluded by a fraudulent pact. It is a dirty trick of the worst sort—one, however, which will not destroy a truly revolutionary organization.

What made the operation possible: while the leaders of the various organizations subscribing to this pact met abroad and made an imaginary revolution, the leaders of the July 26 Movement were in Cuba, leading a very real revolution.

Are these lines superfluous? So be it. I would not have written them were it not for the bitterness and mortification we feel at the way you tried to associate the movement with this pact, even considering that procedural differences should never prevail over the essential. In spite of everything, we would have accepted it—for the positive value unity always offers, for the value of certain Liberation Junta projects, for the aid offered us that we really need—if we did not find ourselves in pure and simple disagreement with some of its essential principles.

Even if our situation became desperate, if the dictatorship mobilized as many thousands of soldiers as it wanted to annihilate us, we would never accept the sacrifice of certain fundamental principles or our conception of the Cuban Revolution.

These principles are clearly stated in the Sierra Manifesto.

To suppress, in a unity pact, the principle of hostility toward foreign intervention in Cuba's internal affairs is an act of the most lukewarm patriotism and of manifest cowardice.

To declare that we are opposed to such intervention, is not only to oppose it on behalf of the revolution—for it would be an offense against our sovereignty and, let it be said, against a principle dear to all the peoples of Latin America; it is also to oppose intervention in support of the dictatorship—in the form of shipments of planes, bombs, modern tanks, and weapons, thanks to which it maintains itself in power and for which no one, with the exception of the peasant population of the Sierra Maestra, has suffered more than we have. To enforce respect for the principle of nonintervention would in itself overturn the dictatorship. Are we going to be so cowardly as not to dare demand the withdrawal of pro-Batista foreign intervention? So insincere as to make a behind-the-scenes request to pull our chestnuts out of the fire? So feeble as not to risk pronouncing a single word on the question? Under these conditions, how can we have the audacity to declare ourselves revolutionaries and endorse the unity pact's claim to historic significance?

The unity declaration has also eliminated our formal commitment to reject any form of military junta as the provisional government of the republic.

However much it may let itself be deluded by the illusion that Cuba's problems will be resolved by eliminating the dictator, the worst thing to befall the nation at this moment would be Batista's replacement by a military junta. Certain contemptible civilians—who were actually accomplices on March 10, [1952], but who subsequently broke away, perhaps because of their all-consuming ambition and immoderate fondness for blackjack—envisage this type of solution, which only the enemies of our country's progress could view with favor.

Latin American experience has proved that all military juntas slip toward autocracy. The worst of the evils that have been a scourge on this continent is the entrenchment of military castes in countries that go to fewer wars than Switzerland and have more generals than Prussia. One of our people's most legitimate aspirations, at this crucial hour when its democratic and republican destiny is being either salvaged or destroyed, is the preservation of the civilian tradition, born in the struggles for emancipation. That tradition, the most precious legacy of its liberators, would be trampled underfoot the very instant a uniformed junta put itself at the head of the republic (something none of our generals in the independence struggle, not even the most vainglorious, was tempted to do, in either war nor peace). Just how far shall we have gone along the road of renunciation if, out of a fear of wounding sensibilities (more imaginary than real among the honest military men who support us), we devote ourselves to suppressing a statement on such an important principle? Or is it not understood that a timely statement would avert the danger of a military junta, a junta which would do nothing more than prolong the civil war?

We have no hesitation in stating that if a military junta replaces Batista, the July 26 Movement will resolutely continue its campaign for liberation. We prefer to struggle harder today, rather than fall into a new, bottomless abyss tomorrow; neither a military junta nor a puppet government played by the military! Civilians to govern with decency and honor; soldiers to their barracks. Each of them fulfilling their duty!

Are we perhaps waiting for the generals of March 10, before whom Batista—on feeling himself strongly menaced—would gladly give way, seeing this to be the most viable means of transferring the necessary powers with a minimum of damage to his own interests and those of his coterie? To what end does this lack of foresight lead? This lack of ideals, this lack of a will to fight?

If you do not have faith in the people, if you do not count on their great reserves of energy and combative spirit, then you do not have the right to lay hands upon their destiny, not in order to block and frustrate its most heroic hopes for a republican existence. Let us not allow the politicos, with their deals, puerile ambitions, desperate greed, and advance division of the spoils, to meddle with the revolutionary process, because in Cuba men are dying for something more. Let the hack politicians become revolutionaries, if they wish! But do not let them transform the revolution into degenerate politics. Too much of our people's blood is being spilled today, too many enormous sacrifices have been made, to deserve such a worthless deception tomorrow.

Aside from these two fundamental principles, which were omitted from the unity pact document, we are also in disagreement on other points:

If we are to accept sub-section B of secret clause II, relating to the powers of the Liberation Junta, which provides for naming "the president of the republic in the provisional government," then we cannot accept sub-section C of the same clause, which includes among those powers, "Approval or disapproval, in its totality, of the cabinet named by the president of the republic, as well as changes that may arise in the case of a total or partial crisis."

How can it be imagined that the president's right to appoint and remove his collaborators should remain subject to the approval of a body not connected with the state power? Is it not clear that inasmuch as the junta is composed of representatives of different parties and regions and, consequently, of different interests, the appointment of cabinet members would be nothing more than the search for the least common denominator, as the only means of reaching agreement on diverse questions? Is it possible to accept a clause that implies the establishment of two executives within the state? The only guarantee that all regions of the country must demand of the provisional government is that its mission be based on a minimum fixed program and that it play its moderator role with absolute impartiality during the transitional stage, leading to complete constitutional normality.

To attempt to interfere in the appointment of each minister is tantamount to wanting to control the public administration so as to subjugate it to political interests. This procedure has meaning only for the parties and organizations which, lacking mass support, can expect to survive only within the canons of traditional politics. It is incompatible with the exalted political and revolutionary goals pursued by the July 26 Movement for the republic.

The mere existence of secret agreements is in itself unacceptable, especially when these agreements are not about organizational questions or plans of action of the resistance, but are about problems on which the nation should have its say, such as the structure of the future government, which is why any agreement should be publicly proclaimed. [José] Martí said, "In the revolution, methods are secret but the ends must always be public."

Another equally inadmissible point for the July 26 Movement is secret clause VIII, which says, "The revolutionary forces, and their weapons, will become part of the regular armed institutions of the republic."

First of all, what is meant by the revolutionary forces? Does this mean that one accepts into the police force, or as a sailor or soldier, those whose weapons are today carefully hidden, who fold their arms while a handful of compatriots fight against the organized forces of the dictatorship, but who will not hesitate to brandish them on the day of victory? Are we thus going to shield, in a revolutionary document, the very virus of gangsterism and anarchy that has been the scourge of the republic in a still recent past?

Experience in the territory we occupy has taught us that maintaining public order is an important problem for the country. Facts have demonstrated that from the time the existing order is suppressed, many bonds are dissolved and delinquency, if it is not stopped in time, flourishes everywhere. It is with the timely application of stringent measures, with the full and total approval of the population, that we have put an end to the first manifestations of banditry. Peasants, who formerly considered agents of authority as enemies of the people, used to offer protection to a fugitive who had problems with the authorities. Today, they see our combatants as defenders of their interests, and order reigns, its best guardian being the citizenry itself.

Anarchy is the worst enemy of the revolutionary process. To combat it from now on is a fundamental necessity. Those who do not understand this should not concern themselves with the fate of the revolution; it is natural that those who have not sacrificed themselves for it should not care about its survival.

The nation must know that justice will be done and that crime will be punished, wherever it appears.

The July 26 Movement claims for itself the duty of maintaining public order and reorganizing the armed institutions of the republic:

1) Because it is the only organization possessing disciplined militia throughout the country and an army in the field which has won more than 20 victories over the enemy.

2) Because our fighters have proven their generosity and their lack of hate toward the soldiers a thousand times, by always sparing their lives, by caring for those wounded in battle, by never torturing an opponent even if it were known he had important information. They have maintained this wartime conduct with a magnanimity that commands admiration.

3) Because it is necessary to infuse the armed institutions with that spirit of justice and nobility the July 26 Movement has spread among its own fighters.

4) Because the equanimity we have displayed in this war is the best guarantee that honorable military men have nothing to fear from the revolution. They will not have to pay for the misdeeds of those who, by their crimes and shame, have brought disgrace to the military uniform.

Certain other aspects of the unity pact remain difficult to grasp. How is it possible to achieve agreement without having defined a strategy of struggle? Were members of the Authentic Organization still thinking of a putsch in the capital? Were they going to continue accumulating arms and more arms, which would surely sooner or later fall into the hands of the police, rather than pass them on to the fighters? Lastly, have they accepted the proposition of the general strike as advocated by the July 26 Movement?

In addition, we have the impression that the military importance of the Oriente struggle has been woefully underestimated. Today in the Sierra Maestra, we are no longer waging guerrilla war but a war of confrontation. Our forces, inferior in number and arms, take as much advantage as possible of the terrain, more rapid movement, and the constant surveillance of the enemy. It is superfluous to stress the unique importance of the moral factor in this struggle. The results have been astonishing and some day they will be known in detail.

The entire population is in revolt. If it were armed, our detachments would not have to worry about even the smallest corner of the country; the peasants would not allow a single enemy to pass. The dictatorship's defeats, as it continues to send large-scale reinforcements, could be turned into disasters. Anything I might say to you concerning the way in which the courage of the people has been aroused would fall short of the reality. The dictatorship is engaging in barbarous reprisals. The mass murder of peasants rivals the butchery perpetrated by the Nazis in Europe. They make the defenseless population pay for each of their defeats. The communiqués of the general staff announcing rebel losses are always preceded by a massacre. Such practices have awakened a spirit of fierce revolt among the people. The heart bleeds and the spirit is afflicted at the thought that no one has sent these people a single gun; at the thought that while the peasants wait, powerless, for their homes to be burned down and their families to be murdered, while they call for guns with all the strength of despair, arms caches exist in Cuba which are not being used to destroy even one miserable lackey, and which await seizure by the police, or the dictatorship's collapse, or the extermination of the rebels.

The conduct of many of our fellow citizens could not have been more ignoble. There is still time to change and to aid those who struggle. From our personal point of view, this has no importance. You should not think that self-interest or pride dictates these words: our fate is sealed and we are not afflicted with doubts. We will either die here, to the last rebel, and in the cities, an entire generation of youth will perish, or we shall triumph over the most incredible obstacles. For us, defeat is not possible; the year of sacrifices and heroic deeds our men have experienced will not be obliterated by anyone or anything. Our victories are real, and cannot easily be erased. Our men, more resolute than ever, will fight to the last drop of their blood.

Those who have refused to help us will suffer defeat; those who were with us at the beginning and have abandoned us; those who, having lacked faith in dignity and ideals, squandered their time and prestige in shameful deals with Trujillo despotism; those who, possessing arms, were led by their own cowardice to hide them at the moment of combat: they have blundered, not us.

We can say one thing loudly and clearly: if we had seen other Cubans fighting for freedom, pursued and on the verge of being exterminated; if we had seen them resisting day after day without surrendering or weakening in their resolve, we would not have hesitated to fly to their assistance and if necessary to die with them. We are Cubans, and Cubans cannot remain unmoved by the struggle for liberty, not in any other country of Latin America. Were the Dominicans mustering their island's forces to liberate their people? For each Dominican there were 10 Cubans. Were Somoza's followers invading Costa Rica? Cubans hastened there to join the battle. It is hard to imagine that today, when their own country is arduously battling for liberty, some Cubans, exiled from their homeland by the dictatorship, deny aid to their brothers and sisters who fight!

If they do aid us, will they set unfair conditions? In order to repay their aid, will we have to offer them the republic as booty? Should we renounce our ideals and make a new art of this war—killing one's fellow men, plunging the country into a useless blood bath—not redeeming the reward the country expects from such a sacrifice?

The leadership of the struggle against dictatorship is, and will continue to be, in Cuba itself and in the hands of revolutionary fighters. Those who, now or later, wish to be considered leaders of the revolution must be inside the country and must directly accept the responsibilities, risks, and sacrifices required by the situation in Cuba today.

The exiles have a role to play in this struggle, but it is absurd that they should attempt to tell us from abroad which peak we should storm, which sugar plantation we are permitted to burn, which acts of sabotage we can carry off successfully, and at which moment, under which circumstances, and in what form we can call a general strike. This is more than absurd, it is ridiculous. Help us abroad by collecting funds among Cuban exiles and émigrés, by leading a publicity campaign for the Cuban cause. Denounce from there the crimes of which we here are victims. But do not try to lead from Miami a revolution that is taking shape in all the cities and fields of the island, amid struggle, turmoil, sabotage, strikes, and the thousand other forms of revolutionary activity which the fighting strategy of the July 26 Movement has set into motion.

The national leadership is ready, as it has repeatedly made known, to enter into talks in Cuba with the leaders of any opposition organization whatsoever, for the purpose of coordinating specific plans and carrying out concrete activities deemed to be useful in overturning the dictatorship.

The general strike will take place with effective coordination of efforts among the Movement for Civil Resistance, the National Workers Front, and any other group which has rejected the spirit of sectarianism and entered into contact with the July 26 Movement, which today finds itself the only opposition organization fighting within the country.

The workers section of the July 26 Movement is organizing strike committees in every industrial center, together with those opposition elements who show support for a work stoppage and who do not seem likely to disappear at the crucial moment. These strike committees will constitute the National Workers Front, which will be the only representative of the proletariat the July 26 Movement will recognize as legitimate.

The overthrow of the dictator necessarily implies the removal of an inglorious congress, the leadership of the Confederation of Cuban Workers, and all the mayors, governors, and other functionaries who, directly or otherwise, relied on the "elections" of November 1, 1954, or on the military coup d'état of March 10, 1952, to win their posts. It also implies the immediate freeing of political prisoners, whether civil or military, as well as bringing to trial all the accomplices of the dictatorship's crimes.

The new government shall rest on the 1940 constitution, guaranteeing all the rights recognized by it, and holding itself aloof from all political sectarianism.

The executive shall assume the legislative functions assigned by the constitution to the congress of the republic, and shall have for its principal task the holding of general elections, in accordance with the 1943 electoral code and the 1940 constitution, and putting into effect the 10-point minimum program of the Sierra Manifesto.

The present supreme court shall be declared dissolved on account of its inability to resolve the illegal situation created by the coup d'état. This does not preclude the subsequent reappointment of some of its present members who have defended constitutional principles or maintained a firm position against the crimes, absolutism, and abuses of these years of dictatorship.

The president of the republic shall determine the manner of constituting the new supreme court and it shall, in its turn, be charged with reorganizing all the courts and autonomous institutions, dismissing those who are convicted of involvement in the shady dealings of the dictatorship. The appointment of new functionaries shall be done according to the law. The political parties, under the provisional government, shall enjoy this sole right: namely, the freedom to defend their program before the people, to mobilize and organize the citizens within the framework of our constitution, and to participate in the general elections.

The necessity of appointing the person called on to occupy the presidency of the republic has already been elucidated in the Sierra Manifesto, and our movement has declared that in its opinion the said person should be chosen by all civic institutions. Be that as it may, although five months have passed, this question has not yet been resolved. It is becoming increasingly urgent to give the nation an answer to the question: who shall succeed the dictator? It is not possible to wait one more day in the face of this giant question mark. The July 26 Movement is answering the question. It presents its proposal to the people, as the only possible formula for guaranteeing legality and developing the preconditions for unity and provisional government. This man must be that upright magistrate of the Oriente court of justice, Dr. Manuel Urrutia. It is not we, but his own conduct, that has singled him out, and we expect that he will not refuse this service to the republic.

The grounds for appointing him are:

1) He is the member of the judiciary who has most respected the constitution by declaring, in court chambers after the trial of the *Granma* expeditionaries, that organizing an armed force against the regime did not constitute a crime and was perfectly legitimate, in accordance with the spirit and the letter of the constitution and the law. This declaration was unprecedented for a magistrate in the history of our struggles for freedom.

2) His life, dedicated to the true administration of justice, assures us that he is professionally and personally sufficiently equipped to maintain the balance between all legitimate interests at the moment the dictatorship is overturned by the people.

3) No one is as free of party spirit as Dr. Manuel Urrutia. By virtue of his position as judge, he does not belong to any political group. No other citizen of equal prestige, without active involvement, has been so identified with the revolutionary cause.

If our conditions—the disinterested conditions of an organization that has agreed to the greatest sacrifices, which has not been consulted before its name has been used in a unity pact it has not ratified—are rejected, we shall continue the struggle alone, as we have always done, with no other arms than those we take from the enemy in each battle, with no other aid than that of the sorely tried people, with no support other than our ideals.

After all, it is the July 26 Movement, and it alone, that has struggled actively throughout the country and continues to do so. The militants of the movement, and nobody else, have brought the revolt from the rugged mountains of Oriente all the way to the western provinces. They alone have carried out sabotage, burned sugarcane fields, and executed the political thugs. The July 26 Movement alone has been able to organize the nation's workers in a revolutionary way. It alone has cooperated in the organization of civil resistance, in which all civic groups from virtually every region of Cuba are united.

Understand that we have withdrawn from bureaucratic entanglements and from participation in the government. But you must understand once and for all that the July 26 militants have not given up and will never give up guiding and leading the people—from the underground, from the Sierra Maestra, or from the graves where the enemy may fling our dead. We will not give this up, because not only we but an entire generation has promised the people of Cuba concrete solutions to their momentous problems.

We shall conquer or die, alone. The struggle will never be harder than it was when we were only 12 men; when we did not have the support of a people inured to war and organized across all the Sierra Maestra; when we did not have a powerful and disciplined nationwide organization, as we have today; when we could not count on the tremendous support of the masses, such as that displayed on the day our unforgettable Frank País died.

In order to die with dignity, company is not necessary.

Fidel Castro
Sierra Maestra
December 14, 1957

PINO DEL AGUA II

By the beginning of 1958 a certain truce had been established between our forces and Batista's troops. The army, nevertheless, continued to issue communiqués reporting eight rebel losses one day, 23 the next—of course suffering no losses themselves. This was their most common tactic, especially in the region where my column was operating, in which Sánchez Mosquera dedicated himself to imaginary battles against rebel forces, murdering peasants whose corpses added to his service record.

At the end of January, censorship was lifted and, for the last time until the war ended, the newspapers printed some news. An air of truce was blowing through government circles. Ramírez León, one of Batista's legislators, made a more or less spontaneous trip accompanied by a legislator from Manzanillo, Lalo Roca, and a Spanish journalist from *París Match*, named Meneses, who conducted a series of interviews in the Sierra Maestra.

In the United States, long statements about the denunciation of the Miami Pact were being published by the committee-in-exile of the July 26 Movement, whose president was Mario Llerena and whose treasurer was Raúl Chibás. (These representatives found their work in that part of the world so good for their health that at present it has apparently become their permanent residence. Perhaps they have careers similar to those they had during the war of liberation, when they seemed to be honest people.)

The interviews with Meneses, published in the magazine *Bohemia,* had international repercussions; but within the country, there was an interesting debate between Masferrer and Ramírez León, during those fleeting days when the Havana press published a little news.

Censorship had been lifted in five of the six provinces. In Oriente, constitutional guarantees were still suspended and censorship continued.

In the middle of January a group of members of the July 26 Movement, taken prisoner as they were leaving the Sierra Maestra, were brought before the press. They included Armando Hart, Javier Pazos, Luis Buch, and a guide named Eulelio Vallejo. This news was of some interest—despite the fact that *compañeros* were taken prisoner, and often assassinated, every day—because it revealed the polemic that had already become more or less public between the two parts of the July 26 Movement. In response to a fairly idiotic letter I had sent *compañero* René Ramos Latour, he wrote me a rejoinder. A copy of my letter, however, was circulated. Armando Hart wrote me a polemical note and intended to send it to me from the Sierra Maestra, where he had gone to see Fidel. Fidel, however, believed that this letter would provoke yet another one, then another, until at some point or other the thing could fall into enemy hands, which would do us no good. With discipline, Armando obeyed the order, but he forgot the note was in one of his pockets, and it was on him when he was arrested.

The lives of Armando Hart and his *compañeros* hung by a

thread during the days they were held incommunicado in prison. The Yankee embassy mobilized to investigate the source of the controversy. As a result of the particular terms expressed in the respective arguments, the enemy sensed something and pricked up its ears.

Independent of this incident, Fidel felt it was important to strike a resounding blow, to take advantage of the lifting of censorship; we prepared ourselves for this.

Once again, Pino del Agua was the spot chosen. We had attacked it once successfully [in September 1957]; from then on, the enemy had occupied it. Even when the troops were not moving about much, their position on the crest of the Sierra Maestra made wide detours necessary, and traffic in the zone was always dangerous. The elimination of Pino del Agua as an army forward position would be of great strategic importance and, given the new press conditions in the country, could resonate nationally.

From the first days in February, feverish preparations and inspections of the area began, mainly by Roberto Ruiz and Félix Tamayo, both from the region and today officers in our army. We also hastened preparations of our latest weapon, the M-26, also called "Sputnik," to which we attributed exceptional importance. It was a small tinplate bomb, which we first launched using a complicated apparatus, a kind of catapult made with the lines from an underwater spear gun. Later we perfected it so that we could launch it using a rifle and cartridges, making the device travel much farther.

These little bombs made a lot of noise and were frightening, but since they had only a tinplate casing, their lethal power was minor and when they exploded close to enemy soldiers, they inflicted only minor wounds. In addition, it was very difficult to time the lighting of the fuse so that the final trajectory and the explosion would coincide perfectly. Because of the impact of the launch, the fuses often went out and the little bombs would not explode, falling intact into enemy hands. When the enemy realized this, they no longer feared them; in this first battle, though, they had their psychological effect.

We made our preparations with infinite care, and the attack took place on February 16, [1958]. Our efforts were reported in *El Cubano Libre*, in which we produced a near-exact synthesis of how the battle took place.

The strategic plan was very simple: Fidel, knowing that an entire company was in the sawmill, doubted that our troops could take the camp. Our goal was to attack, destroy their posts, surround the camp, and watch for reinforcements, for we knew well that troops on the march are more alert than stationary troops. We established various ambushes and expected great results from them, stationing at each an appropriate number of men to deal with the likelihood that enemy forces would pass that way.

The attack was directed personally by Fidel, whose general staff was on a hill to the north, commanding a clear view of the sawmill. The battle plan: Camilo was to advance along the road from El Uvero, passing through Bayamesa; his troops, the forward guard of Column No. 4, were to take the posts, advance as far as the terrain permitted, and hold there. Retreating guards were to be impeded by Captain Raúl Castro Mercader's platoon, situated on the edge of the road to Bayamo; and in case the enemy tried to reach the Peladero river, Captain Guillermo García was waiting for them with some 25 men.

When firing started, our mortar, which Quiala was operating and which had exactly six shells, would enter the fray; then the siege would begin. An ambush led by Lieutenant Vilo Acuña on the Loma de la Virgen would aim to intercept troops coming from El Uvero; and farther away to the north, waiting for troops coming from Yao by way of Vega de los Jobos, was Lalo Sardiñas with some snipers.

In this ambush, we first tested a specialty of mine, with far from successful results. *Compañero* Antonio Estévez (later killed during an attack on Bayamo) had contrived a system for exploding undetonated airplane bombs, using a gunshot as a detonator. We installed the device, foreseeing an army advance through an area in which we had little strength. There was a lamentable mistake: the very inexperienced and highly nervous *compañero* in charge of announcing the arrival of the enemy gave the signal at the approach of a civilian truck. The mine worked, and the driver became the innocent victim of this new weapon that, after it was developed, became so effective.

At dawn on February 16, Camilo moved to take the posts, but our guides had not expected the guards to pull back very close to their camp during the night; there was quite a delay before the attack began. The men thought they were in the wrong place and moved forward very cautiously, not realizing what the enemy had done. It took Camilo and his 20 men no less than an hour to cover the 500 meters between the two positions, walking single file.

They finally reached the settlement. The guards had installed a simple alarm system: some string near ground level with tin cans tied to it. The cans rattled when stepped on or when the string was touched. But they had also left some horses grazing, so that when the column's forward guard brushed the string, the soldiers thought it was just the horses. Camilo was therefore able to get very close to them.

On the other side, our vigil became more anxious as the hours passed before the long-awaited attack began. Finally, we heard the first shot marking the beginning of the battle, and we started our bombardment — the six mortar shells — that ended quickly, with neither pain nor glory.

The guards had seen or heard the first attackers, and with the burst of gunfire that began the battle, they wounded *compañero* [Ángel] Guevara, who later died in our hospital. In a few minutes, Camilo's forces had wiped out any resistance, taking 11 weapons (among them two machine guns) and three prisoners, and killing seven or eight; but resistance inside the barracks was organized immediately and our attacks were held off.

Lieutenants Noda and Capote, and the fighter Raimundo Lien, died one after the other attempting to advance. Camilo was wounded in the thigh, and Virelles had to retreat, abandoning the machine gun he was in charge of operating. Despite his wound, Camilo returned at dawn to try and salvage the weapon. In the first light of dawn he was caught in a hail of fire and wounded again, but luckily the bullet, which penetrated his abdomen, left his body through his side without touching any vital organs. While Camilo was rescued and the machine gun lost, another *compañero* named Luis Macías was wounded and dragged himself through the bushes in the opposite direction from the retreat of his *compañeros*; there he met his death. Some isolated fighters, from positions near the barracks, bombarded it with the Sputniks or M-26s, sowing confusion among the soldiers. Guillermo García could not participate at all in this battle, since the soldiers made no attempt to leave their refuge; as we had foreseen, they immediately radioed for help.

At mid-morning, the situation throughout the zone was calm, but from our command post we heard shouting which filled us with anguish, along the lines of: "Here goes Camilo's machine gun," followed by some volleys. Along with the abandoned tripod machine gun, Camilo had left his cap with his name inscribed on the inside, and the guards were making fun of us. We guessed that something had happened, but for the whole day, we could not make contact with the troops on the other side. Meanwhile, Camilo, attended by Sergio del Valle, refused to retreat and they waited there for further developments.

Fidel's predictions were coming true: the company led by Captain Sierra sent forward guard units from Oro de Guisa to investigate what was happening at Pino del Agua. Waiting for them was Paco Cabrera's entire platoon, about 30 to 35 men stationed by the road, on the hill called El Cable because of the cable to help vehicles make the difficult climb.

Our squadrons were posted, under the command of lieutenants [Eddy] Suñol, Alamo, Reyes, and William Rodríguez. Paco Cabrera was also there as platoon leader, but those in charge of holding off the forward guard were Paz and Duque, facing the road. The small enemy force advanced and was completely destroyed: 11 dead and five wounded prisoners who were treated in a house and left there; Second Lieutenant Laferté, who today is one of us, was also taken prisoner; and 12 rifles were captured, among them two M-1s and a machine gun, as well as a Johnson.

One or two soldiers who were able to flee made it to Oro de Guisa with the news. Receiving word, the people in Oro de

Guisa must have asked for help, but Raúl Castro was stationed, with all his forces, between Guisa and Oro de Guisa. We had presumed the guards would arrive this way to relieve the besieged men at Pino del Agua. Raúl organized his forces so that Félix Pena and the forward guard would close the road to enemy reinforcements; then his squadron, with that of Ciro Frías, would attack the enemy immediately; and then Efigenio would close the encirclement in the rear.

One detail went unnoticed: two inoffensive and bewildered peasants, who passed all our positions with roosters under their arms, turned out to be army soldiers from Oro de Guisa, sent to explore the road. They observed our troop's positions, and reported to their comrades in Guisa. As a result, since they knew his position, Raúl had to bear the brunt of the army's offensive. They attacked him from an elevation and Raúl had to make a long retreat, during which one man was wounded and one man, Florencio Quesada, was killed.

The road from Bayamo, which passes through Oro de Guisa, was the only route taken by the army in its attempt to advance. Although Raúl was obliged to retreat, given his disadvantageous position, enemy troops advanced very slowly along the road and did not appear during the whole day.

That day we were under constant attack by the army's B-26s, which machine-gunned the hills with no greater result than inconveniencing us, obliging us to take precautions.

Fidel was euphoric over the battle; at the same time, he was worried about the fate of our *compañeros* and on various occasions he took greater risks than he should have. Some days later, that fact provoked a group of us officers to send him a letter requesting, in the name of the revolution, that he not risk his life needlessly. This rather infantile letter, although inspired by the most altruistic motives, did not, I believe, warrant even a reading on his part. Needless to say, he did not pay the least attention to it.

That night I insisted that an attack of the kind Camilo had carried out was possible; that we could overcome the guards posted in Pino del Agua. Fidel was not in favor of the idea, but he finally agreed to try it, sending a force under Escalona's command, composed of Ignacio Pérez's and Raúl Castro Mercader's platoons. The *compañeros* approached and did everything possible to reach the barracks, but they were repelled by heavy fire and retreated without trying to attack again. I asked to be given command of the force, and Fidel reluctantly agreed.

My idea was to get as close as possible and, with Molotov cocktails made from the sawmill's own gasoline, set fire to the houses, all made of timber, and oblige the men to surrender or at least come pouring out to face our fire. As we approached the battle site and prepared to take positions, I received this short manuscript from Fidel:

> February 16, 1958. Che: If everything depends on an attack from this side, without support from Camilo and Guillermo, I do not think that anything suicidal should be done, because it runs the risk of too many casualties and failing to achieve the objective.
>
> I recommend, very seriously, that you be careful. You must not take part in the fighting: this is a strict order. You are charged with leading the men well, which at this moment is crucial. F [Fidel].

Almeida, who had brought the message, also told me in person that I could attack, on my responsibility, according to the terms of the note, but that he (Fidel) was not in agreement. The strict order not to enter into combat weighed on me. The likelihood, if not the certainty, that several men would be killed; the chances of taking the barracks; our lack of information concerning the positions of Guillermo's and Camilo's isolated forces; all this, and also taking all the responsibility on my shoulders, was too much for me, and, crestfallen, I took the same path as my predecessor Escalona.

The following morning, amid constant aerial attack, the order for a general retreat was given. After a few shots made using telescopic sights at the soldiers who were beginning to leave their shelters, we began to retreat along the ridge of the Sierra Maestra.

As can be noted in the official dispatch we issued at the time, the enemy suffered between 18 to 25 deaths and we captured 33 rifles, five machine guns, and a lot of ammunition. To the list of casualties the name Luis Macías must be added, whose fate then was not known, and other *compañeros* like Luis Olazábal and Quiroga, wounded in different actions of the prolonged battle. In the February edition of the newspaper *El Mundo,* the following dispatch appeared:

El Mundo. Wednesday, February 19, 1958. The loss of 16 insurgents and five soldiers is reported. It is not known whether Guevara was wounded.

The army's general staff issued a communiqué yesterday at 5 p.m., denying that a significant battle with the rebels had taken place at Pino del Agua, south of Bayamo. The report further admits that "there have been a few skirmishes between army reconnaissance patrols and groups of rebels," and that at the time of the report, "rebel casualties rose to 16, while the army suffered five casualties." The communiqué adds, "as for whether the well-known Argentine communist Che Guevara was wounded, this has not yet been confirmed. Nothing regarding the presence of the insurrectional leader in those encounters has been confirmed, but it is known that he remains hidden in the labyrinth of the Sierra Maestra."

A little later, or perhaps even around this same time, the massacre of Oro de Guisa occurred, directed by Sosa Blanco—the assassin who, in the first days of January 1959, died before a firing squad. While the dictatorship could only confirm that Fidel "remains hidden in the labyrinth of the Sierra Maestra," troops under his personal command begged him not to risk his life needlessly, and the enemy army avoided climbing up to our bases. Some time later, Pino del Agua was abandoned, and we completed the liberation of the western part of the Sierra Maestra.

A few days after that battle, one of the most important actions of the struggle occurred: Column No. 3, under the direction of Commander Almeida, moved toward the region of Santiago, and the "Frank País" Column No. 6, under the direction of Commander Raúl Castro, crossed the eastern plains, penetrated Mangos de Baraguá, went on to Pinares de Mayarí, and then formed the "Frank País" Second Eastern Front.

Report on the second battle of Pino del Agua
from *El Cubano Libre*

Pino del Agua is a settlement in the heights of the Sierra Maestra next to the Bayamesa peak. Defended by Captain Guerra's company, entrenched and well fortified, it is the army's farthest point of advance into the Sierra Maestra. The objective of the attack was not to capture the sawmill, but to establish an encirclement that would force the army to send in reinforcements. The situation of the nearest troops was as follows: in San Pablo de Yao, some 12 kilometers from the sawmill, was Sánchez Mosquera's company. Captain Sierra's company was in Oro, about six kilometers away. The navy garrison at El Uvero was 25 kilometers away. Reinforcements were also expected to arrive from Guisa and Bayamo. Our forces were on each of the roads leading to Pino del Agua from these places, waiting to intercept them.

At 5:30 a.m. on February 16, the forces of Column No. 4 under the command of Captain Camilo Cienfuegos, launched the attack. The attack was launched so violently that the posts were taken without difficulty, causing the enemy eight dead, four prisoners, and a number of wounded. From then on, the enemy's resistance intensified, causing the deaths of lieutenants Gilberto Capote and Enrique Noda, and *compañero* Raimundo Liens, on our side. Comrade Ángel Guevara was badly wounded and died several days later in one of our field hospitals.

The siege continued for an entire day. Reconnaissance forces arrived from Oro: a total of 16 men. These forces were taken by surprise and totally annihilated. Three wounded prisoners were captured but were left behind in peasant houses because of the impossibility of transporting them. The head of the column, Second Lieutenant Evelio Laferté, was taken prisoner. Only two men, apparently wounded, were able to escape; the rest were killed in action.

Our forces defending the roads from Yao and El Uvero had to remain inactive, since these troops did not move out from their bases. The column led by Commander Raúl Castro was forced to engage in combat under critical circumstances. His men were unable to fire on the enemy, since they were advancing behind a shield of peasant women and children. *Compañero* Florentino Quesada was killed in this action. The number of losses suffered by the army is not known.

Hours after Commander Raúl Castro's column withdrew, the army advanced on our positions. A group of terrorized and defenseless peasants had remained there, seeking refuge in some huts to escape the battle. All the refuge seekers were ordered out and then machine-gunned in cold blood. Thirteen individuals were killed, the majority of them women and children. Those wounded in this "victorious" action by the army were attended to in Bayamo, and they are listed in the first unofficial communiqués on the battle.

Despite the foggy day, planes strafed positions occupied by our forces during the entire battle, causing no harm. At midday on February 17, our forces withdrew from Pino del Agua, ending the action with a new attack on Oro by elements of Column No. 6. The results of this encounter on the enemy's part are not known; our forces suffered no casualties.

The final tally is as follows: the enemy suffered between 18 and 25 dead, a similar number of wounded, and five prisoners. These are Second Lieutenant Evelio Laferté, soldiers Erasmo Yera, Francisco Travieso Camacho, Ceferino Adrián Trujillo, and Bernardo San Bartolomé Martínez Carral (the last of whom was wounded). Thirty-three rifles, five machine guns, and a large amount of ammunition was seized. Our troops suffered the casualties mentioned above, plus three slightly wounded men, one of them Captain Camilo Cienfuegos.

The ambitious plan conceived by our army's general staff was not fully realized, but a total victory over the army was achieved. We dealt a further blow to their already declining combat morale, and demonstrated to the entire nation the growing power of the revolution and our revolutionary army, which is preparing to come down to the plains to continue its victories.

Sierra Maestra, February 1958

Letter to Fidel Castro

Sierra Maestra
February 19, 1958

Compañero:

Owing to an urgent necessity, and under the pressing circumstances, the officers, and all responsible members in our ranks, wish to inform you of our troop's concerns with regard to your participation in combat.

We implore you to forsake your practice [of always participating], which unintentionally endangers the success of our armed struggle and, more than that, endangers your goal of a true revolution.

Please understand, *compañero*, that this is not motivated by any kind of sectarianism, and that we do not wish to impose any kind of force. We are only motivated, at all times, by a justified affection and esteem for you, and by a love of our homeland, our cause, and our ideas.

Although you bear no traces of egoism, you must understand the responsibility resting on your shoulders and the dreams and hopes placed in you by the generations of the past, the present, and the future. In light of all this, accept this somewhat authoritative plea, which is slightly bold, and perhaps too demanding. But we do so for Cuba. For the sake of Cuba, we ask one more sacrifice from you.

Your brothers in struggle and ideas,

Che	Juan Almeida
Celia Sánchez	Raúl Castro
Ciro Frías	J. Martínez Páez
Sergio Valle	José Ramón Machado
Luis Crespo	Félix Pena
Paco Cabrera	Guillermo García
Ignacio Pérez	Manuel Fajardo
Vitalio Acuña	Ramiro Valdés

Delio Gómez Ochoa

Camilo Cienfuegos

Efigenio Ameijeiras

Marín

José Quiala

Marcos Borrero

Calixto García Martínez

José Sotomayor

Fernando Virelles Iñiguez

Humberto Rodríguez Díaz

Hermes Cardero

F. Villegas

Eduardo Sardiñas

Raúl Castro Mercader

Luis Orlando Rodriguez

Universo Sánchez

Idelfredo Figueredo Río

Horacio Rodríguez

R. Jiménez Lage

Ernesto Casillas

Abelardo Colomé Ibarra

J. Diz

Olvein Botello

Armando Velis

INTERLUDE

In the months of April and June 1958 two poles could be seen in the insurrectional wave.

Beginning in February, after the battle at Pino del Agua, this wave gradually increased until it threatened to become an uncontainable avalanche. People were rising in insurrection against the dictatorship throughout the country, and particularly in Oriente province. After the failure of the [April 9] general strike called by the July 26 Movement, the wave subsided until it reached its lowest point in June, when the dictatorship's troops more and more tightened their encirclement of Column No. 1.

In the first days of April, Camilo had left the protection of the Sierra Maestra for the area of El Cauto, where he was appointed commander of "Antonio Maceo" Column No. 2, and carried out a series of impressive feats in the plains of Oriente. Camilo was the first army commander who went out on to the plains to fight with the morale and effectiveness of the army of the Sierra Maestra, putting the dictatorship in hard straits until several days after the April 9 failure, when he returned to the Sierra Maestra.

Taking advantage of the situation, during the height of the revolutionary wave, many camps were set up composed of some people who were yearning to fight, and others who were thinking only of keeping their uniforms clean so as to enter Havana in triumph. After April 9, when the dictatorship's counteroffensive began to step up, those groups disappeared or joined the *Sierra* forces.

Morale fell so much, that the [enemy] army considered it opportune to offer pardons, and it prepared some leaflets, which it dropped by air in the rebel zones. The leaflets read:

> Compatriots: If by having become involved in insurrectional plots, you are still in the countryside or in the mountains, you now have the opportunity to make amends and return to your family.
>
> The government has issued orders to offer respect for your life and your home if you lay down your weapons and abide by the law.
>
> Report to the governor of the province, the mayor of your municipality, the friendly congressman, the nearest military, navy, or police post, or to any ecclesiastical authority.
>
> If you are in a rural area, come with your weapon on one shoulder and with your hands up.
>
> If you come forward in an urban zone, leave your weapon hidden in a safe place so that it may be collected immediately after you report it.
>
> Do this without losing time, because the operation for total pacification will continue with greater intensity in the area where you find yourself.

Then they published photos of people who had turned themselves in, some real, others not. It was clear that the counterrevolutionary wave was growing. Eventually, it would crash against the peaks of the Sierra Maestra, but at the end of April and the beginning of May, it was in full ascent.

Our mission, in the first phase of the period we are discussing, was to hold the front occupied by Column No. 4, which extended to the outskirts of the town of Minas de Bueycito. Sánchez Mosquera was stationed there, and our struggle consisted of fleeting clashes without either side risking a decisive battle. At night, we fired our M-26s at them, but they already knew the scant killing power of that weapon and had simply erected a large mesh netting of wire, against which the TNT charges exploded in their shells of condensed milk cans, causing only a lot of noise.

Our camp was situated about two kilometers from Minas, in a place called La Otilia, in the house of a local landowner. From there we kept watch on Sánchez Mosquera's movements, curious skirmishes occurring every day. Henchmen would go out at dawn, burning peasant huts, looting all their belongings, and withdrawing before we intervened. At other times, they would attack some of our rifle units scattered through the area, making them flee. Any peasant suspected of having an understanding with us was assassinated.

I have never been able to find out why Sánchez Mosquera allowed us to be settled comfortably in a house, in a relatively flat area with no vegetation, without calling on the enemy air force to attack us. Our conjecture was that he was not interested in fighting, and did not want the air force to see how close the troops were, because he would then have to explain why he did not attack. Nevertheless, there were repeated skirmishes, as I have said, between our forces.

One of those days, I left with an assistant to see Fidel, who was then located in El Jíbaro. It was a long walk, practically a whole day. After spending a day with Fidel, we left the following day to return to our camp in La Otilia. For some reason I don't remember, my assistant had to stay behind and I had to accept a new guide. Part of the route ran along a road and later it entered rolling pastures. In this last part of the trip, nearing the house, a strange spectacle presented itself in one of the rolling fields. In the light of a full moon, clearly illuminating the surrounds and the scattered palm trees, a line of dead mules appeared, some with their harnesses on.

When we got down from our horses to examine the first mule, and saw the bullet holes, the guide's expression as he looked at me was straight out of a cowboy film: the hero of the film arrives with his partner and sees a horse killed by an arrow. He says something like, "The Sioux," and makes a special face for the occasion. That's what the man's face was like and perhaps my own as well, but I did not bother to look at myself. A few meters farther on was the second, then the third, then the fourth or fifth dead mule. It had been a supply convoy for us, captured by one of Sánchez Mosquera's expeditions. I think I remember that a civilian was also murdered. The guide refused to follow me. He claimed he did not know the terrain and simply got on his mount; we separated amicably.

I had a Beretta, and with it cocked, I took the horse by the reins and entered the first coffee field. On reaching an abandoned house, a tremendous noise startled me so much I almost fired, but it was only a pig, also frightened by my presence. Slowly, and very carefully, I covered the few hundred meters left to reach our position, which I found totally abandoned. After much searching, I found a *compañero* who had stayed sleeping in the house.

Universo, who had remained in command of the troops,

had ordered the house evacuated, foreseeing some nocturnal or dawn attack. As our troops were well spread out, defending the place, I lay down to sleep with my lone companion. That whole scene has no significance for me other than the satisfaction I experienced at having overcome fear during a journey that seemed eternal until at last, alone, I reached the command post. I felt brave that night.

But the toughest confrontation with Sánchez Mosquera took place in a very small village, or hamlet, called Santa Rosa. As always at dawn, we were told Sánchez Mosquera was there and we quickly headed to the place. I had a touch of asthma and was therefore riding a bay horse I had made good friends with. The fighting spread out in a fragmented manner; I had to abandon my mount. With the group of men that was with me, we took up position on a small hill, scattering ourselves at two or three different heights. The enemy was firing some mortars, without much success.

For a moment, the shooting became more intense to my right, and I set off to check the positions, but halfway there it also began on my left. I sent my assistant off somewhere, and remained alone, between the two lines of fire. To my left, Sánchez Mosquera's forces, after firing some mortar shells, climbed the hill amid tremendous shouting. Our people, with little experience, managed to fire only one or two isolated shots, and took off running down the hill. Alone, in an open field, I saw soldiers' helmets begin to appear. A henchman began to run down the hill in pursuit of our fighters, who were heading into the coffee fields. I fired my Beretta at him, missed, and immediately several rifles found me and opened fire. I began a zigzagging race, carrying a thousand bullets in an awesome leather cartridge belt on my shoulders, greeted by the derisive shouts of some enemy soldiers. As I got close to the shelter of the trees, my pistol fell. My only insolent gesture of that sad morning was to stop, retrace my steps, pick up the pistol, and take off running, greeted this time by the small dust clouds the rifle bullets kicked up like darts around me.

When I felt I was out of danger, without knowing the fate of my *compañeros* or the result of the offensive, I stopped to rest, barricaded behind a large rock in the middle of the woods. My asthma, mercifully, had let me run a few meters, but it was taking its revenge and my heart was jumping inside my chest. I heard branches breaking as someone approached, but it was no longer possible to keep fleeing (which was what I really felt like doing). This time, it was another *compañero*, lost: a recruit who had recently joined our troop. His consolation was more or less, "Don't worry, commander, I will die with you." I had no desire to die and felt tempted to say something about his mother; I don't think I did. That day I felt cowardly.

At night, we recounted all the events. A magnificent *compañero*—Mariño was his last name—had been killed in one of the skirmishes. Other than that, the result was very poor for the enemy. The body of a peasant shot through the mouth— murdered who knows why—was all that remained in the army's abandoned positions. There, with a small box camera, the Argentine journalist Jorge Ricardo Masetti—who was visiting us in the Sierra Maestra for the first time and with whom we later sustained a deep and lasting friendship—took a photograph of the murdered peasant.

After those battles, we withdrew a bit farther back from La Otilia, but I was already being replaced as commander of

Column No. 4 by Ramiro Valdés, who had been promoted. I left the area, accompanied by a small group of fighters, to take charge of the school for recruits, where the men crossing from Oriente to Las Villas would receive their training. Furthermore, we had to prepare for what was already imminent: the army's offensive. All the following days, of late April and early May, were devoted to preparing defensive positions and trying to cart the largest possible quantity of food and medicine into the hills to be able to resist what we saw coming: a large-scale offensive.

As a parallel task, we were trying to collect a tax on the sugar plantation owners and cattle ranchers. Remigio Fernández came up to see us; he was a cattle rancher who offered us the moon and the stars, but he forgot his promises when he reached the plains. The sugar plantation owners also gave us nothing. Later, when our strength was solid, we got even, but we spent the days of the offensive without the necessary elements for our defense.

A short time later, Camilo was recalled to better cover our small territory, which contained countless riches: a radio station, hospitals, munitions depots, and, on top of that, an airstrip located among the hills of La Plata, where a light plane could land.

Fidel maintained the principle that what mattered was not the enemy soldiers, but the number of people we ourselves needed to make a position invulnerable, and that this was what we should focus on. This was our tactic, and why all our forces gathered around the command post to form a compact front. There were not many more than 200 working rifles when the anticipated offensive began on May 25, in the middle of a meeting Fidel was having with some peasants, discussing the conditions under which the coffee harvest could be carried out, since the army did not allow day laborers to go up to pick the crop.

He had called together some 350 peasants, who were very interested in resolving their crop problems. Fidel had proposed creating a Sierra Maestra currency to pay the workers, to bring the straw and the bags for packing, to set up producer and consumer cooperatives, and a supervisory commission. He also offered the Rebel Army's help for the harvest. Everything was approved, but just as Fidel himself was about to end the meeting, the machine gunning began. The enemy army had clashed with Captain Ángel Verdecia's men, and its air force was punishing the area.

A DECISIVE MEETING

Throughout the entire day of May 3, 1958, a meeting took place in the Sierra Maestra, in Los Altos de Mompié. This gathering, almost unknown until now, was nonetheless of extraordinary importance in guiding our revolutionary strategy. From the early hours of the day until 2 a.m. the following morning, the meeting analyzed the consequences of the April 9 failure and why that defeat took place. It also took the necessary measures to reorganize the July 26 Movement and to overcome weaknesses resulting from the dictatorship's victory.

Although I was not a member of the national committee, I was invited to participate in the meeting at the request of *compañeros* Faustino Pérez and René Ramos Latour (Daniel), whom I had strongly criticized earlier. In addition to those named, also present were Fidel, Vilma Espín (Débora in the underground), Ñico Torres, Luis Buch, Celia Sánchez, Marcelo Fernández (Zoilo at that time), Haydée Santamaría, David Salvador, and Enzo Infante (Bruno), who joined us at midday. The gathering was tense, since it had to assess the actions of the *Llano compañeros*, who in practice had run the affairs of the July 26 Movement until that moment.

At the meeting, decisions were taken that confirmed Fidel's moral authority, his indisputable stature, and the conviction among the majority of revolutionaries present that errors of judgment had been committed. The *Llano* leadership had underestimated the enemy's strength and subjectively over-estimated their own, without considering the methods neces-sary to unleash their forces. But most importantly, the meeting discussed and judged the two conceptions that had been at odds throughout the whole previous stage of the leadership of the war. The guerrilla conception would emerge triumphant from that meeting. Fidel's standing and authority were consoli-dated, and he was named commander-in-chief of all forces, including the militias — which until then had been under *Llano* leadership. Fidel was also named general secretary of the July 26 Movement.

There were many heated debates when the meeting analyzed each person's participation in the events under discussion. But perhaps the most agitated was the discussion with the workers' representatives, who were opposed to any participation by the Popular Socialist Party in the organization of the struggle. The analysis of the strike demonstrated that subjectivism and putschist conceptions permeated its preparation and execution. The formidable apparatus that the July 26 Movement seemed to have in its hands, in the form of organized workers' cells, fell apart the moment the action took place. The adventurist policy of the workers' leaders had failed in the face of an inexorable reality. But they were not the only ones responsible for the defeat. Our opinion was that the largest share of the blame fell on the workers' delegate David Salvador; on Faustino Pérez, who was responsible for Havana; and on the leader of the *Llano* militias, René Ramos Latour.

The fault of the first was having held and put into practice his conception of a sectarian strike, in which the other revolutionary movements would be forced to follow our lead. Faustino's failure was his lack of perspective in thinking that it would be possible to seize the capital with his militias, without closely examining the forces of reaction inside their principal bastion. Daniel was criticized for the same lack of vision but in reference to the *Llano* militias, which were organized as parallel troops to ours but without the same training or the combat morale, and without having gone through the rigorous process of selection through war.

The division between the *Sierra* and the *Llano* was real. There were certain objective bases for this, given the greater maturity achieved in the course of the guerrilla struggle by the *Sierra* representatives and the lesser maturity of the *Llano* combatants. But there was also an extraordinarily important element, something that might be called an occupational hazard. The *Llano compañeros* had to work in their environment and little by little they became accustomed to viewing the work methods required in those conditions as ideal, and as the only methods possible for the movement. Furthermore, logically enough from a human standpoint, they began to consider the *Llano* as having a greater relative importance than the *Sierra*.

After the failures in confronting the dictatorship's forces, there now arose only one capable leadership, that of the *Sierra*, and, concretely, one sole leader, one commander-in-chief: Fidel Castro. At the end of an exhaustive and often violent discussion, the meeting resolved to relieve Faustino Pérez of his duties, replacing him with [Delio Gómez] Ochoa, and to relieve David Salvador of his duties, replacing him with Ñico Torres. This last change did not amount to a substantive step forward as far as the conception of the struggle was concerned. For when the meeting raised the need for unity of all working-class forces to prepare the next revolutionary general strike, which would be called from the Sierra Maestra, Ñico expressed his readiness to work in a disciplined manner with the "Stalinists," but said that he did not think this would lead to anything. He referred to the *compañeros* of the Popular Socialist Party in those terms. The third change, regarding Daniel, did not lead to a replacement, since Fidel directly became commander-in-chief of the *Llano* militias.

The meeting also decided to send Haydée Santamaría to Miami as a special representative of the July 26 Movement, putting her in charge of finances in the exile community. In the political sphere, the national committee was to be transferred to the Sierra Maestra, where Fidel would occupy the position of general secretary. A secretariat of five members was constituted, with one person each in charge of finances, political affairs, and workers' affairs. I don't remember now who the *compañeros* assigned to these positions were. But everything related to arms shipments, or decisions about arms, and foreign relations, would from then on be the responsibility of the general secretary. The three *compañeros* relieved of their duties were to go to the Sierra Maestra, where David Salvador would hold a post as workers' delegate and Faustino and Daniel would be commanders. The latter was given command of a column that participated actively in the fight against the army's final offensive, which was about to be unleashed. He died at the head of his troops while attacking a retreating enemy column. His revolutionary career earned him a place in the select list of our martyrs.

Faustino asked for and obtained authorization to return to

Havana and take care of some of the movement's affairs, to hand over the leadership, and later reintegrate himself into the struggle in the Sierra Maestra. This he did, finishing the war in the "José Martí" Column No. 1 commanded by Fidel Castro. Although history must relate the events just as they occurred, it is necessary to make clear the high opinion we have always had of this *compañero*, who at one moment was our adversary within the movement. Faustino was always considered an irreproachably honest *compañero*, and he was extremely daring. I was a witness to his fearlessness the time he burned a plane that had brought us weapons from Miami, but that had been discovered by enemy aircraft and damaged. Under machine-gun fire, Faustino carried out the operation necessary to prevent it from falling into army hands, setting it on fire with gasoline pouring out of the bullet holes. His whole history shows his revolutionary quality.

At that meeting, other decisions of lesser importance were made, and a whole series of obscure aspects of our reciprocal relations were clarified. We heard a report by Marcelo Fernández on the organization of the movement in the cities, and he was assigned to prepare another report for the movement's cells, detailing the results and decisions of the national committee's meeting. We also heard a report on the organization of the civil resistance, its formation, its work methods, its composition, and how to broaden and strengthen them.

Compañero Buch reported on the committee-in-exile: on Mario Llerena's half-hearted position and his incompatibility with Urrutia. It was decided to ratify Urrutia as our movement's candidate for president and transfer to him a stipend that, until then, Llerena had been receiving as the movement's only professional cadre in the exile community. In addition, the meeting decided that if Llerena continued interfering he would be relieved of his position as president of the committee-in-exile. There were many problems abroad; in New York, for example, the groups of [Arnaldo] Barrón, [Ángel] Pérez Vidal, and Pablo Díaz worked separately, and at times clashed or interfered with each other. It was resolved that Fidel would send a letter to the emigrant and exile groups recognizing the committee-in-exile of the July 26 Movement as the sole official body.

The meeting analyzed all the possibilities for the support of the Venezuelan government headed at that time by Wolfgang Larrazábal. He had promised to support the movement, which in fact he did. The only complaint we might have with Larrazábal is that along with a planeload of weapons, he sent us the "worthy" Manuel Urrutia. But actually, we ourselves were the ones who had made such a deplorable choice.

Other agreements were reached during the meeting. In addition to Haydée Santamaría, who would go to Miami, Luis Buch was to travel to Caracas, Venezuela, with precise instructions regarding Urrutia. Carlos Franqui was ordered to the Sierra Maestra to take charge of the leadership of Radio Rebelde. Contacts would be made by radio, via Venezuela, using codes composed by Luis Buch that worked until the end of the war.

As can be appreciated from the decisions made, this meeting was of capital importance. Various concrete problems of the movement were finally clarified. In the first place, Fidel would lead the war, militarily and politically, in his dual role as commander-in-chief of all forces and as general secretary of the organization. The *Sierra* line would be followed, that of direct armed struggle, extending it to other regions and in that way taking control of the country. We did away with various naive illusions of attempted revolutionary general strikes when the situation had not matured sufficiently to bring about that type of explosion, and without having laid the adequate groundwork for an event of that magnitude.

In addition, the leadership would lie in the Sierra Maestra, which objectively eliminated some practical decision-making problems that had prevented Fidel from exercising the authority he had earned. In fact, this did nothing more than register a reality: the political predominance of the *Sierra* fighters, a consequence of their correct position and interpretation of events. The meeting corroborated the correctness of our earlier doubts, when we considered the possibility of a failure of the movement's forces in attempting a revolutionary general strike, if carried out in the manner outlined at a meeting prior to April 9.

Certain very important tasks still remained: above all, resisting the approaching offensive, since the army's forces were taking up positions in a ring around the revolution's principal bastion—the command post of Column No. 1 led by Fidel. Afterward, the tasks would be the invasion of the plains, the seizure of the central provinces, and finally, the destruction of the regime's entire political-military apparatus. It would take us seven months to complete those tasks in full.

Most urgent was to strengthen the Sierra Maestra front, and to ensure that a small bastion could continue speaking to the people of Cuba and sowing the seed of revolution among them. It was also important to maintain communications abroad. A few days earlier, I had witnessed a radio conversation between Fidel and Justo Carrillo, who represented the Montecristi Group, that is, a group of aspiring thugs including representatives of imperialism such as Carrillo himself and [Ramón] Barquín. Justo offered the moon and the stars, but asked that Fidel make a declaration supporting the "pure" military men. Fidel answered that while this was not impossible, it would be difficult for our movement to understand a call of this nature. Our people were falling victim to soldiers, and since they were all lumped together, it was difficult to distinguish the good from the bad. In short, the declaration was not made. Llerena was also spoken with, I seem to recall, as well as Urrutia. An attempt was made to issue a call for unity to try to prevent the breakup of the flimsy grouping of disparate personalities [the Caracas Pact]. From Caracas, they were trying to capitalize on the armed movement for their own gain, but they represented our aspirations for international recognition, and we therefore had to be careful.

Immediately after the meeting, the participants scattered. It was my task to inspect a whole range of zones, trying to create defensive lines with our small forces to resist the army's push. The really strong resistance would begin in the most mountainous areas, from the Caracas peak, where the small and poorly armed groups of Crescencio Pérez would be located, to the zones of La Botella or La Mesa, where Ramiro Valdés's forces were distributed.

This small territory had to be defended, with not much more than 200 functioning rifles, when a few days later Batista's army began its "encirclement and annihilation" offensive.

THE FINAL OFFENSIVE AND THE BATTLE OF SANTA CLARA

[The general strike of] April 9 [1958] was a resounding defeat that never endangered the regime's stability. Furthermore, after that tragic date, the government was able to transfer troops and gradually place them in Oriente province, spreading its destruction to the Sierra Maestra. More and more our defense had to be from within the Sierra Maestra, and the government kept increasing the number of regiments it placed in front of our positions, until there were 10,000 men. With these forces it began the May 25 offensive in the town of Las Mercedes, which was our forward position.

There, Batista's army gave proof of its ineffectiveness in combat, and we showed our lack of resources: 200 working rifles to fight against 10,000 weapons of all sorts — an enormous disadvantage. Our troops fought bravely for two days, with odds of one against 10 or 15; fighting moreover, against mortars, tanks, and the air force, until the small group was forced to abandon the town. It was commanded by Captain Ángel Verdecia, who one month later would courageously die in battle.

By that time, Fidel Castro had received a letter from the traitor Eulogio Cantillo, who, true to his charlatan's politicking attitude, wrote as the enemy's chief of operations to the rebel leader, saying that the offensive would be launched in any case, but that "The Man" (Fidel) should take care to await the final result. The offensive, in fact, ran its course, and in two and a half months of hard fighting, the enemy lost over 1,000 men, counting dead, wounded, prisoners, and deserters. They also left 600 weapons in our hands, including a tank, 12 mortars, 12 tripod machine guns, over 200 submachine guns, and countless automatic weapons; also, an enormous amount of ammunition and equipment of all sorts, and 450 prisoners, who were handed over to the Red Cross when the campaign ended.

Batista's army came out of that last offensive in the Sierra Maestra with its spine broken, but it had not yet been defeated. The struggle continued. It was then that the final strategy was established, attacking at three points: Santiago de Cuba, which had been under a flexible siege; Las Villas, where I was to go; and Pinar del Río, at the other end of the island, where Camilo Cienfuegos was to march as commander of Column No. 2, named "Antonio Maceo" in memory of the historic invasion by the great leader of 1895, who crossed the length of Cuban territory with epic actions, culminating at Mantua. Camilo Cienfuegos was not able to fulfill the second part of his program, as the exigencies of the war forced him to remain in Las Villas.

Once the regiments assaulting the Sierra Maestra had been wiped out, the front had returned to its normal intensity, and our troops had increased their strength and morale, it was decided to begin marching on the central province of Las Villas. My orders specified our main strategic task: to systematically cut off communications between both extremes of the island. I was also ordered to establish relations with all political groups that might be operating in the mountains of the region, and I was given broad powers to militarily govern my assigned area.

We were to set off by truck on August 30, 1958, with these instructions and believing the trip would take four days. Then an unexpected accident disrupted our plans. A pickup truck was arriving that night, carrying uniforms and gasoline for the otherwise prepared vehicles. A cargo of arms also arrived, by air, at an airstrip close to the road. But the plane was sighted just as it landed, even though it was dark, and the airstrip was bombed systematically from 8 p.m. until 5 a.m. At that point, we ourselves burned the plane to prevent it falling into enemy hands or having the bombardment continue by day, with even worse results. Enemy troops advanced on the airstrip, intercepting the pickup truck carrying the gasoline and leaving us on foot.

So it was that we began the march on August 31, without trucks or horses, hoping to find them after crossing the highway from Manzanillo to Bayamo. In fact, having crossed it we found the trucks, but also — on the first day of September — we encountered a fierce hurricane that made all roads impassable except for the central highway, the only paved road in this region of Cuba, forcing us to give up on vehicle transport. From that moment on we had to use horses, or walk. We were loaded down with a lot of ammunition, a bazooka with 40 shells, and everything necessary for a long march and for rapidly setting up camp.

Days passed, and it was already becoming difficult, even though we were in the friendly territory of Oriente: crossing overflowing rivers and streams that had become rivers, struggling with difficulty to prevent our ammunition, arms, and shells from getting wet; looking for horses and leaving tired horses behind; avoiding inhabited zones as we moved away from the eastern province.

We walked through difficult, flooded terrain, suffering the attacks of mosquito swarms that made periods of rest unbearable, eating little and poorly, drinking water from swampy rivers or simply from swamps. Each day of travel became longer and truly horrible. A week after leaving camp, by the time we crossed the Jobabo river, which marks the border between Oriente and Camagüey provinces, our forces were greatly weakened. This river, like all the previous ones and those we would cross later, was flooded. We were also feeling the effects of the lack of footwear among our troops, many of whom were walking barefoot through the mud of southern Camagüey.

On the night of September 9, as we were approaching a place known as La Federal, our forward guard fell into an enemy ambush, and two valuable *compañeros* were killed. But the most lamentable consequence was being noticed by the enemy forces, who from then on gave us no respite. After a brief clash, the small garrison there surrendered and we took four prisoners. Now we had to march very carefully, since the air force knew our approximate course. One or two days later, we reached a place known as Laguna Grande, together with Camilo's force — much better equipped than ours. The area stands out for its extraordinary number of mosquitoes, which made it absolutely impossible for us to rest without a mosquito net, and not all of us had one.

These were days of tiring marches through desolate expanses

of only water and mud. We were hungry, thirsty, and could hardly advance because our legs felt like lead and the weapons were tremendously heavy. We continued advancing with the better horses Camilo had left us when his column took their trucks, but we had to give them up near the Macareño sugar mill. The guides they were supposed to send us did not arrive and we set off on the adventure as we were.

Our forward guard clashed with an enemy outpost in a place called Cuatro Compañeros and the exhausting battle began. It was daybreak, and with great effort we managed to gather a large part of our troop in the largest woods in the area. But the army was advancing along its edges and we had to fight hard to make it possible for some of our men, who had fallen behind, to cross some railroad tracks into the woods. The air force then sighted us and the B-26s, the C-47s, the big C-3 reconnaissance planes, and the light planes began bombing an area no more than 200 meters wide. Finally, we withdrew, leaving one man killed by a bomb and carrying several wounded, including Captain Silva, who went through the rest of the invasion with a broken shoulder.

The picture the following day was less desolate, since many of those who had fallen behind showed up, and we managed to gather the whole troop, minus the 10 men who were to join Camilo's column and with him get to the northern front of Las Villas province, in Yaguajay.

Despite the difficulties, we were never without the encouragement of the peasants. We always found someone who would serve as a guide, or who would give us the food without which we could not go on. Naturally, it was not the unanimous support of the whole people we had enjoyed in Oriente, but there was always someone who helped us. At times we were reported to the enemy as soon as we crossed a farm, but that was not because peasants were acting directly against us. Rather, their living conditions made these people slaves of the landowners and, fearful of losing their daily subsistence, they would report to their master that we had passed through the region. The latter would take charge of graciously informing the military authorities.

One afternoon we were listening on our field radio to a report by General Francisco Tabernilla Dolz, who with the typical arrogance of a thug was announcing that Che Guevara's hordes had been destroyed. He was giving extensive details about the dead, the wounded, names, and all sorts of things — based on items taken from our backpacks after that disastrous encounter with the enemy a few days earlier. All this was mixed in with false information cooked up by the army's high command. News of our passing produced great merriment among our troop, but pessimism was getting hold of them little by little. Hunger and thirst, exhaustion, feeling impotent against the enemy forces closing in on us, and more than anything, the terrible foot disease the peasants call *mazamorra* — which turned each step our soldiers took into an intolerable torment — had made us an army of shadows. It was difficult, very difficult, to advance. Our troop's physical condition worsened day by day, and the meals — today yes, tomorrow no, the next day maybe — in no way helped alleviate the misery we were suffering.

We spent the hardest days besieged in the vicinity of the Baraguá sugar mill in pestilent swamps, without a drop of drinking water; attacked constantly by the air force; not a single horse to carry the weakest across barren marshes; our shoes totally destroyed by the muddy seawater; and plants injuring our bare feet. Our situation was really disastrous when, with difficulty, we broke out of the encirclement at Baraguá and reached the famous Júcaro–Morón trail, an historically evocative place, the scene of bloody fighting between patriots and Spaniards during the war of independence.

We did not have time to recover even a little when a new downpour, bad weather, enemy attacks, or reports of their presence forced us to march on. The troop was increasingly tired and disheartened. When the situation was most tense, however, when insults, pleas, and sharp remarks were the only way to get the weary men to advance, a sight far away in the distance lit up their faces and instilled a new spirit in the guerrillas. That sight was a blue streak to the west, the blue streak of the Las Villas mountain range, seen for the first time by our men. From that moment on, the same or similar hardships became more bearable and everything seemed easier. We slipped through the last encirclement by swimming across the Júcaro river, which divides the provinces of Camagüey and Las Villas, and it already seemed that a new light was illuminating us.

Two days later we were in the heart of the Trinidad–Sancti Spíritus mountain range, safe, ready to begin the next stage of the war. We rested for another two days; we had to be on our way immediately and prepare ourselves to prevent the elections scheduled for November 3. We had reached the mountains of Las Villas on October 16. Time was short and the task was enormous. Camilo was doing his part in the north, sowing fear among the dictatorship's men.

Our task, upon arriving for the first time in the Escambray mountains, was clearly defined: we had to harass the dictatorship's military apparatus, above all its communications; and, as an immediate goal, we had to prevent the elections from taking place. But this work was made difficult because time was scarce, and because of the disunity among the revolutionary forces, which translated into internal quarrels that cost us dearly, including human lives.

We were supposed to attack the neighboring towns to prevent the elections, and plans were elaborated to do this simultaneously in the cities of Cabaiguán, Fomento, and Sancti Spíritus, in the rich plains of the center of the island. Meanwhile, the small garrison at Güinía de Miranda — in the mountains — surrendered; later the Banao garrison was attacked, with few results. The days prior to November 3, the date of the elections, were extraordinarily busy. Our columns were mobilized everywhere, almost totally preventing voters in those areas from going to the polls. Camilo Cienfuegos's troops in the northern part of the province paralyzed the electoral farce. Basically, from the transport of Batista's soldiers to commercial traffic, everything stood still.

There was practically no voting in Oriente; the percentage was a little higher in Camagüey; and in the western region, in spite of everything, mass abstention was evident. This abstention was achieved spontaneously in Las Villas, as there had not been time to synchronize the passive resistance of the masses with the activity of the guerrillas.

In Oriente, successive battles were taking place on the first and second fronts, as well as on the third, with the "Antonio Guiteras" Column No. 9 relentlessly exerting pressure on Santiago de Cuba, the provincial capital. Except for municipal seats, the government had nothing left in Oriente.

The situation was also becoming very serious in Las Villas, with intensified attacks on communications. On arrival, we completely changed the system of struggle in the cities; we rapidly sent the best militia members from the cities to the training camp to receive instruction in sabotage, which proved effective in urban areas.

During the months of November and December 1958, we gradually closed the highways. Captain Silva totally blocked the highway from Trinidad to Sancti Spíritus, and the island's central highway was seriously damaged when the bridge across the Tuinicú river was dynamited, although it did not collapse completely. The central railroad was blocked at several points; moreover, the southern route had been cut by the second front and the northern route had been closed by Camilo Cienfuegos's troops. The island was divided into two parts. The region most in upheaval, Oriente, received aid from the government only by air and sea, and this became increasingly insecure. The symptoms of the enemy's disintegration were increasing.

An extremely intense campaign for revolutionary unity had to be carried out in the Escambray mountains, because already operating there was a group led by Commander [Eloy] Gutiérrez Menoyo (Second National Front of the Escambray), another of the Revolutionary Directorate (led by commanders Faure Chomón and Rolando Cubela), another smaller one of the Authentic Organization, another of the Popular Socialist Party (commanded by [Félix] Torres), and us. In other words, there were five different organizations operating under different commands and in the same province. After laborious talks I had to have with their respective leaders, we reached a series of agreements and it was possible to go on to form a more or less common front.

From December 16 onward, the systematic cutting off of bridges and all kinds of communications had made it very difficult for the dictatorship to defend its forward positions and even those on the central highway. Early that day, the bridge across the Falcón river, on the central highway, was destroyed, and communications between Havana and the cities to the east of Santa Clara, the capital of Las Villas province, were virtually cut off. Also, a number of towns — the southernmost being Fomento — were besieged and attacked by our forces. The commander of the city defended his position more or less effectively for several days. Despite the air force's punishment of our Rebel Army, the dictatorship's demoralized troops would not advance overland to support their comrades. Realizing that all resistance was useless, they surrendered, and more than 100 rifles joined the forces of freedom.

Without giving the enemy any respite, we decided to paralyze the central highway immediately, and on December 21 we simultaneously attacked Cabaiguán and Guayos, both on the central highway. The latter surrendered in a few hours, and during the following days, so did Cabaiguán with its 90 soldiers. (The surrender of the garrisons was negotiated on the political basis of letting the soldiers go free, on the condition that they leave the liberated territory. In this manner, they were given the opportunity to surrender their weapons and save themselves.) Cabaiguán once again proved the dictatorship's ineffectiveness, as it never sent infantry units to reinforce those under siege.

In the northern region of Las Villas, Camilo Cienfuegos was attacking several towns, which he was subduing at the same time as he was laying siege to Yaguajay, the last bastion of the dictatorship's troops. Yaguajay was under the command of a captain of Chinese ancestry who resisted for 11 days, immobilizing the revolutionary troops in the region. At the same time our troops were already advancing along the central highway toward Santa Clara, the provincial capital.

After Cabaiguán had fallen, we set out — in active collaboration with the forces of the Revolutionary Directorate — to attack Placetas, which surrendered after only one day of struggle. After taking Placetas, we liberated in rapid succession Remedios and Caibarién on the northern coast, the latter an important port. The picture was becoming gloomy for the dictatorship, because in addition to continuous victories scored in Oriente, the Second National Front of the Escambray was defeating small garrisons, and Camilo Cienfuegos controlled the north.

When the enemy withdrew from Camajuaní without offering resistance, we were ready to launch the definitive attack on the capital of Las Villas province. (Santa Clara is the hub of the island's central plain, with 150,000 inhabitants, it is the center of the railroad system and all communications in the country.) It is surrounded by small, bare hills, which were previously occupied by the troops of the dictatorship.

At the time of the attack, our forces had considerably increased our weaponry, as we had taken several positions and some heavy weapons, which were lacking ammunition. We had a bazooka without shells, and we had to fight against some 10 tanks. We also knew that for us to fight most effectively, we had to reach the city's populous neighborhoods, where a tank is much less efficient.

While the troops of the Revolutionary Directorate were taking the Rural Guard's No. 31 garrison, we set about besieging almost all of Santa Clara's fortified positions. Fundamentally, however, our fight was focused against the guards of the armored train stationed at the entrance of the Camajuaní road. The army, which was well equipped, tenaciously defended these positions.

On December 29, we began the struggle. At first, the university served as our operations base. Later, we established our headquarters closer to the city's downtown area. Our men were fighting against troops supported by armored units and were forcing them to flee, although many paid for their boldness with their lives. The dead and wounded began to fill the improvised cemeteries and hospitals.

I remember an episode that highlights the spirit of our forces in those final days. I had admonished a *compañero* because he was sleeping in the midst of battle, and he replied that he had been disarmed for accidentally firing his weapon. I responded with habitual dryness, "Get yourself another rifle by going disarmed to the front line ... if you're up to it." In Santa Clara, while speaking to the wounded in the Sangre Hospital, a dying man touched my hand and said, "Remember, commander? In Remedios you sent me to find a weapon ... and I earned it here." He was the combatant who had accidentally fired his weapon. He died a few minutes later, I think content for having proven his courage. Such was our Rebel Army.

The hills of Cápiro continued to resist, and we continued fighting there the whole day of December 30, at the same time gradually taking different points in the city. By then, communications between the center of Santa Clara and the armored train had been cut off. Those in the train, seeing they were surrounded on the hills of Cápiro, tried to escape by rail with all their magnificent cargo. Arriving at the spur we had already destroyed previously, the locomotive and some carriages were derailed. A very interesting battle began, in which our Molotov cocktails forced the men out of the armored train. They were very well protected but only willing to fight at a distance, from comfortable positions, against a virtually unarmed enemy, in the style of the colonizers against the Indians of the North American west. Assaulted by men who, from nearby positions and adjoining carriages, threw bottles of burning gasoline, the train became—thanks to its armored plating—a veritable oven for the soldiers. In a few hours, the whole lot surrendered with their 22 carriages, their antiaircraft guns, their machine guns of the same type, and their fabulous quantity of ammunition (fabulous, of course, compared with our meager supply).

We had been able to take the power station and the city's whole northwest side. We went on the air to announce that Santa Clara was almost in the hands of the revolution. In the announcement, which I made as commander-in-chief of the armed forces in Las Villas, I remember I had the sorrow of informing the Cuban people of the death of Captain Roberto Rodríguez, "Vaquerito," small in stature and years and leader of the "suicide squad," who had played with death a thousand and one times fighting for freedom. The "suicide squad" was an example of revolutionary morale, and only selected volunteers joined it. But whenever a man died—and that happened in every battle—and when the new aspirant was named, those not chosen would be grief-stricken and even cry. Strange to see those seasoned, noble figures showing their youth in their tears of despair, because they did not have the honor of being in the front line of combat and death.

The police station fell next, surrendering the tanks that

defended it. And in rapid succession No. 31 garrison surrendered to Commander Cubela, while the jail, the courthouse, the provincial government palace, and the Grand Hotel—where snipers on the 10th floor had kept up fire almost until the end of combat—surrendered to our forces.

At that moment, only the Leoncio Vidal garrison, the largest fortress in central Cuba, had not surrendered. But by January 1, 1959, there were already growing signs of weakness among the forces defending it. That morning, we sent captains [Antonio] Núñez Jiménez and [Alfonso] Rodríguez de la Vega to negotiate the surrender of the garrison.

Reports were contradictory and extraordinary: Batista had fled that day, leaving the high command of the armed forces in complete disarray. Our two delegates established radio contact with [General Eulogio] Cantillo, telling him of the offer of surrender. But he indicated he could not accept because it constituted an ultimatum, and because he had taken over command of the army in accordance with precise instructions from the leader Fidel Castro. We contacted Fidel immediately, telling him the news, but giving our opinion of Cantillo's treacherous attitude—an opinion with which he absolutely agreed. (In those decisive hours, Cantillo let all the main figures in Batista's government escape. His attitude was even more saddening considering he was an officer who had contacted us; we had trusted him as a military man of honor.)

The results that followed are known to everyone: Castro's refusal to recognize Cantillo's authority; Fidel's order to march on the city of Havana; Colonel Barquín seizing command of the army after leaving the Isle of Pines prison; the seizure of Camp Columbia by Camilo Cienfuegos and of La Cabaña fortress by our Column No. 8; and the final installation, within a few days, of Fidel Castro as prime minister of the provisional government. All this belongs to the country's present political history.

We are now in a position in which we are much more than the simple instruments of one nation. We are now the hope of the unredeemed Americas. All eyes—those of the great oppressors and those of the hopeful—are firmly on us. In great measure, the development of the popular movements in Latin America depends on the future stance that we take, on our capacity to resolve so many problems. And every step we take is being observed by the ever-watchful eyes of the big creditor and by the optimistic eyes of our brothers and sisters in Latin America.

With our feet planted firmly on the ground, we are beginning to labor and produce our first revolutionary works; we confront the first difficulties. But what is Cuba's main problem if not the same as all of Latin America, the same even as enormous Brazil with its millions of square kilometers and with its land of marvels that is a whole continent? The one-crop economy. In Cuba, we are slaves to sugarcane—the umbilical cord that binds us to the large northern market. We must diversify our agricultural production, stimulate industry, and ensure that our minerals and agricultural products, and—in the near future— our industrial production, go to the markets that are best suited for us and by our own methods of transportation.

The government's first big battle will be the agrarian reform, which will be audacious, thorough, but flexible: it will destroy the large estates in Cuba, although not Cuba's means of production. It will be a battle that will absorb a great part of the strength of the people and the government during the coming years. The land will be given free to the peasant. Landowners who prove that they came by their holdings honestly will be compensated with long-term bonds. But the peasantry will also be given technical assistance; there will be guaranteed markets for the products of the soil. And production will be channeled with a broad national sense of development in conjunction with the great battle for agrarian reform, so that within a short time the infant Cuban industries can compete with the monstrous ones of the countries where capitalism has reached its highest level of development. Simultaneously with the creation of the new domestic market that the agrarian reform will bring about, and the distribution of new products to satisfy a growing market, there will arise the need to export some products and to have the adequate instrument to take them to this or that part of the world. That instrument will be a merchant fleet, which the already approved Maritime Development Law envisages.

With these elementary weapons, we Cubans will begin the struggle for our territory's total freedom. We all know it will not be easy, but we are all aware of the enormous historic responsibility of the July 26 Movement, of the Cuban Revolution, of the nation in general, to be an example for all the peoples of Latin America, whom we must not disappoint.

Our friends of the indomitable continent can be sure that, if need be, we will struggle no matter what the economic consequence of our actions may be. And if the fight is taken further still, we shall struggle to the last drop of our rebel blood to make this land a sovereign republic, with the true attributes of a nation that is happy, democratic, and fraternal with its brothers and sisters of Latin America.

Appendices

TO FIDEL CASTRO
(ABOUT THE INVASION)

September 3, 1958

Fidel, I write to you from the open plains, no aircraft about, relatively few mosquitoes, and without having eaten, solely due to the rapid pace of our march. I will give you a brief account.

We left during the night on August 31 with four horses, since it was impossible to leave in trucks because Magadan took all the gasoline and an ambush was feared in Jibacoa. We passed without incident through the area — soldiers had abandoned it — but were unable to continue for more than a couple of leagues, sleeping in a little grove of trees on the other side of the highway. I recommend establishing a platoon permanently in Jibacoa, to enable shipments of supplies from the area, which until now has been closely watched.

On September 1 we passed the highway and took three cars that broke down with alarming frequency. We reached a spot called Cayo Redondo, where we spent a day as the hurricane approached. The soldiers came near, numbering 40, but they withdrew without a battle. We continued on with the trucks, aided by four tractors, but this became impossible and we had to abandon them the following day, September 2, and continue on foot with a few horses, reaching the banks of the Cauto river, which we couldn't cross by night because of rising water. We spent eight hours the next day in the crossing, and that night reached the house of the "Colonel" [Arcadio Peláez], following the route we had planned. We are without horses but can get more along the way, and I intend to arrive at the assigned zone of operations with everyone in the saddle. It is not possible to calculate exactly how long we will be delayed owing to the numerous inconveniences along these devilish tracks.

I will try to keep you informed along the way, by creating an efficient mail system, and will send you reports on the people we meet. In this region I recommend only two people up to now: Pepín Magadan, who has his weaknesses but is surprisingly effective and who could be put in charge of obtaining supplies and money; and Concepción Rivero, who is a very serious man, from what has been seen.

Nothing more for now. An embrace to the distant world that from here is barely visible in the distance.

September 8, 1958
1:50 a.m.

After exhausting marches by night, I finally write to you from Camagüey. It is not immediately possible to accelerate the march, which averages three to four leagues a day. Half the troops are on horseback though without saddles. Camilo is in the area and we are waiting for him here, at the Bartles rice plantation; he has not yet arrived. The plains are formidable, not so many mosquitoes, we have not seen even a single soldier, and the airplanes seem like inoffensive doves. Radio Rebelde can be heard with great difficulty via Venezuela.

Everything indicates that the enemy does not wish to fight

and neither do we. I confess that I'm afraid of the thought of retreating with 150 inexperienced recruits through unknown parts, although an armed guerrilla unit of 30 men could work wonders in this zone, and revolutionize it. Passing through, I laid the groundwork for a rice workers' union in Leonero, and spoke about the tax, but that idea got nowhere. It's not that I capitulated to the owners, but the quota seems excessive to me. I told them it could be discussed and left it for the next person who comes. Someone with a social consciousness could work miracles in this area, and there are plenty of trees to hide behind.

I can't tell you about my future plans, in terms of our route, because I don't know myself. It depends more on particular circumstances and luck. We're currently waiting for some trucks to see if we can free ourselves of the horses, perfect for [Antonio] Maceo's pre-aviatory days, but which are highly visible from the air. If it weren't for the horses, we could travel by day in peace.

There is mud and water everywhere, and the Fidelisms I've had to make so we can arrive with the shells in good condition, are straight out of the movies. We have had to swim across various creeks — barbarous work — but the troops are conducting themselves well, even though the punishment squadron is growing fast and promises to be the largest one in the column. The next report will come to you over the airwaves, if that's possible, from the city of Camagüey.

Nothing more, except to repeat the fraternal embrace to those of the Sierra Maestra, which can no longer be seen.

September 13, 1958
9:50 p.m.

After several haphazard marches, I'm still writing you from the middle of Camagüey, where today we are about to cross through the most dangerous part, or one of the two most dangerous parts, of the journey. Camilo crossed last night with a number of technical difficulties but no military problems.

Since the last report I sent you, we have been through some unpleasant things. Owing to a lack of guides, we fell into an ambush at Remigio Fernández's farm in La Federal, in which Marcos Borrero, a captain, was killed. We overcame the eight soldiers, killing three and taking four prisoner. We planned to keep them with us until finding an opportunity to release them; one escaped and blew the whistle. About 60 soldiers arrived, and on Camilo's advice, who was close by, we retreated almost without combat, but we lost another man, Dalcio Gutiérrez, of the Sierra Maestra. [Mark] Herman was slightly wounded in the leg, and Enriquito Acevedo somewhat seriously in both arms. The same Acevedo distinguished himself, as did Captain Ángel Frías and Vaquerito, Lieutenant Roberto Rodríguez.

Later, they tried to advance again and we surprised a truck, with only four of our men in the ambush, causing them at least two casualties. We withdrew to La Federal then left rapidly, taking Enrique for treatment. The next day, the B-26s came to strafe. Camilo was able to follow more quickly, and we are waiting for the trucks I ordered to be fetched.

Strange things are happening around here, suggesting the immediate arrival of an experienced, "tough" leader to these parts would be worthwhile. On no account should it be more than 30 armed men, but they could gather everything necessary here, in every sense. It would be worthwhile operating in the region of Naboas, where the climate is very good owing to the spoils from the Francisco sugar mill. There is constant vegetation from Santa Beatriz as far as Santa Cruz, enough for this number of men. They should follow what the leadership in Camagüey is doing, promising to incorporate everybody; we have been inundated by unarmed men asking to enlist. I investigated the matter of the crazy guy: effectively, the man has a terrible case of war psychosis.

There are many other questions I would like to raise with you, but time is not on my side and I must leave. It's said there are many enemy soldiers along the way, but by the time this report arrives, you will have found this out by other means.

A SIN OF THE REVOLUTION

Revolutions, radical and accelerated social transformations, are made in specific circumstances. They rarely, if ever, emerge fully ripe, and not all their details can be scientifically foreseen. They are made from passion, from the improvisation of human beings in their struggle for social change, and they are never perfect. Our revolution was no exception. It committed errors, and some of these cost us dearly. Today, evidence of another such error has been shown to us, that although it has had no repercussions, still demonstrates the truth of the popular sayings: "Birds of a feather flock together" and "A leopard never changes its spots."

When the troops of the invading column reached the foothills of the Escambray, after 45 days on the march—in great pain, their feet bloodied and lacerated by fungal diseases, continuing on faith alone—they were greeted by an unusual letter. It was signed by Commander Carrera, and it stated that the column of the Rebel Army under my command was prohibited from entering the Escambray without a clear explanation of our intentions. Before ascending, I was to stop marching and explain myself. Stop on the open plains, in the conditions we found ourselves in, under the constant threat of enemy encirclement, which we could only escape through rapid movement! This was the essence of the long, insolent letter.

We continued ahead, perplexed, sorry because we could not wait for those who described themselves as our comrades-in-struggle, but determined to resolve any problems and carry out the express orders of commander-in-chief Fidel Castro, who had clearly ordered us to work for the unity of all combatants.

We reached the Escambray and made camp near Del Obispo peak, visible from Sancti Spíritus with a cross on its summit. We were able to establish our first camp there, and immediately looked for the house where we were supposed to find the guerrilla's most precious item: shoes. There were no shoes; they had been taken by the forces of the Second National Front of the Escambray, despite the fact they had been obtained by the July 26 Movement. A storm was brewing. Nevertheless, we succeeded in maintaining our calm, and talked with a captain, who later informed us he had murdered four combatants who wished to abandon the second front and join the revolutionary ranks of the July 26 Movement. We had a discussion with Commander Carrera, unfriendly but not heated. He had already drunk half a bottle of liquor, about half his daily quota. He was not as gross and aggressive in person as was his missive a few days earlier, but we saw in him an enemy.

Later we met Commander Peña, famous in the region for rustling the peasants' cattle. He emphatically prohibited us from attacking Güinía de Miranda, because the village belonged to his zone. When we argued that the region belonged to everyone, that it was necessary to fight, and that we had more and better weapons and more experience, he simply said that our bazooka was matched by 200 shotguns, and that 200 shotguns had the same effect as a bazooka. End of discussion. Güinía de Miranda was to be taken by the second front, and we could not attack it. Naturally we paid no attention, but we knew we faced dangerous "allies."

After many trials and tribulations, too long to relate, where our patience was tested infinitely — and where, according to the just critique of *compañero* Fidel, we put up with more than we should have — we reached a "truce." They permitted us to make the agrarian reform in the entire area belonging to the Second National Front of the Escambray, as long as we permitted them to collect taxes. Collect taxes — that was their watchword!

The story is a long one. In a bloody and unrelenting struggle we occupied the principal cities of the nation, counting on the support of fine allies in the Revolutionary Directorate, whose members, although fewer and with less experience, did everything possible to assist in our common success. On January 1, the revolutionary command demanded that all troops be placed under my command in Santa Clara. The Second National Front of the Escambray, through the mouth of its leader Gutiérrez Menoyo, immediately placed itself at my orders. No problem whatsoever. We then ordered them to wait for us, because we had to arrange some administrative tasks in the first big city we had conquered.

It was difficult to control things during those days, and we soon learned that the second front, following behind Camilo Cienfuegos, had entered Havana "heroically." We thought it might be some maneuver to try to gain strength, to occupy some position, to create a provocation. We already knew them, but with each day we got to know them better. They did in fact occupy the most important strategic positions, from their point of view ... A few days later the first bill arrived from the Hotel Capri, signed by Fleitas: it was for $15,000 in food and drink for a small number of beneficiaries.

When it came time to assign ranks, almost 100 captains and a good number of commanders aspired to comfortable state jobs, in addition to a huge, "select" group of men put forward by the inseparable Menoyo and Fleitas, who aspired to a whole range of jobs in the state apparatus. These were not particularly well-paying positions, but they had one characteristic: they had all been sources of graft during the pre-revolutionary regime. Housing inspectors; tax collectors; all the places where money changed hands and passed through avid fingers—these posts were the objects of their desires. This was a part of the Rebel Army with which we had to coexist.

From the very first days, serious disagreements arose that sometimes culminated in violent words. But our apparent revolutionary good sense always prevailed, and we gave way for the sake of unity. We maintained our principles. We did not permit theft, and we did not give out key positions to those we knew to be potential traitors. But neither did we eliminate them; we made allowances, always on behalf of some vague and poorly understood idea of unity. This was a *sin of the revolution.*

The same sin led us to pay succulent salaries to people like Barquín, Felipe Pazos, Teté Casuso, and so many other domestic and foreign freeloaders the revolution kept to avoid conflict, trying to buy their silence with a tacit understanding: a salary that was already parasitical, from a government they were waiting to betray. But the enemy has more money and more means of bribery than the people do. When all is said and done, what could we offer a Fleitas or a Menoyo except a position of work and sacrifice?

They, who lived off the tales of a struggle in which they did nothing, were deceiving people, looking for jobs, always trying to get closer to where money was ripe for the picking, rabble-rousing in all the cabinet ministries. All pure revolutionaries scorned them, yet we allowed them to function, gritting our teeth. They were an insult to our revolutionary conscience. Their presence constantly revealed to us our sin: the sin of flexibility in the face of a lack of revolutionary spirit; in the face of potential traitors; in the face of weakness of spirit, cowardice, thievery, "cattle-rustling."

Our conscience has now been cleared because together they have all left, sent by God in little boats to Miami. Thank you, "cattle-rustlers" of the second front. Thank you for relieving us of the execrable presence of self-appointed commanders, ridiculous captains, heroes unfamiliar with the rigors of battle but not the easy seizure of peasant homes. Thank you for this lesson you have given us, for demonstrating that consciousness cannot be bought with revolutionary generosity, that we must be strict and demanding with everyone. Thank you for showing us the need to be inflexible in the face of errors, weakness, and bad faith, and for allowing us to rise up, denounce, and punish, wherever it occurs, any vice that goes against the high ideals of the revolution.

Let the example of the second front, the example of our good, dear friend, the ex-thief Prío, call us back to reality. Let us not be afraid to call a thief a thief, because we ourselves, honoring what we loosely called "revolutionary tactics," referred to the thief as "ex-president" during the days when the "ex-president" did not refer to us as "despicable communists," as he does now, but as "saviors of Cuba."

A thief is a thief, and he'll die a thief — at least the high-level ones. Not the desperate person who in certain countries must steal a crust of bread so their children can eat. The other one, who robs to get himself women, drugs, or drink, or to satisfy the base instincts that drive him—he'll be a thief his whole life.

Now they are together over there, those who assaulted our conscience, like Felipe Pazos, who sold his honesty as if it were a gold coin to put at the disposal of "serious" institutions. People like Rufo López and Justo Carrillo, who took a baby step to accommodate themselves to the situation in order to get a little further. People like [José] Miró Cardona, eternal optimists. The incurable thieves, complicit in murders against the people. The "cattle-rustlers," whose "great deeds" were carried out against the masses of peasants they murdered in the Escambray, sowing more terror than Batista's army itself. They are part of our conscience. They remind us of our sin, a sin of the revolution that must not be repeated, a lesson we must learn.

Revolutionary conduct is a mirror of revolutionary faith. When someone who calls himself a revolutionary does not behave as such, he is no more than a charlatan. Let them all embrace one another: the Venturas and Tony Varonas, who fight so much among themselves; the Príos and Batistas; the Gutiérrez Menoyos and Sánchez Mosqueras; killers who murder to satisfy immediate cravings, and who do so in the name of freedom. Thieves and traders in honesty; opportunists of all stripes; presidential candidates—a pretty package.

How much you have taught us! Thank you.

LIDIA AND CLODOMIRA

I met Lidia some six months after we had begun our revolutionary activities. I was new in the role of commander of Column No. 4, and in search of provisions we went down for a lightning raid on the little village of San Pablo de Yao, near Bayamo, in the foothills of the Sierra Maestra. One of the first houses in the village belonged to a family of bakers. Lidia, a woman of some 45 years, was one of the owners of the bakery, whose only son had been a member of our column. From the first, she threw herself into revolutionary work enthusiastically and with exemplary devotion.

When I call her name to mind, I feel more than just affectionate appreciation for this irreproachable revolutionary, for she showed a particular devotion to me and preferred working under my orders, regardless of the front I might be assigned to. Innumerable were the occasions Lidia acted as special messenger, for me or for the movement. She carried to Santiago and to Havana the most compromising documents, all of our column's communiqués, and issues of our newspaper, *El Cubano Libre*; to us she brought paper, medicines, whatever we needed, whenever we needed it.

Her limitless audacity was such that male messengers avoided her company. I will always remember the opinion—somewhere between admiration and resentment—of one of them, who told me, "That woman has more ... than [Antonio] Maceo, but she's going to get us all killed. The things she does are crazy, this is no time for games." Lidia, however, went on crossing the enemy lines, again and again.

I was transferred to the zone of Minas del Frío, in Las Vegas de Jibacoa, and she followed. This meant leaving the auxiliary camp that she had commanded gallantly and slightly tyrannically for some time, causing a certain resentment among the Cuban men, since they were not accustomed to taking orders from a woman. Her camp, at Las Cuevas between Yao and Bayamo, was the revolution's most forward position; we wanted to remove her from that command because it was too dangerous a base. After the enemy had located it, our men often had to leave it under fire. I tried to have Lidia transferred from there once and for all; but I succeeded only when she followed me to the new front.

Among the anecdotes that reveal Lidia's character, I remember now the day that Geilín, one of our best fighters—a mere boy from Cárdenas—was killed. He was stationed at Lidia's forward post at that time. Returning from a mission, Lidia observed some soldiers advancing stealthily toward the post, a result no doubt of some informer's tip-off. Lidia's reaction was unhesitating. She took out her little .32 revolver to give a couple of warning shots in the air; but friendly hands stopped her in time, for it would have cost the lives of all of them. Meanwhile, the soldiers advanced and surprised Geilín, the camp sentry. Guillermo Geilín defended himself bravely until, twice wounded and knowing what would happen to him if he were to fall into the hands of these thugs, he committed suicide. The enemy soldiers advanced, burned everything flammable, and left.

The following day, I met Lidia. Her expression revealed the

greatest despair over the death of the young fighter and also resentment against the person who prevented her from warning him. "Me, they would have killed," she said, "but the boy would have been saved. Me, I'm an already old woman, but he wasn't even 20." She returned to this subject again and again. At times there seemed to be a kind of boasting in her constant expressions of contempt for death. The missions entrusted to her, however, were always carried out to perfection.

Lidia knew how fond I was of puppies and she was always promising to bring one from Havana, without ever doing so.

During the days of the great army offensive, Lidia carried out her missions to the letter. She came and went from the Sierra Maestra, bringing and taking highly important documents, establishing our connection with the outside world. She was accompanied by another fighter of the same caliber I know only by name, a name known and revered by the entire Rebel Army: Clodomira. Lidia and Clodomira had already become inseparable comrades-in-danger; they came and went, always together by each other's side.

I had asked Lidia to contact me as soon as I arrived from Las Villas, after the invasion, since she was to be our principal means of communication with Havana and with the general staff in the Sierra Maestra. I arrived and soon found her letter in which she announced she had a puppy ready to give me and that she would bring it on her next trip.

This was the trip Lidia and Clodomira never took. Soon after, I learned that the incapacity of a man—a hundred times their inferior as a fighter, as a revolutionary, as a human being—had resulted in Lidia and Clodomira being located. Our *compañeras* defended themselves to the death; Lidia was wounded when she was captured. Lidia's and Clodomira's bodies have disappeared; they are sleeping their last sleep, together, no doubt, as they were when they fought during the last days of the great battle for freedom.

Someday, maybe, their remains will be found, perhaps in some lonely field in the enormous cemetery the island became.

But within the Rebel Army, among those who fought and made sacrifices in those anguished days, the memory will live forever of the women who, by the risks they took daily, made communication with the rest of the island possible. Among all of us — for us on the first front, and for me personally — Lidia occupies a favored place. This is why I offer these words of remembrance in homage to her today, like a modest flower laid on the vast grave this once joyful island became.

Glossary

GLOSSARY

ACEVEDO GONZÁLEZ, ENRIQUE (Enriquito) (1942–). Born in Las Villas. Incorporated into the first front of Column No. 4 of the Rebel Army. Member of Column No. 8. Reached the rank of captain.

ACOSTA FERRALS, CLODOMIRA (1937–58). Born in Yara. Member of the July 26 Movement. Member of the Rebel Army as messenger. Clodomira and Lidia Doce were inseparable *compañeras*. On September 12, 1958, on a mission to Havana, Clodomira was captured, tortured, and killed.

ACUÑA NÚÑEZ, JUAN VITALIO (Vilo) (1925–67). Born in Granma province. A peasant from the Sierra Maestra who enlisted as guerrilla fighter in Column No. 1, on the first front. Later transferred to Column No. 4 on the first front, then to Column No. 3 on the third front. Reached the rank of commander of the Rebel Army.

ALMEIDA BOSQUE, JUAN (1927–). Born in Havana. Participated in the attack on the Moncada garrison on July 26, 1953, and was subsequently imprisoned. Member of the *Granma* expedition. Reached the rank of commander. Head of Column No. 3. Today a commander of the revolution.

AMEIJEIRAS DELGADO, EFIGENIO (1931–). Born in Las Tunas. Member of the *Granma* expedition. Guerrilla fighter in Column No. 1, then in Column No. 6 on the second front. Reached the rank of commander.

April 9, 1958. The July 26 Movement calls a general strike throughout Cuba. It is announced without adequate preparation, and the strike fails. Batista's forces increase their repression and offensive action.

ÁRBENZ, JACOBO (1914–71). Democratically elected president of Guatemala from 1951–54. Overthrown by a CIA-backed coup in 1954.

August 1, 1957. A general strike begins in Santiago to protest the July 30 murder of Frank País. On July 31, 60,000 Cubans had attended a funeral march for País in Santiago. The August 1 protest rapidly spreads throughout Oriente province and then to the entire island.

Authentic Organization. Part of the bourgeois opposition to Batista's regime, formed by members of the Cuban Revolutionary Party (the Authentic Party). After 1959 its leaders opposed the revolution and left Cuba.

Authentic Party. See Cuban Revolutionary Party.

BATISTA, FULGENCIO (1901–73). Army sergeant who seized control of the Cuban government in 1934. He left office in 1944, and on March 10, 1952, he led a coup d'état which overthrew the government of Carlos Prío Socarrás. He fled Cuba on January 1, 1959.

Bay of Pigs. Location of US-backed invasion on April 17, 1961; the last invaders surrendered at Playa Girón on April 19.

BORDÓN MACHADO, VÍCTOR (1930–). Born in Quemado de Güines. Member of the Orthodox Party youth and later the July 26 Movement. Participated in the April 9, 1958, strike. The first to form a guerrilla group in Las Villas province in the region of Sagua La Grande. Incorporated into Column No. 8 in October 1958.

Caracas Pact. An agreement that united opposition political currents announced on July 20, 1958, and signed by a broad range of the anti-Batista opposition, including Fidel Castro for the July 26 Movement. Called for an armed uprising to establish a provisional government and for an end to US support for Batista's dictatorship.

CARRILLO, JUSTO. Founded the Montecristi Group in 1956. Fled to the United States after the revolution and helped organize counterrevolutionary activities.

CASILLAS, JOAQUÍN (d. 1959). Army official notorious for his brutality. Tried and executed after the revolution.

CASTILLO ARMAS, CARLOS (1914–57). Guatemalan colonel. Installed as dictator by a US-backed coup in Guatemala against President Árbenz in 1954.

CASTRO MERCADER, RAÚL (1937–). Born in Las Tunas. Member of the July 26 Movement. Member of the first contingent of reinforcements sent by Frank País to the Sierra Maestra. Member of columns No. 1 and No. 4 on the first front. Reached the rank of captain in the column led by Che Guevara.

CASTRO RUZ, FIDEL (1926–). Led the attack against the Moncada garrison on July 26, 1953, and was subsequently imprisoned. Released in 1955 as a result of a public defense campaign. Organized the July 26 Movement and went to Mexico to organize the rebel forces. A *Granma* expeditionary and commander-in-chief of the Rebel Army. Cuban Prime Minister from February 1959 until December 1976; now president of the Council of State and Council of Ministers; first secretary of the Cuban Communist Party.

CASTRO RUZ, RAÚL (1931–). Participant in the 1953 Moncada attack and subsequently imprisoned. A *Granma* expeditionary and commander of the Rebel Army's Second Eastern Front. A minister of the Revolutionary Armed Forces from 1959 until the present. Vice-premier 1959–76. In 1976, he became the first vice-president of the Council of State and Council of Ministers. Second secretary of the Cuban Communist Party since 1965. Brother of Fidel Castro.

CHIBÁS, EDUARDO (1907–51). Founded the Orthodox Party in 1947. Elected senator in 1950. Committed suicide in 1951 at the conclusion of a radio address as a protest against government corruption.

CHIBÁS, RAÚL. Orthodox Party leader and brother of Eduardo Chibás. Signed the Sierra Manifesto in 1957 and was subsequently the treasurer of the July 26 Movement committee-in-exile. Fled to the United States after the revolution.

CHOMÓN MEDIAVILLA, FAURE (1929–). Leader of the Revolutionary Directorate. Participated in the March 13, 1957, attack on the presidential palace. In 1958 he arrived back in Cuba in an armed expedition on the boat *Scapade*. Organized a guerrilla detachment and joined the Rebel Army in the Escambray mountains.

CIENFUEGOS GORRIARÁN, CAMILO (1932–59). Born in Havana. Member of the *Granma* expedition. Commander of the "Antonio Maceo" Column No. 2. In January 1959 he was designated commander of the Rebel Army. Killed in a plane accident on October 28, 1959.

CONTE AGÜERO, LUIS (1924–). Journalist and leader of the Orthodox Party. Took an oppositionist stand against Batista, but opposed the revolutionary struggle. Went to the United States in 1960.

CRESPO CASTRO, LUIS (1923–2002). Born in Matanzas. Member of the *Granma* expedition. Member of the Rebel Army in Column No. 1 on the first front. Reached the rank of commander. Che refers to him as the *guajiro* Crespo.

Cuban Revolutionary Party. Founded in 1934, it took the name used by José Martí's party in the 19th century struggle against Spain. Formed government in 1944–52. Opposed Batista, then opposed the revolutionary government.

CUERVO NAVARRO, PELAYO (1901–57). Born in Guantánamo. Distinguished lawyer and soldier in the Orthodox Party. Killed hours after the assault of the March 13, 1957, presidential palace; his body was found in the El Laguito country club.

DEL VALLE JIMÉNEZ, SERGIO (1927–). Member of the July 26 Movement. Physician incorporated into the guerrilla army in Column No. 1 on the first front. Medical commander of Column No. 2.

Diario de la Marina. Right-wing Cuban daily. Closed by the revolutionary government on May 13, 1960.

DÍAZ GONZÁLEZ, JULIO (Julito) (1929–57). Born in Havana. Participated in the 1953 attack on the Moncada garrison. Exiled to Mexico and member of the *Granma* expedition. Killed in the El Uvero combat on May 28, 1957, with the rank of captain.

DOCE SÁNCHEZ, LIDIA (1912–58). Born in Holguín. Member of the July 26 Movement. Signed up for the Rebel Army in columns No. 1 and No. 4 as a messenger. Tortured and killed on September 12, 1958.

ECHEVERRÍA, JOSÉ ANTONIO (Manzanita). President of the Federation of University Students. When the Revolutionary Directorate attacked the presidential palace and Radio Reloj on March 13, 1957, he died in a gunfight with police.

El Cubano Libre. Name of the newspaper published by the Rebel Army, initially from the Sierra Maestra. A newspaper with this name was also published by the *Mambís*, independence fighters against colonial Spain.

El Uvero. Site of the May 27–28, 1957, battle in Oriente province. The Rebel Army overran a well-fortified army outpost.

ESCALONA ALONSO, DERMIDIO. Incorporated into the second front of the Rebel Army. Distinguished in the battle of Blanquizal and the second battle of Pino del Agua. Designated to open a guerrilla front in the Órganos mountains, Pinar del Río, in 1958. Finished the war with the rank of commander.

ESPÍN GUILLOIS, VILMA (Débora) (1930–). Born in Santiago de Cuba. Member of the national leadership of the July 26 Movement in Santiago under the command of Frank País. Eastern coordinator of the movement. In 1958 she joined the Rebel Army's Column No. 6 on the second front.

FAJARDO RIVERO, MANUEL EUGENIO (Piti) (1930–60). Born in Granma province. Physician. Incorporated into the Rebel Army in Column No. 1, and later in Column No. 12 on the fifth front. Reached the rank of commander.

FAJARDO SOTOMAYOR, MANUEL ENRIQUE (1932–95). Born in Granma province. One of the first peasants to enlist in 1956 in the first front, later moving to the second front. Reached the rank of commander.

FERNÁNDEZ FONT, MARCELO (Zoilo) (1932–2004). Born in Havana. National coordinator of the July 26 Movement in Havana.

GARCÍA FRÍAS, GUILLERMO (1928–). Born in Granma province. One of the first peasants to offer help and enlist in the Rebel Army in Column No. 1. Founder of the third front. Reached the rank of commander of the revolution.

GARCÍA MARTÍNEZ, CALIXTO (1931–). Born in Matanzas. Participated in the attacked on the Carlos Manuel de Céspedes garrison in Bayamo. Exiled, then became a member of the *Granma* expedition. Commander of the Rebel Army's Column No. 1.

Granma. Yacht used by revolutionaries to travel from Mexico to Cuba, November–December 1956.

HART DÁVALOS, ARMANDO (1930–). Born in Havana. Lawyer. Member of the National Revolutionary Movement. Founder of the July 26 Movement. Organized the uprising of November 30, 1956. Arrested and imprisoned on the Isle of Pines (since renamed the Isle of Youth), until the triumph of the revolution.

HERNÁNDEZ, MELBA (1922–). A lawyer who participated in the 1953 Moncada attack and was subsequently imprisoned. A member of the national leadership of the July 26 Movement and a leader of the underground movement. Joined the Rebel Army in the Sierra Maestra.

IGLESIAS LEYVA, JOEL (1941–). Born in Santiago de Cuba. Signed up for Column No. 1 of the guerrilla forces, then Column No. 4, and later, the "Ciro Redondo" Column No. 8. Fought in the Las Villas invasion under the leadership of Che Guevara. Reached the rank of commander.

INFANTE URIBAZO, ENZO (Bruno) (1930–). Born in Santiago de Cuba. Member of the provincial committee of the July 26 Movement in Santiago de Cuba. Coordinator of the July 26 Movement in Camagüey and responsible for its national publicity. Fought in the November 30, 1956, uprising, after which he was imprisoned until January 1959.

July 26 Movement. Founded in 1955 by veterans of the Moncada attack and youth activists from the left wing of the Orthodox Party, and others. Broke officially with the Orthodox Party in

March 1956. During the revolutionary war it was composed of the Rebel Army in the mountains (*Sierra*) and the urban underground network (*Llano*). Fused in 1961 with the Popular Socialist Party and the Revolutionary Directorate to form the Integrated Revolutionary Organization (ORI).

LAFERTÉ PÉREZ, EVELIO. Second lieutenant in Batista's army. Taken prisoner by the Rebel Army at the second battle of Pino del Agua. Joined the guerrilla forces in 1958 under Fidel's orders, and reached rank of captain.

LAMOTTE CORONADO, HUMBERTO (1919–56). Exiled to Mexico and subsequent member of the *Granma* expedition. Killed in Alegría de Pío on December 5, 1956.

La Plata. Site of the first Rebel Army victory against Batista's forces, on January 17, 1957, in Oriente province.

Llano. See July 26 Movement.

LÓPEZ FERNÁNDEZ, ANTONIO (Ñico) (1934–56). Born in Havana. Led the assault on the Carlos Manuel de Céspedes barracks. While in exile in Guatemala he befriended Che Guevara. Member of the national leadership of the July 26 Movement. Member of the *Granma* expedition. Assassinated in Boca del Toro on December 8, 1956.

MACEO, ANTONIO (1845–96). Prominent military leader and strategist in the three Cuban independence wars. Opposed the 1878 treaty that ended the first war. Led a march from the east to the west of island in 1895–96. Killed in battle.

MACHADO VENTURA, JOSÉ RAMÓN (Machadito) (1930–). Member of the July 26 Movement. Soldier and physician of the Rebel Army. Member of Column No. 6 on the second front. Reached the rank of commander.

HERMAN, MARK. US citizen who enlisted in the first front of the Rebel Army. Instructor at the recruit training school in Minas del Frío in 1958. Member of Column No. 8. Reached the rank of captain.

Mambís. Independence fighters against colonial Spain.

March 13, 1957. Armed units of the Revolutionary Directorate attack the presidential palace in Havana in an attempt to assassinate Batista. The attack fails and a number of revolutionaries are killed, including the directorate's leader, José Antonio Echeverría.

MÁRQUEZ RODRÍGUEZ, JUAN MANUEL (1915–56). Born in Havana. Member of the July 26 Movement. Played an important role in preparing the *Granma* expedition, of which he was second-in-command. Assassinated at La Norma farm on December 16, 1956, after disembarking from the *Granma* at Las Coloradas beach.

MARTÍ, JOSÉ (1853–95). Cuban national hero. Noted poet, writer, speaker, and journalist. Founded the Cuban Revolutionary Party in 1892 to fight Spanish rule and oppose US plans. Launched the 1895 independence war. Killed in battle.

MÁS LÓPEZ, CARLOS (Carlitos) (1939–58). Born in Granma province. Peasant collaborator with the guerrilla fighters. Signed up with the Rebel Army in Column No. 4 on the first front.

Reached the rank of captain. Mortally wounded at the battle of Naranjo and died on July 14, 1958, in the La Plata hospital.

MASETTI BLANCO, JORGE RICARDO (Segundo) (1929–64). A journalist born in Argentina. He visited the guerrilla fighters in the mountains, interviewing Fidel Castro and Che Guevara. He and Che Guevara sustained a deep and lasting friendship. Killed while leading a guerrilla force in northern Argentina.

MATOS, HUBERT. Commander in the Rebel Army. In October 1959 he attempted to organize a counterrevolutionary rebellion in Camagüey province. He was arrested and imprisoned until 1979.

Miami Pact. Announced on November 1, 1957, by forces including leaders of the Authentic Organization, the Cuban Revolutionary Party, the Orthodox Party, the Revolutionary Directorate, and others, who falsely claimed the document had been signed by authorized representatives of the July 26 Movement. It created the Cuban Liberation Junta, dominated by Carlos Prío Socarrás. It was denounced by the Rebel Army and the July 26 Movement in a letter drafted by Fidel Castro.

MIRÓ CARDONA, JOSÉ (1902–74). A leader of the bourgeois opposition to Batista. Prime minister of Cuba, January–February 1959. Left for the United States in 1960, and served as the president of the counterrevolutionary Cuban Revolutionary Council in exile.

MONTANÉ OROPESA, JESÚS (1923–99). Born in Nueva Gerona on the Isle of Pines. One of the leaders of the 1953 attack on the Moncada garrison, after which he was arrested and tried. Exiled to Mexico, he joined the *Granma* expedition. After the guerrillas were dispersed at Alegría de Pío, he was taken prisoner on December 12, 1956, and remained in prison until after the triumph of the revolution.

Montecristi Group. Group including officers in Batista's army, formed in 1956 by Justo Carrillo, with the goal of encouraging a military coup against Batista.

MORA MORALES, MENELAO (1905–57). Born in Pinar del Río. An active fighter against the Machado dictatorship. Killed in the March 13, 1957, assault on the presidential palace.

MORALES HERNÁNDEZ, CALIXTO (1929–). Born in Camagüey. Member of the *Granma* expedition and columns No. 1 and No. 8 of the Rebel Army, where he reached the rank of captain.

November 30, 1956. The July 26 Movement organizes an uprising in Santiago de Cuba, led by Frank País, to coincide with scheduled arrival of the *Granma*. The rebellion is crushed, and in its wake, Batista's police begin a wave of arrests and murders, especially in Santiago and throughout Oriente province.

NÚÑEZ JIMÉNEZ, ANTONIO (1923–). Born in Havana. Combatant in the Rebel Army. Helped prepare the April 9, 1958, strike. Worked on the creation of the Escambray front.

Orthodox Party. Formed in 1947 by Eduardo Chibás, on a platform of honesty in government. After Chibás's death in 1951, members of the youth wing under Fidel Castro's leadership provided initial cadres for the July 26 Movement. Its official leadership moved to the right and fragmented.

PAÍS GARCÍA, FRANK (David or **Carlos)** (1934–57). Born in Santiago de Cuba. Founder and head of the action and sabotage group of the July 26 Movement in Santiago. Directed the uprising on November 30, 1956. Killed on July 30, 1957, in his hometown, with his *compañero* Raúl Pujol.

PAÍS GARCÍA, JOSUÉ (1937–57). Born in Santiago de Cuba. Brother of Frank País. Captain of the July 26 Movement clandestine militias. An outstanding participant of the November 30, 1956, uprising. Killed in his hometown on June 30.

PARDO GUERRA, RAMÓN (Guile) (1939–). Combatant of the Rebel Army from 1957. Member of Column No. 4 on the first front. Later joined Column No. 8.

PEÑA TORRES, HERMES. Soldier of the Rebel Army. Member of Column No. 8.

PÉREZ HERNÁNDEZ, FAUSTINO (1920–92). Born in Cabaiguán in Las Villas province. Physician. Exiled to Mexico where he joined the *Granma* expedition. Played a key role in the urban resistance. National head of the action and sabotage group of the July 26 Movement. After the April 9, 1958, strike he fought in the Sierra Maestra, where he reached the rank of commander.

PÉREZ MONTANO, CRESCENCIO (1895–1986). Born in Granma province. Founder of the July 26 Movement. With Celia Sánchez, he supported the arrival of the *Granma*. A member of Column No. 1 on the first front, he later led Column No. 7. Reached the rank of commander.

PONCE DÍAZ, JOSÉ (1926–). Born in Havana. Participated in the attack on the Moncada garrison. Member of the *Granma* expedition.

Popular Socialist Party (PSP). Founded in 1925 as the Communist Party of Cuba, later changed its name to the Popular Socialist Party in 1944. After the revolution's victory, it fused with the July 26 Movement and the Revolutionary Directorate, in 1961.

PRÍO SOCARRÁS, CARLOS (1903–77). Leader of the Cuban Revolutionary Party and Cuban minister of labor 1944–48. Elected president in 1948. Overthrown by Batista's coup d'état in 1952. Opposed the revolution and went to the United States in 1961.

RAMOS LATOUR, RENÉ (Daniel) (1932–58). Born in Holguín. Member of the July 26 Movement, working in the northern zones of Mayarí, Cauto, Antilla, and Nicaro. On the national leadership of the movement's action and sabotage group. Arrived in the Sierra Maestra in 1957, with Column No. 1. Reached rank of commander.

Rebel Army. Armed force of the July 26 Movement in the revolutionary war against Batista. Became the Revolutionary Armed Forces in 1959.

REDONDO GARCÍA, CIRO (1931–57). Born in Havana. Participated in the attack on the Moncada garrison, after which he was arrested and tried. Exiled to Mexico, he later joined the *Granma* expedition. Member of the general staff in Column No. 4, he reached rank of captain. Killed in the battle of Mar Verde on November 29, 1957, and posthumously promoted to commander.

Revolutionary Directorate. Formed in 1955 by José Antonio Echeverría and other leaders of the Federation of University Students. The directorate led the March 13, 1957, attack on the presidential palace, later adding that date to its name. Organized a guerrilla column in the Escambray mountains in February 1958. Fused with the July 26 Movement and the Popular Socialist Party in 1961.

RODRÍGUEZ CORDOVÍ, GEONEL (1934–58). Born in Palma Soriano. Member of the July 26 Movement. Captain of Column No. 4 on the first front. He was hit by a mortar shell on July 11, 1958, in Naranjo, and died in the La Plata hospital on July 12.

RODRÍGUEZ CRUZ, RENÉ (El Flaco) (1931–90). Born in Cárdenas. Member of the July 26 Movement and a *Granma* expeditionary. Combatant in Column No. 8.

RODRÍGUEZ DE LA VEGA, ALFONSO (Cuco). Rebel Army fighter. Physician in the Las Villas campaign as captain of Column No. 8.

RODRÍGUEZ FERNÁNDEZ, ROBERTO (Vaquerito) (1935–58). Born in Sancti Spíritus. Member of columns No. 1 and No. 4 on the first front. Chief of the "suicide squad" of Column No. 8. Died in the attack on the Santa Clara police station on December 30, 1958.

RODRÍGUEZ PÉREZ, FRUCTUOSO (1933–57). Born in Las Villas. Vice-president of the Federation of University Students. Participated in the March 13, 1957, attack on the presidential palace. After José Antonio Echeverría's death he became president of the Federation of University Students and general secretary of the Revolutionary Directorate. He was assassinated on April 20, 1957, after a betrayal.

ROQUE NÚÑEZ, ROBERTO (1915–89). Born in Cienfuegos. Member of the navy and the July 26 Movement. Captain of the *Granma* expedition. He was arrested after the guerrillas were dispersed at Alegría de Pío, and remained in prison until the triumph of the revolution.

SÁNCHEZ ALVAREZ, UNIVERSO (1919–). Born in Matanzas. Member of the July 26 Movement and the *Granma* expedition. Reached the rank of commander.

SÁNCHEZ MANDULEY, CELIA (1920–80). Born in Granma province. Founder of the July 26 Movement in Manzanillo. Supported the arrival of the *Granma* expeditionaries. With Frank País, she organized the first reinforcement contingent sent to the Sierra Maestra. She joined the Sierra Maestra struggle and became a member of the general staff of the Rebel Army, with Fidel Castro.

SÁNCHEZ MOSQUERA, ÁNGEL. Colonel in Batista's army. Notorious for his brutality against peasants.

SÁNCHEZ WHITE, CALIXTO (1924–57). Born in Nueva Escocia. A pilot and mechanic who fought in World War II. Exiled to Miami. Organized and led a group of expeditionaries, who disembarked from the *Corinthia* at Mayarí, which resulted in the May 28, 1957, massacre of almost all the participants.

SANTAMARÍA CUADRADO, HAYDÉE (Yeyé) (1922–80). Born in Las Villas. Participated in the attack on the 1953 Moncada garrison, after which she was arrested, tried, and imprisoned.

A member of the national committee of the July 26 Movement. Sent by the July 26 Movement to fulfill missions outside of Cuba in support of the revolutionary struggle.

SARDIÑAS MENÉNDEZ, GUILLERMO (1916–64). Catholic priest who enlisted in the Rebel Army and reached the rank of captain.

Sierra. See July 26 Movement.

Sierra Manifesto. Announced on July 12, 1957, by Fidel Castro, Felipe Pazos, and Raúl Chibás. Called for a united effort to overthrow Batista and support the Rebel Army. Outlined elements of agrarian reform and opposed foreign interference in Cuban affairs.

SOTO ALBA, PEDRO (Pedrín). Born in Granma province. A member of the July 26 Movement and the *Granma* expedition. After the battle of Alegría de Pío, he went underground, then rejoined the Rebel Army in the first contingent sent to the Sierra Maestra by Frank País. Member of Column No. 1 on the first front. Killed in combat on June 26, 1958, and posthumously promoted to commander by Raúl Castro.

SUÁREZ MARTÍNEZ, RAÚL (1935–56). Born in Cienfuegos. Participated in the underground student struggle. Exiled to Mexico, he became member of the *Granma* expedition. He was killed in Boca del Toro, on December 8, 1956.

SUÑOL RICARDO, EDDY (1926–71). Born in Holguín. Member of the July 26 Movement in Santiago under Frank País. Soldier in Column No. 1, and subsequent head of Column No. 14 on the fourth front. Reached the rank of commander.

TRUJILLO, RAFAEL (1891–1961). Dictator of the Dominican Republic from 1930 until his assassination.

URRUTIA, MANUEL (1902–81). A magistrate at the trial of captured *Granma* expeditionaries, where he publicly criticized Batista's regime. He became Cuban president in January 1959, resigned in July the same year, and went to United States.

VALDÉS MENÉNDEZ, RAMIRO (Ramirito) (1932–). Born in Artemisa. Participated in the attack on the Moncada garrison, after which he was arrested and tried. Exiled to Mexico, he became a member of the *Granma* expedition. When Che Guevara went to lead Column No. 8 in Minas del Frío he became head of Column No. 4. Today he is a commander of the revolution.

WESTBROOK ROSALES, JOSÉ (Joe) (1937–57). Born in Havana. Member of the Revolutionary Directorate. Participated in the March 13, 1957, attack on the presidential palace. Killed on April 20 the same year, after a betrayal.

Also available as an audiobook from

HarperCollinsAudioBooks

www.harpercollins.co.uk

Also by Ernesto 'Che' Guevara

The Motorcycle Diaries

In January 1952, two young men from Buenos Aires set out to explore South America on 'La Poderosa', the Powerful One: a 500cc Norton. One of them was the 23-year-old Che Guevara.

Written eight years before the Cuban Revolution, these are Che's diaries – full of disasters and discoveries, high drama, low comedy and laddish improvisations. During his travels through Argentina, Chile, Peru and Venezuela, Che's main concerns are where the next drink is coming from, where the next bed is to be found and who might be around to share it.

Within a decade the whole world would know his name. His trip might have been an adventure of a lifetime – had his lifetime not turned into a much greater adventure ...

'*Easy Rider* meets *Das Kapital*'   *The Times*

'A revolutionary bestseller'   *Guardian*

The Bolivian Diary
The Authorised Edition

With an Introduction by Fidel Castro

This is Che Guevara's famous last diary, found in his backpack when he was captured, arrested and subsequently executed by the Bolivian army in October 1967. Published after his death, it catapulted Che to iconic status throughout the world.

In November 1966, Che arrived in Bolivia to lead a guerrilla force, fighting that country's military dictatorship. At first, they won their battles, outwitting the vastly superior forces surrounding them. Gradually, however, the army began to surround them, and their situation became more and more desperate.

Here, in Che's own words, are the events leading up to those final days. Told with honesty and humility, it is a remarkable record of heroism and bravery.

'Guevara was a figure of epic proportions. These diaries, stark and moving, will be his most enduring monument'   *Observer*

'Vivid and compelling'   *Economist*

Guerrilla Warfare

The Authorised Edition

Che Guevara remains one of the world's most iconic political and revolutionary figures. Fascinating to admirers and adversaries alike, he captured the minds of millions with his leadership and his belief in guerrilla warfare as the only effective agent to achieve political change.

Here, in his own classic text on revolution, Che draws on his first-hand experience of the Cuban campaign to document all aspects of guerrilla warfare.

This is the definitive, authorised version of Che's manifesto on revolution and includes his final revisions, completed just before his death. It is both an incisive handbook and an invaluable historical source.

'A how-to manual for guerrillas and a manifesto for revolutionary idealists ... Che's political testament'   *Observer*